Curriculum and Instruction for Emerging Adolescents

Curriculum and Instruction for Emerging Adolescents

THOMAS E. CURTIS AND WILMA W. BIDWELL

State University of New York at Albany

ADDISON-WESLEY PUBLISHING COMPANY

Reading, Massachusetts • Menlo Park, California
London • Amsterdam • Don Mills, Ontario • Sydney

ISBN 0-201-00902-1
ABCDEFGHIJ-MA-7987

Preface

The primary purpose of this text is to present a curriculum and instruction focus devoted to the education of emerging adolescents in the middle schools of the United States. Much has been written in recent years supporting the development of an organizational structure in the middle between the elementary and the secondary school. The concepts presented here have import for all who are concerned with these schools. Graduate students, inservice teachers, administrators, and knowledgeable laypersons should find its pragmatic approach and its reference to basic principles useful. It should give direction to those who are concerned with providing a broad-based education for emerging adolescents.

We believe that a middle school has unique purposes which are different from those of either the elementary school or the high school. The middle school is a transitional school which should be devoted to the personalization of purposes, standards, and methods which promote the growth and development of each individual pupil. A commitment to personalization is the major premise upon which a middle school program should be built.

There are a number of arguments regarding appropriate grade levels for a middle school, and, while appropriate grade division is an important issue, it is our opinion that the crucial question to be considered relates to the education program for the pupils themselves. Thus, the question of whether to retain a traditional seven-nine pattern or to change to a five-eight or six-eight organization may hinge upon other issues or problems unique to each district, and no major defense is tendered here for any particular pattern of grades. Our focus is upon curriculum and instruction rather than upon organizational structure, except as structure within a school relates to program. It is our contention that a study of current practice indicates that the guidelines and principles presented here can be applied within any pattern for any grades devoted to emerging adolescent education.

Our first chapter enunciates the middle school concept with definitions, purposes, and corollaries. The first unit presents the unique characteristics of the emerging adolescent in the middle school and stresses the phases of his or her growth and development—the physical, the socio-emotional, and the intellectual. In the second unit the educational antecedents of public education, the culture which surrounds the school, and appropriate learning theory upon which to base education for the emerging adolescent are considered.

The curriculum guidelines for middle schools are in the third unit and are supported by a strong argument for a systematic plan for achievement of a balanced program to include the acquisition of learning skills, an intensification of exploration as a basic function, and provision for a wide range of equivalent but alternative content.

The fourth unit is devoted to instructional procedures which support this balance and achieve its goals for individual pupils. This makes imperative an increase in flexibility and alternatives in both curriculum and instruction—so that individual needs and purposes of individual learners can be met.

In Chapter 14 most commonly utilized curricular organizations are analyzed and their applications in facilitating differing purposes of individual pupils during this period of emerging adolescence are discussed.

In the Appendix is contained a series of recommendations for practices in a middle school. Those activities are recommended which have been proven in practice in various transitional schools throughout the United States. In addition, logical extensions of these practices are proposed as possible for a middle school of the future.

Albany, New York   T.E.C.
October 1976   W.W.B.

Contents

CHAPTER 1

Purposes of the Middle School

The purposes of education for emerging adolescents have remained relatively stable through the various stages of evolution of the middle school from the first junior high school in 1910 to the present. This chapter presents a rationale for the education of emerging adolescents with guidelines for curriculum and instruction focused upon personalization, an approach designed to meet the varied, individual needs of learners. Middle school purposes have been of continuing concern among educators and, as designed for a particular group of pupils, subject to intense discussion. Reasons given for the existence of the middle school range from an interest in shortening the educational experience leading to an earlier mastery of content to a concern for providing the most effective educational experiences for pupils progressing through the developmental stages of emerging adolescence. We will explore these motives in an historical and sociological context at a later point.

It is our position that the middle school should be primarily concerned with the goal of providing an environment for personal, social, and emotional growth as students develop from childhood to adolescence. Further, functioning as a transition between elementary and high school, it should provide opportunities for extending basic skills, exploring new uses for skills, and extending and expanding conceptual frameworks in knowledge areas.

The middle school therefore has a set of unique functions and responsibilities. These basic principles are set forth in this introductory chapter. The corollaries and implications derived from them will be elaborated in succeeding chapters for the development of programs, instructional systems, and organizational patterns within which education of the emerging adolescent may be facilitated.

DEFINITION OF THE MIDDLE SCHOOL

The middle school is a transitional school responsible for providing the most appropriate program designed to assist pupils in coping with personal and educational development needs during emerging adolescence.

Clarification of terms follows in order to make the above definition and its concepts more understandable in terms of operations implied for the middle school. A *transitional school* is one in which the articulation between elementary and senior high school is achieved. The major purposes of elementary and secondary schools are different. Historically, the elementary school has furnished general education for all, while the secondary school has served as a preparatory school for the colleges. The middle school has faced problems because of this dichotomy. Particularly since Sputnik, secondary schools have placed an even greater stress upon intellectual endeavor. A transitional school which serves the unique needs of the youngsters enrolled in it cannot be dominated by demands from other educational institutions. In order to serve the students fully in the transitional status, the middle school should intensify individualization of instruction and personalize programs to meet the needs of emerging adolescents more effectively. Emphasis in the middle school should be upon growth of the learner toward self-reliance, both social and intellectual, which should lead more naturally toward the choice of an appropriate secondary program for each individual.

The term *program* refers to the organized learning experiences of the emerging adolescent within the total curriculum of the middle school and the instructional procedures involved in developing those experiences. This implies maximum attention in the school to social and emotional interaction between pupil and pupil, pupil and teacher, and pupil and environment in its broadest sense, as well as focus and development of conceptual structures within each pupil. In other words, all types of development in an ideal program—physical, socio-emotional, and intellectual—would have equal stress. A framework for emerging adolescent education must assist the pupil in maintaining an equilibrium among multiple growth factors.

The term *personal* emphasizes the variability within and among individuals at this stage of development and forces upon those responsible for their education a concern beyond the traditional "three Rs" to the purposes perceived by the emerging adolescent, and to the needs exacted by and related to the rapidly changing culture.

The term *educational* as used here extends beyond the traditional acquisition of subject matter to include "learning how to learn." Learning how to learn is essential in order to cope with rapidly expanding knowledge and societal change; it is a skill which the student will constantly use. For implementation, the general education content to be mastered by the individual must be judiciously selected, appropriately structured, and effectively utilized. Expending effort to develop broad-based learning skills and encourage more individual exploration in areas beyond general education is strongly recommended. Deletion of irrelevant content from the curriculum is required.

The term *emerging adolescence* within the framework of this book refers to the period immediately preceding, the period immediately contiguous to, and the period most immediately subsequent to puberty. The extreme variability of ages at which puberty is reached by different individuals in our society is a cause of one of the major educational problems in middle school theory. Some girls achieve puberty as early as 10 years of age, while some boys will not achieve this stage until age 15. Thus, a theory of education for this group must take into account extreme heterogeneity among emerging adolescents. Support for middle school theory, attendant implications for education, and application of educational methodologies all are focused on the wide range of variabilities within and among emerging adolescents—which is one of the chief justifications for a middle school.

PRIMARY FUNCTIONS OF A MIDDLE SCHOOL

The primary functions are seen to be three-fold in nature. They are:

1. development of a cultural transition from childhood to later adolescence,
2. establishment of an educational transition from elementary to secondary school philosophies, and
3. recognition of and appropriate consideration for the extreme variabilities within and among the emerging adolescent group.

The primary functions of the middle school should be based upon the assumptions of complete personalization of purposes, of criteria for achievement, and of instructional procedures for the emerging adolescent.

The *cultural transition* from childhood to later adolescence is significantly affected by the physical development of the child, regardless of the culture or subculture in which he or she lives. The child is oriented toward the family and is primarily parent-centered in ideals, with some values being developed through association with peers. By later adolescence, through the development of a set of completely individualistic ideals, this individual has become established as an operative unit among his or her peers. The period of cultural transition in emerging adolescence is probably the single most crucial period of one's life. Changes occur which include important transitions such as the recognition of one's sex role, the development of emotional independence from adults, the acquisition of new sets of values, as well as many others.

The concern for *educational transition* is in terms of a developmental approach. According to the studies of Piaget, children become capable of engaging in differing types of learning operations at different ages, developing from concrete to more complex forms of operations in thought as they become older. The idea of educational transition is founded on the understanding of growth of cognitive development. If the elementary child is capable of working with concrete operations and becomes capable of working in abstract operational terms and formal operational terms at a later date, educational methods appropriate to the level of functioning of the emerging adolescent should be used in the middle school. Thus both the middle school and secondary school instructional procedures should vary according to the cognitive level at which each child functions. The issue is not elementary versus secondary procedures but rather a focus on the importance of the transitional stage of education for the middle school. Instructional procedures intended to achieve cognitive growth in the middle school years should be based on appropriate experiences, methods, and materials which are neither elementary nor secondary in their fundamental nature, but developed for middle school pupils.

The *variability* within the emerging adolescent group makes personalization within the middle school an overriding concern. Appropriate consideration for the variabilities within socio-emotional, physical, and intellectual development must become one of the chief functions of a middle school. While most teachers have some idea of the variabilities in intellectual and academic achievement among their students, and although differences in academic achievement may be recognized, the question arises as to what actual curricular changes can be made as a result. One rather common answer has been homogeneous grouping, where the primary attempt is to reduce differences in order to lessen the teaching task. It is one of the major theses of this book that rather than attempting to narrow the range of variabilities for the convenience of the school staff, more careful attention should be given to them. If each child is to develop to the full extent of his or her capacities in each of the three areas of developmental growth, differences should be expected to increase in direct proportion to the success of our recognition and provision for developmental experiences for each individual. This variability in the purposes and needs of individual emerging adolescents should become the governing factor in curriculum and instruction, rather than a vain attempt to mold the group into a convenient amalgam. The emphasis should be upon the personalization of instruction.

Such personalization of instruction should not be confused with individualization, where each pupil is assigned individual tasks separate and distinct from what others may be doing at that moment. Personalization of instruction involves the systematic meeting of the needs, purposes, and desires of individuals. In some cases this may involve large groups if all have a common need. In other situations small groups may be appropriate, based upon the meeting of similar purposes experienced by lesser numbers of pupils. In other words, personalization of instruction can occur in any setting if the personal needs, purposes, and desires of each emerging adolescent are being met by a wide range of learning experiences presented by the teacher from which the pupil may select the most appropriate.

DESCRIPTION OF AN ORGANIZATIONAL UNIT FOR MIDDLE SCHOOLS

A middle school is a school which combines into one organization certain intermediate grades in the school system which may have been customarily assigned to either elementary or secondary structures. School years assigned to this organization have ordinarily consisted of various combinations of grades between five and nine; i.e., five-eight, six-eight, seven-eight, or seven-nine. The difference between this organizational description and that given in the definition of the middle school is obvious. Here the chief emphasis is placed upon administrative organization. Clarity of structure and administrative independence are essential in order to develop the educational program which is recommended. Nevertheless, we maintain that the *only purpose of an organizational structure is to facilitate the development of the pupils within that structure.* This can best be accomplished when a genuine concern exists for curriculum and instruction within whatever educational context has been developed by the district as an administrative structure for emerging adolescents.

COROLLARIES TO MIDDLE SCHOOL FUNCTIONS

In order to accomplish the functions of a middle school, certain corollaries, expressed in terms of the development of the pupils in the school toward certain desired goals, must be achieved. This is because a school can be effective only insofar as it helps the pupils within it to achieve both their own individual goals and those goals set for them by society. Although the educational philosopher and/or middle school administrator may be primarily concerned with the achievement of the three unique functions of the middle school previously mentioned, the faculty and staff who are working directly with the emerging adolescents may be more concerned with the corollaries which are devoted to the needs of individual pupils within the school. These corollaries are developed as follows:

1. development from dependence to independence in all areas,
2. development of a viable value system,
3. development of a process orientation,
4. development of individual self-evaluation,
5. development of alternative paths for individual purposes,
6. development of basic content structure as preparation for adult life, and
7. development of restructured content for increase of cognitive knowledge.

These seven corollaries are stated in terms of individual development with emphasis placed on each pupil's personal developmental processes and patterns. The faculty will have three major goals added to the dimensions listed above. Goals within the framework of the functions of the school must be established, and sets of criteria for measuring the growth and achievement of these goals for individual students within the program must be developed. In addition, the over-all effectiveness of the total school program must be assessed. General principles and implications from each of the corollaries follow.

The *development from dependence to independence in all areas* is extremely important to the basic three functions of the middle school. In the current American culture children are expected to be dependent upon the strengths and desires first of their parents and then of their teachers; while in their adult years they are expected to be independent, to make decisions based upon their own judgment, and to accept responsibility for those decisions. This is expected in matters of intellect, emotion, and physical development. It is during the period of emerging adolescence that this independence is first expected to appear. A secondary school student is expected to be able to make decisions with some assistance from adults. The faculty of a middle school must work within all aspects of the curriculum to help the emerging adolescent develop this ability, along with self-understanding and understanding of others, in order to achieve the goals of adolescence in the search for independence.

One aspect of this growth toward independence is the *development of a viable value system.* A value system, to be viable, must allow for growth and continued re-examination of both societal and individual values. Because emerging adolescence is the stage of development during which individuals move from an acceptance of the value system of others to the emergence of self with an individually held value system, this area is of utmost importance to a middle school program. If the emerging adolescent learns the essence and process of valuing and accepts the possibility of alternative values for the self and others in society, it could be expected that a value system might be developed within each individual which would be acceptable in relation to both society and each person. The aim of this process is fundamental to democracy.

The *development of a process orientation* within the framework of the thinking operations of the emerging adolescent is most important. This approach aids not only the educational transition from elementary to secondary school approaches, which is the obvious application, but should also be seen as a way toward a better cultural transition to adult life. Participation in current society demands continuous learning, which is dependent upon an individual command of the processes of learning. In a changing world milieu, it is no longer an adequate approach to education to assume it to be completed at the culmination of the formal school years. The adult must continue learning throughout life, and learning operations thus assume a great importance in the continuous need to orient oneself in the rapidly changing culture.

It is now widely accepted that different individuals learn by different processes. Hence, variabilities found in the emerging adolescent should be encouraged so that each pupil develops not only his or her own best style of learning and problem solving, but understands the need to augment other styles of learning. The orientation toward the learning process is particularly vital to middle school education since the development of learning skills is a significant part of the curriculum during this period of education.

The *development of individual self-evaluation* is probably as important, if not more important, than the teacher evaluation. The concept of self-actualization is extremely important here, since the way in which emerging adolescents see themselves as growing and maturing entities will certainly affect their future socio-emotional and intellectual growth. Emerging adolescents, then, should be helped with an evaluation of their individual strengths and weaknesses which is at once realistic and self-accepting. To be realistic without being self-accepting might be ruinous to the self-concept of many, while to be self-accepting without being realistic might be equally disastrous for others. Thus, criticism of a *constructive* nature by teachers and other professionals is not only acceptable but mandatory.

If a teacher is to diagnose the needs and evaluate the progress of individual emerging adolescents it is first necessary to *develop alternative paths for individual purposes.* Each emerging adolescent may be assumed to have unique goals which may be achieved through unique approaches. These approaches and educational alternatives may or may not be the same for each individual as for others within the class. At the times that the paths of individuals do coincide with others the teacher could certainly aid the pupils simultaneously. At those times when the individual is following a particular valid path which is unique, then the teacher must be sure to allow this freedom of choice. As an example, if three students are working to develop understanding and more emotional independence, it may be that all of them would reach some level of this goal but possibly through different pathways. Thus the task of the faculty member or professional staff member might be the development and design of experiences based upon certain objectives clearly stated, with many separate and discrete paths toward those goals.

In order to accomplish the functions of a middle school, the traditional structure of curriculum content must be considerably edited and revised. This restructuring must take into account the purposes of the emerging adolescent in preparation for adult life, and the increase of cognitive skills and knowledges. The *restructuring of content in preparation for adult life* should take into account three facets of the content of the curriculum for middle school: (1) a new critical view of the traditional structures of the disciplines as a viable alternative for educating middle school pupils, (2) a more discerning look at the scope and sequence of any innovative structures or traditional structures with a view to the effectiveness of that scope and sequence, and (3) a most critical evaluation of all content included within the educational program. There is a pressing need to determine what content might be deleted as a result of more effective structuring or lack of utility if learned in its present form.

In utilizing these criteria for a new view of content in preparation for adult life it is necessary to ensure that all students receive such general knowledge as is necessary for them to become and remain effective adults in American society. Thoughtful and innovative approaches are necessary when determining which particular content could be most effective in accomplishing this. Emphasis on the content to be offered and criteria for its selection must be a continuous process in the middle school of the future.

Restructuring content in order to increase cognitive skills and knowledges is to be stressed because the need in a changing society is for individuals who are able to understand not only what now is, but what may be and what can be. An individual in the late twentieth century must be prepared to continue learning throughout life. To achieve this goal, the pupil should strive to the utmost to increase skills and knowledges; the learning process does not cease when current formal school experiences have been completed.

The two corollaries which pertain to the deletion of irrelevant content and the restructuring of the remaining content are not to be construed as anti-intellectual. On the contrary, the ability to utilize the intellect is crucial in the innovative educational program suggested here. The over-arching issue in these particular corollaries is that one needs to accumulate only that content which is relevant to the needs and purposes of emerging adolescents and which will strongly correlate with their purposes and coping behavior in the future.

Personalization does not necessitate an isolation of the individual from the group or complete individualization of instruction. Personalized purposes may be achieved by the pupil while working alone, in small groups, or in large groups. Differing purposes may be achieved in each of these organizational structures. In fact, the greater the differences in instructional procedures and organizational methods utilized, the greater the possibility of achieving this recommended personalization.

PROGRAMMATIC PURPOSES

If middle schools are to assume their rightful place in the educational structure of American education in the future, strong emphasis must be placed upon their three unique and discrete primary functions in addition to the continuation of those functions which they hold in common with elementary and secondary schools. Experience has shown that school administrators, school boards, and patrons tend to make decisions based upon practical concerns. Therefore, middle school proponents must stress and support those functions, curricular and instructional as well as organizational, which are vital to the program for the emerging adolescent and which cannot be satisfactorily achieved by the elementary or the high schools to the degree that they can be achieved by a dynamic and adequately supported middle school. These have been divided into programmatic purposes based upon the developmental needs of emerging adolescents in the psychomotor, affective, and cognitive domains.

Psychomotor domain

Physical development as an aspect of the growth of the emerging adolescent must be stressed in the middle school program. Emerging adolescents learn from observation as well as formal instruction those precepts most important to their elders. Hence practices, in addition to instruction, which emphasize the importance of physical development should be encouraged. In the concern for physical development of the middle school pupil, five general areas seem to be worthy of note. These are:

1. recognition and acceptance of the appropriate sex role by the pupil,
2. recognition and acceptance of the physical body by the pupil,
3. adequate health diagnoses,
4. adequate diagnosis of physical abilities, and
5. appropriate development of individual physique.

Most modern curricula stress sex education in some form or other in almost all grades. The importance of the *recognition and acceptance of the appropriate sex role* by the individual pupil during the period of emerging adolescence is well documented. Interest in sex as a personal phenomenon is present at all levels of development. The extreme variability in the ages of reaching puberty makes this intense preoccupation with the sex role a major aspect in the development of the middle school child. At the emerging adolescent level of education, when sex first becomes an important factor in the life of the individual, a recognition of the differences between boys and girls and an acceptance of a more mature male or female role is at times vital. The experience certainly is of utmost importance to the individual pupil in the middle school. The teacher may, in an indirect manner, help each individual develop a natural acceptance, understanding, and interpretation of the meaning of the change of bodily functions. Thus an understanding on the part of the teacher of the changes within the children as they are taking place and the teacher's empathy form an important aspect in the pupil's life. Any pupil not achieving self-recognition and acceptance of his or her sex role in the middle school is at a vast social and emotional disadvantage entering the upper grades of the secondary school.

The onset of puberty creates within the individual an increasing awareness of the physical body, with all of the intricacies associated with it. Prepubertal layers of fatty tissue and possible acne during the slightly later period are only two examples of problems characteristic of this age which may distress the emerging adolescent far out of proportion to their actual importance. The importance of this particular problem is clearly delineated by the contrast between the lean youth and the heavy one at puberty who each experience these differences with perhaps little understanding. All possible efforts should be made to assist the pupil during this period when the development of the physical body is so personally important. Much more can and should be done by the staff of the middle school to develop the physical body of the student. The *pupil's recognition and acceptance of the physical body* with its unique advantages and disadvantages must be considered one of the primary tasks of the middle school.

Every emerging adolescent should have a continuing series of *health diagnoses* during the middle school years. If the home cannot furnish such reports the school should assume the responsibility for the administration of a health diagnosis for the individual to assure that every pupil has adequate attention. The purpose of this diagnosis should be to determine any health and physical problems which may have developed earlier or may have been developing during this middle school period. The Greek maxim of "a sound mind in a sound body" would seem appropriate. An individual who is physically sound is more capable of utilizing cognitive and affective abilities.

A healthy, adequately functioning body is of prime importance from both a humanitarian and a utilitarian viewpoint.

In addition to a diagnosis of the health of the individual, an *adequate diagnosis of the physical abilities*, both micro and macro, is recommended. In an ideal middle school program much greater emphasis should be placed upon physical activities and the development of physical abilities. It is unreasonable, however, to expect similar physical activities from pupils with dissimilar physical abilities. Worries about health and sports competencies are quite common at this stage of development. Attention should be given to the welfare and well-being of all children. Steps should be taken to alleviate health and physical problems. Physical fitness in all aspects is important. Hence, a diagnostic and prescriptive program for the development of physical abilities is considered equally as important as the diagnosis and development of mental abilities.

The *appropriate development of individual physique*, a sound and healthy body, has been an object of little concern in the American school system. Physical education should be considered as only a beginning toward this goal even though it may be a well-conceived and well-executed program. Continuous and intensive effort throughout the middle school program must be stressed to achieve this.

Affective domain

The purposes of emerging adolescents in the affective domain may be delineated in the following areas:

1. development of self-realization,
2. development of aesthetic perception,
3. development of socially responsible behavior, and
4. recognition of ethics.

The *development of self-realization*, the beginning of understanding one's self within the framework of one's environment and an acceptance of the uniqueness that is the individual, is an area of concern more crucial during the emerging adolescent years than at any other time in the individual's life. As the child changes from immaturity to the relative maturity of adolescence it is vital that he or she understand, insofar as possible, the emotions and their development and be able to accept this emotional self without excessive pride or self-criticism. Each pupil should move from middle school into the secondary schools with a greater self-knowledge.

Aesthetic appreciation contributes to a complete, harmonious, and fruitful life for an individual. Therefore it is recommended that a middle school develop a strong sense of *aesthetic perception* so that emerging adolescents may acquire a full sense of individuality and awareness in an increasingly technological society. More and more emphasis will be placed on leisure and service activities. In order to derive the most value from activities which stress the individual and his or her relation to the surroundings a more acute sense of beauty should be developed. The school and the community must provide for each emerging adolescent the varieties of experience necessary to assist each to accept the need and ability to appreciate various types of aesthetic creations. Attempts to standardize perceptions at any stage of development are not appropriate to the middle school. One role of the teacher is to sensitize the student to varieties in perceptions and aesthetic needs—the teacher may help pupils to further their own individual development in these areas. Real appreciation is assumed to be much deeper and to come from the inner self. It is assumed to be best developed through encouragement of broader and deeper perception of artistic creations rather than from mere exposure. An opportunity for the student to participate in aesthetic activities for full expression of self is also recommended.

The development of *socially responsible behavior* should follow from the encouragement of self-development within the individual in all the previously stated categories. The middle school should, however, have an explicit commitment to the development of socially responsible behavior. The school is responsible for preparing the child to accept the responsibilities derived from the general mores of the culture. Emerging adolescents, with their strong idealism and search for themselves, may be expected to seek desperately for behaviors which are socially acceptable. The middle school should provide a social environment which encourages behaviors which are not only socially acceptable, but which are socially responsible as well. This goal should have high priority and should be emphasized more strongly than in the past. Many problems of society now and in the future require citizens with a strong sense of responsibility for self and for others. The emphasis here is on socially responsible behavior rather than on the socially acceptable behavior which is the more common practical goal of middle schools.

In the multi-valued society which currently is the United States, *ethics* has become a controversial area of concern. In general education all emerging adolescents should be involved in processes for clarification of values (valuing as a process) and experiences with formal statements of ethics and their implications. Recognition of the tenets of the ethics generally held most dear by individuals and groups should be recognized by each emerging adolescent, although not necessarily accepted.

Cognitive domain

Most traditional schools stress their capacity to enhance pupil development in the cognitive domain. It becomes necessary to examine the extent of cognitive development more closely, however. The amassing of facts has been accepted as evidence of achievement, but we believe that this represents an unwarranted delimitation of the facets of this domain. A middle school program, in order to realize· the corollaries attendant to middle school functions, should enhance the progress of all pupils in the following areas during the emerging adolescent years:

1. development of self-evaluative processes,
2. development of exploration experiences,
3. development of basic skills of learning,
4. development of learning skills,
5. development of learning modalities, and
6. development of knowledge of content base for future study.

The *self-evaluation of learning* in all aspects is perhaps most important in personalization of purposes. It involves an understanding of individual strengths and weaknesses and a growth in responsibility for learning tasks. The middle school must cultivate in the student the capacities of self-direction and self-evaluation. As the emerging adolescent begins to develop the ability to work with cognitive abstractions, it becomes important to develop processes for analyzing those abstractions. Since elementary school learning processes are more concrete in nature, the inauguration of formal thought in the middle school necessitates this greater concern for self-evaluation for emerging adolescents.

The usefulness of the concept of personalization of purposes becomes most evident in the area of *exploration experiences.* A good middle school must, of necessity, present to each student the opportunity to grow outward in individual interests, skills, and other educational attainments. By exploration we mean that learning which the individual pupil absorbs to satisfy his or her own unique purposes. It might lie within the framework of what is usually considered general education, or in extra-curricular activities, or in individual study. However it may be provided, exploration is based upon the personal needs and purposes of the emerging adolescent, and not upon those of society or the school.

This type of learning need not be formalized into courses of study, but might better be considered in terms of periods of study appropriate to the evanescent interests of emerging adolescents. The guidance of a versatile and flexible teacher becomes most important as pupils attempt to discover and develop their own educational interests.

The greatest possible development of the *command of basic skills of learning* should be a commitment of the middle school. Different individuals achieve at different rates and reach certain goals at different ages. A sizable group of pupils might be expected to have mastered basic skills by the time they had entered middle school. Others, however, may not have reached this stage of learning. Under the principles of personalization of purposes it becomes the duty of the middle school faculty to continue work in this crucial area. Individuals have differing needs which may affect their work in basic skill areas. Those who have exhibited a weakness in these areas may have had varying motivational problems based upon differences in background. Basic skills should be related to individual pupil interests and motives if they are to be most effectively developed by the emerging adolescent.

Another cognitive concern of a middle school stresses the development of *learning skills*. These skills differ in both kind and degree from the basic skills just mentioned. By learning skills we mean the application of the basic skills (i.e., reading, arithmetic, composition, and speech) to learning in subject areas and to the achievement of the higher cognitive processes. They are usually divided into three general areas: development of library skills, development of media skills, and development of thought processes.

A wide variety of materials should be available to meet the needs and interests of widely differing students. Some pupils are more capable of working in those subject areas such as arithmetic which are sequential in nature with one topic leading logically to the next. Those whose interests tend toward social studies or such find their thought processes moving in less sequential patterns. Each individual's development of learning skills is unique, not only as a function of native ability but also as a function of the purposes (both transitory and lasting) for utilizing the particular type of learning at a given moment.

With the development of exploratory experiences available for the application of learning skills, the increase in self-direction on the part of the individual student within the school will be optimized. Each emerging adolescent must become an independent learner by the time he or she has reached the secondary schools insofar as intellectual capability permits. Learning skills must be especially emphasized in an innovative middle school because these abilities are not innate; they must be systematically encouraged, enhanced, and developed within each pupil.

In addition to skills, different *learning modalities* must be considered in the learning of emerging adolescents. Different pupils utilize different modes of thinking and styles of learning to achieve different objectives depending upon different purposes. Many modes of thinking and learning are present. Most objectives are achieved through a type of rote learning which is relatively ineffective. Learning modes must be utilized in a practical operation in which students are presented with alternatives rather than a single question with a single right answer. Some individuals will learn best by programmed textbooks utilizing stimulus-response theory; others will learn best in a concrete operational procedure; and yet others will learn best in a very theoretical framework in which abstract thinking is most utilized. All modes need to be encouraged so that the high school and college pupil will be able to employ whatever mode of learning is most effective within a particular situation.

The last area of development to be considered at this point is that of a *knowledge content base for future study*. Much has been written about learning modes and skills, the individuality and uniqueness of emerging adolescents, and other equally important points. Statements have been made concerning the deletion and restructuring of content in the middle school. We do not suggest that content is not important in the middle school. In order for continuing learning in later school and nonschool settings to occur certain basic content elements of structure and concepts are necessary. In both sequential and less-sequential areas some general knowledge must be gained in the elementary school and the middle school. One of the goals of the middle school is to diagnose the development of each individual pupil in many areas of development for specific educational content, and to assist the pupil in growing as far as possible in many areas. Increasing breadth and depth of educational content and advancement into the secondary schools with the best possible base for future study is a major concern for each middle school.

Encouraging the emerging adolescent to seek alternative paths to learning and alternative solutions to problems will foster the development of creativity in the thought processes. The middle school, with its emphasis upon exploration and learning skills, is well equipped to develop this crucial attitude toward learning. The adolescent who has a "creative approach" will be in a better position to assume the learning tasks which lie ahead in the secondary schools and in life.

Given the basic premise of purposiveness as one of the prime essentials of education, new approaches to middle school education are necessary. Since purposes are, of necessity, personal and unique to the individual, the primary task of the teacher becomes that of diagnostician, guide, and assessor. The teacher must diagnose the needs and purposes of each individual pupil, present whatever alternative paths would be effective for that pupil, and then assist that pupil in assessing whether the purposes have been achieved. Throughout this process, strong support should be given to the emerging adolescent in his or her efforts to evaluate the extent to which his or her purposes have been met.

RELATED READINGS

Alexander, William M., et al. *The Emergent Middle School*. 2d. ed. New York: Holt, 1969.

Bondi, Joseph. *Developing Middle Schools: A Guidebook*. 1972. Mss. Info.

Bossing, Nelson L., and Cramer, Roscoe V. *The Junior High School*. Boston: Houghton Mifflin, 1965.

Curtis, Thomas E., ed. *The Middle School*. Albany, New York: Center for Curriculum Research and Services, State University of New York at Albany, 1968.

Eichhorn, Donald H. *The Middle School*. New York: The Center for Applied Research in Education, 1966.

Gruhn, William T., and Douglass, Harl R. *The Modern Junior High School*. 3d. ed. New York: Ronald, 1971.

Hansen, John, and Hearn, Arthur. *The Middle School Program*. Chicago: Rand McNally, 1971.

Howard, Alvin W., and Stoumbis, George C. *The Junior High and Middle School: Issues and Practices*. Scranton, Pa.: Intext Educational Publishers, 1970.

Leeper, Robert R., ed. *Middle School in the Making: Readings from Educational Leadership*. Washington, D. C.: Association for Supervision and Curriculum Development, 1974.

Overly, Donald E., et al. *Middle School: Humanizing Education for Youth*. Worthington, Ohio: Charles A. Jones, 1972.

Van Til, William; Vars, Gordon F.; and Lounsbury, John H. *Modern Education for the Junior High School Years*. 2d. ed. Indianapolis, Ind.: Bobbs-Merrill, 1967.

UNIT I

Characteristics of Emerging Adolescence

To be most effective an educational system must be based upon the growth and developmental characteristics of the pupils involved in that organization. A primary rationale for the existence of middle schools is the meeting of needs of youth passing through the stage of emerging adolescence. Only the presence of unique developmental characteristics at this stage of development can justify the necessity of a unique type of school best suited to interact with those characteristics.

The middle school, as a separate entity, may thus be justified by observation of how emerging adolescents vary from younger children enrolled in elementary school and from older adolescents attending high school. Having identified such differences, both in kind and degree, school officials may develop a program best suited to the needs, purposes, and desires of emerging adolescents. Such a program should deviate from typical elementary and secondary programs to such a degree that a discrete administrative unit seems appropriate.

Extensive study of growth patterns has led to new insights into the developmental characteristics of emerging adolescents. The occurrence of earlier puberty, greater height and weight, and other physical phenomena now as compared to the beginning of the twentieth century, combined with the more specific research information about physical growth and motor skills made available in recent years have presented more extensive and effective insights for middle school staffs. Changing social patterns have created new and crucial problems in the development of an educational milieu best fitted for learning for emerging adolescents. Current theories about cognitive development as espoused by Piaget present implications which must be rigorously examined and evaluated in order to organize cognitive development in middle school years.

CHAPTER 2

Physical Development in Emerging Adolescence

PHYSICAL CHANGES AT PUBERTY

The onset of puberty is accompanied by tremendous changes within the body of each individual, whether male or female. The primary change is one of rapid acceleration in growth patterns. From a period of relative stability during the middle-childhood years, the child's body rather suddenly begins to change; bones lengthen, muscles increase, glands begin to produce hormones. These changes create a condition of continuous change referred to as the adolescent growth spurt, and are accompanied by such changes as increased height, body breadth and depth, heart size, lung capacity, and other structural changes. The onset of these changes can occur at any time between ages 8 and 20—a spread of 12 years covering the outside extremes.[1] The age range covering the significant proportion of the cases is shown in material derived from Bossing and Cramer.[2] The 1959 statistics indicate that 88 percent of girls are pubescent at the age of 14 and 97 percent are mature at the age of 15, while 83 percent of boys are either pubescent or postpubescent by age 14 and 96 percent are either pubescent or postpubescent by age 15. Thus, it would seem that nine out of ten girls are pubescent by the time they are in the eighth grade (which is ordinarily at age 14), while more than four out of five boys also have reached pubescence by this time.

Hormonal changes

From the biological point of view, the endocrine glands and the hormones they secrete are an important phenomenon of growth at this age. One of the characteristic processes in sexual maturation is the development of sex hormones. Gonadotrophins, while present at birth, are found in the urine in increasing amounts approximately two and one-half years before sexual maturation. This release of gonadotrophins seems to be under the control of the hypothalamus.[3]

In addition, it has been noted that estrogens, the female hormone, and andro-gens, the male hormone, begin to be secreted within the bloodstream at approximately the same time as gonadotrophins. These sex hormones are but two of many hormones that are sent throughout the body by the endocrine glands.

It might be hypothesized that when appropriate stimuli reach the thalamus from the perceptions of the emerging adolescent, and this stimula-tion is transported to the hypothalamus, that organ might release hormonal substances into the blood, which might then be carried to the pituitary gland thus stimulating it to greater activity. Under these circumstances the nervous system might be able to affect the endocrine glands in such a way as to indicate an extremely close correlation between the endocrine function and the nervous system.[4]

This interrelationship between the hormonal balance of the body and the nervous system of the brain has certain implications for the development of the educational system for emerging adolescents. The possibility of extreme changes in mood and volatility found in many emerging adolescents becomes much more easily explained when the possibility of temporary chemical imbalance due to temporarily uneven hormonal secretions is noted. The con-cerns of the emerging adolescent about his or her physical body may create psychosomatic problems which, while not noted by adult observers, may have great impact upon the emotions of the emerging adolescent. Last, since the emotions are affected to some extent by the hypothalamus, it is not unrea-sonable to expect that the emotions of the emerging adolescent might be less predictable than in childhood or in later adolescence when hormonal secre-tions become less of a factor in the physical development of the youngster.

Sexual development

The question of the exact timing of emerging adolescence has been complicated by the fact that it is primarily determined by the physical development of the sexual organs. According to Espenschade and Eckert,

> The onset of puberty is difficult to assess in males and is usually based up-on the development of the secondary sex characteristics and the growth of the genitalia. In females the menarche, or first menstrual period, is usually taken as the onset of puberty....[5]

According to Forbes,

> ...the girl experiences all of the phenomena of adolescence, including the growth spurt, about two years earlier than the boy. For a short while she

may even exceed the boy in both weight and height.... The earlier
maturation of the female is shown in other ways: dentition is more rapid,
myopia occurs earlier, and skeletal maturation is more advanced.... Girls
reach their peak performance in motor abilities at an earlier age than
boys.... [6]

Growth spurt

While hormonal secretions are of tremendous importance in the physiological
development of emerging adolescents, they are not so readily evident as the
rapid growth in skeletal and muscular development found at this stage of
growth. Data compiled by Shuttleworth indicates that

> ... in girls, this growth spurt lasts from about 11 to 13½ years of age
> during which time the peak height gain averages 3¼ inches per year while
> in boys the growth spurt begins about two years later from 13 to 15½
> years, and has a peak gain in height growth of about 4 inches per year.[7]

Among boys,

> Age 14 marks the apex of the height spurt, the larynx enlarges, and axil-
> lary hair soon makes its appearance. Within a year or so there is rapid in-
> crease in muscular strength and a decided betterment in muscular
> coordination.[8]

Forbes, although well aware of the variations between individuals, was
attempting to establish a series of mean times at which certain physical phenomena might be expected. For example, Espenschade and Eckert indicated
that, although the sequence of physical development tended to be relatively
consistent in boys, the ages at which they occurred were so variable that the
development of boys of 13 and 14 years of age might vary from childhood to
almost complete maturity.[9]

This growth spurt is characterized not only by significant increases in
height and weight, but also in the sequence of the increase for the various parts
of the body. For example, Reynolds and Schoen used longitudinal data on
males and found:

> Leg length tends to reach its peak first and is followed four months later
> by hip width and chest breadth. A few months after the peak of hip width
> and chest breadth gain, shoulder breadth reaches its peak with trunk
> length and chest depth being the last of the skeletal measurements to
> achieve their peak gain. Since approximately one year separates the peaks

of leg length and trunk length gains, the peak gain in stature consequently lies between the two.[10]

The emerging adolescent who has grown accustomed to certain muscular actions achieving certain results finds that his intended actions now often yield completely different results which he may not actually understand. The resultant confusion may create a disturbed ego unsure of self or surroundings. Lengthened bone structure in legs, for example, alters feedback through the previous nervous and muscular system giving the emerging adolescent constant problems in predicting his physical action patterns. He often appears awkward and graceless. By the time he is able to accomplish control of the legs with their greater length, the trunk lengthens. New dimensions of compensation must continuously take place during this period.

At the same time that changes in the bone structure of the growing body are confusing the youngster, other changes are occurring. Male adolescence is a period of great augmentation in lean tissue and a corresponding moderate decline in body fat, thus creating changes in what the muscles can achieve.[11]

Structural differences

Girls differ from boys in their physical development in the ratio of bone and muscle and fat as well as in height and weight increase. While in both bone and muscle growth girls seem to gain equally with boys during the pubertal growth spurt, they do not seem to have as long a period of such gain. Girls also seem to lose some fat during adolescence, but not nearly so much as boys do. This would seem to give boys a considerably different ratio of bone, muscle, and lean body mass in relation to fat compared to girls.[12] These physical changes affect the metabolic rate and dietary requirements of emerging adolescents.

While cell numbers increase in the male throughout his growing years, there is a tremendous acceleration of increase which begins at about 10.5 years and lasts until 16 years. During this time muscle-cell number doubles. For girls the muscle-cell number increases on a relatively straight line until it reaches a plateau at about 10.5 years of age. For a period between the years of about 10.5 to 14.5 the girls have a greater number of muscle cells than boys do.

Cell size for boys seems to show a sustained increase from infancy through adolescence, whereas cell size for girls seems to increase until it reaches a plateau at about 10.5 years of age. Between the periods of 10.5 and 14.5 years of age the girls would seem to have larger muscle cells than boys. After this time the cell size in boys becomes larger.[13] In addition to the rather surprising muscular discrepancy between 10.5 and 14.5 years of age, the matter is further complicated by the fact that according to Tanner the muscles seem to grow first in size and then later in strength.[14]

Prior to and during puberty girls may surpass the physical efforts of boys. But boys tend to do better in certain areas of physical endeavor. For example, they are especially superior at various acts of agility such as jumping full turns and rapid changes of position.[15] Nevertheless, in the period during which boys are at the prepubertal stage and girls have passed this stage (i.e., approximately ages 11 to 13) a relatively strong physical advantage for girls is seen.

SECULAR TRENDS IN SEXUAL MATURATION

The ages at which characteristic physical developments occur in adolescents are not stable. Although the range of ages at which puberty occurs may remain generally the same, current research reveals a number of changes in secular trends in sexual maturity, one of the prime indicators of the onset of adolescence.

A considerable amount of research has been done, most of which indicates a marked and continuing trend over the years of a lowering in the age of menarche, the first menstrual period, in girls. Mills, as early as 1950, noted this change in the age at menarche.[16] Probably the most complete work done on the question of earlier female sexual maturity was written by Tanner, *Growth at Adolescence* (1962), which was concerned with many different facets of the adolescent physical process. For example, Tanner noted that ". . . age at menarche has been getting earlier by some four months per decade in Western Europe over the period of 1830 to 1960."[17]

In a study of six different countries, including the United States, and ranging from 1830 until 1960, Tanner noted the continuing decrease in the age of menarche for girls. For example, the average age for menarche for girls in Norway in 1840 was more than 17 years of age, and had decreased to approximately 13.5 by 1950. Six nations studied showed almost exactly the same trend and rate of change. For example, the statistics quoted for the United States showed an average for the age of menarche of a little over 14 years of age in 1910 and an average of under 13 years of age in 1955. This would indicate approximately 15 months difference in approximately 50 years, or approximately 3/10 of a year for each decade.[18]

A study by Gould and Gould conducted in the early 1930s tends to confirm this finding. They found that daughters were reaching menarche .38 years sooner than their mothers had approximately 25 years earlier.[19] While the statistics vary to some degree, the long-term trend noted previously seems to be established.

Both Tanner and Shuttleworth[20] note that the period for menarche in the United States is much earlier than that in other countries, varying as much as a year in some cases. Espenschade and Eckert contend that,

On the basis of a number of studies, it would appear that these regional variations in the menarche tend to be caused by climatic, nutritional, and racial differences. A survey of the average age at first menstruation for girls in the Americas, Europe, and Asia indicates that the menarche occurs consistently earlier in the central temperate areas and tends to be delayed in the colder northern and southern regions.[21]

While research information concerning the sexual maturation of boys is much more difficult to obtain, such data as are available would seem to indicate that a similar trend toward earlier maturity is present. The work of Kiil (1939) indicated that peak height gain in the adolescent growth spurt in males immediately following puberty occurred at age 17 in 1800, whereas data in the 1930s indicated 14 and 15 years of age for the same phenomenon.[22]

Kiil's work was concerned primarily with Swedish boys. Similar work in 1957 conducted by Jones and Jones for American children indicated a similar secular trend in increased body size and weight for the period from 1892 to 1932. Further, girls between the ages of 12 and 18 were approximately two inches taller and ten pounds heavier; boys were slightly more than two inches taller at 11 years of age and more than three inches taller at 16 years of age.[23]

Several reasons have been advanced to explain the earlier sexual maturation during the last 50 years. Forbes listed four: first, a rebound from a period prior to the industrial revolution when children were the same size, but were stunted due to a multitude of factors brought on by the industrial revolution; second, the vigor due to our situation as a nation of genetic hybrids; third, a decline in chronic diseases; and fourth, improved nutrition.[24] Forbes cites improved nutrition as being the most important or the most likely of these four for the development of earlier maturation. Mills noted some of the same factors. He also reported a phenomenon experienced in ancient Greece where stature and body build were the approximate equivalent of today's, followed by a considerable diminution of size during the Middle Ages.[25] He also noted the effect of climatic influence upon earlier maturation with heat seeming to have a slowing tendency upon menarche.[26]

IMPLICATIONS FOR EDUCATION

Recent research concerning physiological norms and deviations among individuals at pubescence indicates several means by which middle schools might best accommodate the unique physical status found among emerging adolescents. Studies concerning growth patterns, physical plateaus, early and late maturation, and other such phenomena would seem to point to specific needs on the part of emerging adolescents which are unique and which can best be met within a school framework.

Those who favor a separate middle school consider the psychomotor domain as one area of concern which would receive more attention in a school especially organized for the needs of emerging adolescents. These needs can and should be considered from two frames of reference: (1) in terms of a physical education program, and (2) for their importance in the classroom situation.

Physical education activities

There are five major aspects to be considered within the physical education program of the middle school which, while not exhaustive in nature, can, in the hands of a skilled and creative instructor, provide a strong physical education experience for emerging adolescents. These five principles are as follows:

1. personalization of physical activities,
2. increased emphasis upon directed physical activity,
3. de-emphasis on competition,
4. increased emphasis upon individual activities, and
5. acceptance of lower physical skill and proficiency requirements during the stage of puberty.

The most overwhelming insight to be derived from the research material is the immense variation in pupils during the time of puberty. The manner in which puberty affects the physical status of each individual, and the differences in physical ability evinced between and among individual pupils at the same age and grade indicate the imperative necessity for *personalization of physical activity*.

Placing groups of 25 to 100 pubescent boys and/or girls into one class for identical routines and physical experiences is a practice which ignores the requirements of individual students. It is essential that the physical education teacher look into the physical status of each individual under his or her jurisdiction so as to select those activities which develop knowledges and skills appropriate for each individual pupil at a particular time. For example, a game of basketball which might be intended to serve the traditional needs stated in many physical education curriculum guides might be appropriate for a relatively small percentage of the group at a given time. Some pupils at prepubescent stage might find themselves at a tremendous disadvantage in competing with other members of the class who were at a more mature stage. Boys experiencing the rapid skeletal and muscular changes of the growth-spurt stage might be at even more of a disadvantage caused by inability to adjust in agility and balance due to a sudden lengthening of bones. The clumsiness inherent within the stage of puberty among boys and the inability to develop stable motor skills which ensure accuracy should be considered by the understanding instructor. He can then share knowledge and develop self-confidence in a youth participating in the activity.

Competition between boys in pubescent stages and those either prior to or after this period would seem to serve little advantage to any of the three groups. An appropriate solution would seem to be one in which each pupil, either boy or girl, could be placed in the position of competing against his or her own previously established standard in whatever the physical activity might be.

An increased emphasis upon *directed physical activity* would seem to be desirable during this stage. While games and other activities have been favored in some middle school physical education programs because of their extrinsic motivational factors, it is recommended that intrinsic motivation be developed so that the individual can develop at a pace based on the premise of self-competition. In such a program the teacher serves as diagnostician of the various physical capabilities of the emerging adolescent and prescribes activities to sequence the student through each appropriate stage of physical development. In other words, each activity would stress development of certain psychomotor abilities and could be prescribed for each individual pupil according to the diagnosed level of ability and stage of development. The development of a set of criteria based upon a biological age concept setting specific psychomotor skills which could be expected of individuals at particular stages of individual development is important to a viable physical education program.

The unique growth patterns experienced by each individual necessitate a *de-emphasis on competition*. To place all eighth-grade youth in a position where they compete against each other ignores the individuality of physical development. For example, the late-maturing boy is seldom found on a junior high school or a ninth-grade basketball team. It is the early-maturing male who usually makes the team. The effect of unequal competition due to varying stages of development places a heavy burden of social and emotional strain upon the late-maturing boy.

Emphasis should be placed only on those types of competition which each emerging adolescent can carry on with standards appropriate to the attained stage of development. Examples among individual sports are golf, bowling, and swimming. De-emphasis rather than deletion of competition is suggested. While children and youth always compete against each other, the important aspect during pubescence is to take much of the pressure of this competition off emerging adolescents as they go through a most difficult physical stage of development.

An increased emphasis upon *individual activity* would seem to be one of the more important justifications for a stronger emphasis upon physical education in the middle school. Emerging adolescents should be placed in a position where certain psychomotor skills are valued, and where their development is encouraged. Specific abilities, particularly those which a pupil might be able to measure individually, should be stressed. This position places a premium upon more specific standards. These may or may not be any more rigorous, but they should be well understood by both teacher and pupil. Specific skills are necessary for a desired proficiency on the part of the player.

Careful analysis of the nature and component elements of these skills and careful measurement are more appropriate than trial and error or undirected practicing. As the individual pupil practices specific and varied psychomotor skills which are within his or her capabilities, progress should be evident and self-evaluation of the progress should be possible. In case of pupil difficulty with self-evaluation, the teacher should be immediately available to make a careful diagnosis of progress or reasons for lack of progress in specific skills, such as basket shooting, which can be taught in a team, or a group, or an individual situation. Without individualization, a teacher would be hard pressed to diagnose and correct individual difficulties which might escape attention in a group situation.

An understanding and *acceptance of lower physical skill and proficiency requirements during the stage of puberty* should be a goal of both the pupil and the teacher in the middle school. Probably the one physical phenomenon which is least often considered in physical education classes is that of the leveling of psychomotor skills during the stage of pubescence. While most physical educators are aware of the obvious advantages that the well-developed adolescent has over the less-developed child, less attention seems to be given to the leveling, or even decrease, in psychomotor skills evident during the stage of pubescence. The importance of this situation is such that immediate and intense attention should be given to it in the middle school physical education classes.

The physical differences between sixth- and eighth-grade boys and/or girls are no greater than the differences to be found between eighth-grade boys and/or girls due to early or late pubescence. To expect that the various skills necessary in physical education should progress in a linear fashion throughout the middle schools for all pupils is not only incorrect, but can lead to traumatic experiences for both children and instructor. A specific set of diagnostic devices based upon psychomotor skills which take into account this lag at puberty is essential to the most effective facilitation of the physical development of the middle school pupil.

Physical activities in the classroom

In addition to implications for the physical education program which should be drawn from evidence concerning the physical development of emerging adolescents, other factors should be taken into account in classrooms and

**Physical development is a crucial purpose of middle school education.
Alton Farnsworth Middle School**

(Courtesy of Guilderland, New York, Central Schools)

general program planning in middle schools. These implications are important
for all staff associated with the education of emerging adolescents, administrators, teachers, staff, and parents. These implications are:

1. recognition of importance of sex differences,
2. sex education,
3. knowledge of the range of physical variance,
4. concern for physical stress,
5. need for physical movement, and
6. recognition of correlations between physical, socio-emotional, and intellectual development.

The *recognition of importance of sex differences* as a necessary part of experience in a middle school is obvious. Since it is at precisely the period of puberty that individuals are attending the middle grades in the school system, it is extremely important to each individual to realize the physical and emotional changes which are taking place within. It is equally important for the teacher to recognize this phenomenon inasmuch as the self-perception of pupils changes considerably during this period. If the teacher is able to characterize this dramatic physical change in a positive manner, the educational process will enhance the development of the individual emerging adolescent.

Closely related to this area is *sex education.* Pubescence is inevitable, but its import and influence may not be understood either by the individual child or by those with whom he or she works and experiences school life. Knowledge should be imparted and dealt with in such a manner as to facilitate the comprehension of the child regarding his or her physical changes. Education which facilitates acceptance and understanding should be a part of all schooling from elementary through high school. It is especially desirable during middle school years that appropriate stress be placed upon the sexuality phenomena of puberty and maturing as they become more important in the lives of youth undergoing pubescence.

Sex education should include more than a study of physiological aspects of sex. The sex roles of the male and the female should be stressed so that individuals at this stage can relate and interrelate both physical and socio-emotional development. The need for each individual to develop an appropriate sex role can be most effectively accomplished during this period of maturing physical development. Hence social, emotional, and physical aspects of this change must be equally stressed in formal classes, in informal learning situations, and in counseling sessions as provided and sponsored by the school.

A *knowledge of the range of physical variance* inherent in the middle school age group as well as within a single class is most important. Both teachers and pupils should have access to this knowledge, and it should be shared for the primary purpose of assisting emerging adolescents to accept the changes in their physical bodies. The impact on their changed roles and status both as individuals and as a member of their age group and in their families become important aspects of such learning. For example, the prepubescent boy should come to understand that he cannot perform or cope with physical tasks at the same level of skill and proficiency as a postpubescent boy; on activities which require effective use of muscle coordination for skill and speed he may not be able to match the prepubescent girl's performance in physical activities. All emerging adolescents should recognize that they are developing on their own growth continuum and that they are unique as individuals in all aspects of their being. Acceptance of one's own individuality is important rather than competition with other members of the class. These points need to be stressed to the point of acceptance by pupils in this stage of physical development. All pupils should be helped to exert every effort to achieve maximum competence given their unique physical characteristics and stage of development. Unrealistic expectations should not be exacted of adolescents either by themselves, their peers, teachers, or parents.

A *concern for physical stress* is inherent in the questions of physical variance raised above. Research on physiological development presented in a previous section has shown that at certain stages emerging adolescents not only can be expected to perform poorly on psychomotor skills, but that some damage to internal organs can result from over stress on certain physical activities. When muscles, heart, and lungs are growing at disproportionate rates, as they do at this period, heavy physical tension and stress can well result in weakness or interference with development within the physical body creating either present or later physical problems. The very act of growing coupled with the continuous need to generate energy both physical and nervous throughout a typical school day for a middle school child may consume all of the child's available energy. An emerging adolescent might well become exhausted following a rigorous physical education activity. Thus, it is important for each teacher to observe pupils continually for signs of such physical exhaustion. Signs of strain are sometimes difficult to detect. For example, nervous strain is many times evinced by hyperactivity rather than by obvious weariness. The important point here is that the teacher must be continually aware of these possibilities when dealing with emerging adolescents.

The basis for the adolescent's *need for physical movement* creates a problem of a similar nature. The varying and uneven growth and development within the emerging adolescent makes sitting for extended periods without sufficient movement contrary to the physical well-being of the individual. Such factors as rapidly lengthening bones and changes in muscle cells result in a need for movement. Clumsiness is an outward sign of rapidly changing body structure, as is an acute physical need for exercise and utilization of bones and muscles. These needs for movement also may be socially and emotionally related, but the underlying physical elements must be understood.

The *recognition of correlations between physical, socio-emotional, and intellectual development* is essential. Almost all existing studies show marked correlation in the growth patterns of the emerging adolescent. The physical development of pubescence seems to be partially responsible for, as well as correlating with, the social and emotional development of the emerging adolescent. The work of Piaget and others also seems to support the fact that a change in mode of thinking and an academic-learning plateau seem to occur at about the same time as the plateau in physical growth. Thus the indications of correlation among and between various aspects of development need to be further studied and considered by faculty and staff. Ramifications of the relationships may not be obvious to the staff. Nevertheless, such relationships and the ways in which they are considered in developing overall programs for emerging adolescents by teachers, peers, and parents are of great importance in the transition through the emergent stage into later adolescence.

REFERENCES

1. Herbert R. Stolz and Lois Meek Stolz, "Adolescent Problems Related to Somatic Variations," in *The Forty-Third Yearbook of the National Society for the Study of Education, Part I, Adolescence,* ed. Nelson B. Henry (Chicago: University of Chicago Press, 1944), p. 81.

2. Nelson L. Bossing and Roscoe V. Cramer, *The Junior High School* (Boston: Houghton Mifflin, 1965), pp. 68–69.

3. Donald B. Cheek, Claude J. Migeon, and E. David Mellits, "The Concept of Biologic Age," in *Human Growth—Body Composition, Cell Growth, Energy, and Intelligence,* by Donald B. Cheek (Philadelphia: Lea & Febiger, 1968), chap. 38, p. 549.

4. William T. Keeton, *Biological Science* (New York: Norton, 1967), p. 340.

5. From *Motor Development* by Anna S. Espenschade and Helen M. Eckert, Charles E. Merrill Publishing Co., Columbus, Ohio © 1967, p. 173. Reprinted by permission of the publisher.

6. Gilbert B. Forbes, M.D., "Physical Aspects of Early Adolescence," in *The Middle School,* ed. Thomas E. Curtis (Albany, N. Y.: Center for Curriculum Research and Service, SUNYA, 1968), p. 27. Reprinted by permission.

7. F. K. Shuttleworth, "The Physical and Mental Growth of Girls and Boys Age Six to Nineteen in Relation to Age at Maximum Growth," *Monogr. Society for Research in Child Development* 4(3) (1939): 1–291. Reprinted by permission © Society for Research in Child Development, Inc.

8. Forbes, "Early Adolescence," p. 27. Reprinted by permission.

9. Espenschade and Eckert, *Motor Development,* p. 175.

10. E. L. Reynolds and G. Schoen, "Growth Patterns of Identical Triplets from Eight Through Eighteen Years," *Child Development* 18 (1947): 130–151. Reprinted by permission © Society for Research in Child Development, Inc.

11. Forbes, "Early Adolescence," p. 30.

12. Reynolds and Schoen, "Growth Patterns," pp. 130–151.

13. Donald B. Cheek, *Human Growth,* p. 350.

14. J. M. Tanner, *Growth at Adolescence* (Oxford: Blackwell Scientific Publications, 1955).

15. Espenschade and Eckert, *Motor Development,* p. 215.

16. C. A. Mills, "Temperature Influence Over Human Growth and Development," *Human Biology* XXII (Feb. 1950), pp. 71–74.

17. J. M. Tanner, *Growth at Adolescence,* 2d. ed. (Oxford: Blackwell Scientific Publications, 1962), p. 43.

18. Ibid., p. 152.

19. H. N. Gould and M. R. Gould, "Age of First Menstruation in Mothers and Daughters," *Journal of the American Medical Association* XCVIII (1932): 1349–1352.

20. F. K. Shuttleworth, "The Adolescent Period: A Graphic Atlas," *Monogr. Society for Research in Child Development* 14 serial no. 49, no. 1, 1949.

21. From *Motor Development* by Anna S. Espenschade and Helen M. Eckert, Charles E. Merrill Publishing Co., Columbus, Ohio © 1967, p. 179. Reprinted by permission of the publisher.

22. V. Kiil, "Stature and Growth of Norwegian Men During the Past 200 Years," *Skr. norske Vidensk Akad.*, no. 6, 1939.

23. H. E. Jones and M. C. Jones, *Adolescence* (Berkeley: University Extension, University of California, 1957).

24. Forbes, "Early Adolescence," pp. 35–38.

25. C. A. Mills, "Geographic and Time Variations in Body and Age at Menarche," *Human Biology* IX (Feb. 1937), pp. 53–54.

26. C. A. Mills, "Temperature Influence," pp. 71–74.

RELATED READINGS

Cheek, Donald B. *Human Growth—Body Composition, Cell Growth, Energy, and Intelligence*. Philadelphia: Lea & Febiger, 1968.

Epps, Edgar G., ed. *Cultural Pluralism*. Berkeley, Calif.: McCutchan, 1974.

Espenschade, Anna S., and Eckert, Helen M. *Motor Development*. Columbus, Ohio: Merrill, 1967.

Hurlock, Elizabeth B. *Adolescent Development*. 2d. ed. New York: McGraw-Hill, 1955.

Stolz, Herbert R., and Stolz, Lois Meek. "Adolescent Problems Related to Somatic Variations." In *The Forty-Third Yearbook of the National Society for the Study of Education, Part I, Adolescence*. Edited by Nelson B. Henry. Chicago: University of Chicago Press, 1944.

Tanner, J. M. *Growth at Adolescence*. 2d. ed. Oxford: Blackwell Scientific Publications, 1962.

CHAPTER 3

Socio-emotional Aspects of Emerging Adolescence

This section focuses on those emotional characteristics related to healthy social and emotional development of emerging adolescents. While recognizing variations due to individual differences and variances in developmental stages which are most marked at this period of life, a stereotypical image should not be construed from the various characteristics cited. Each of the characteristics mentioned is present in every individual to some degree, but its relative importance varies. Particular emotional stereotypes do not exist in reality; each individual is unique with his or her own set of variations of emotional characteristics.

EMOTIONAL CHARACTERISTICS

We have described adolescence in terms of the behavioral and emotional characteristics of individuals at this stage of development. Although, obviously, individuals differ greatly both in development and in range of expressions, there are many characteristics which we can identify as common to some degree to almost all emerging adolescents. The following characteristics have been observed:

1. tension due to developmental differences,
2. ambivalence,
3. sex-role conflicts,
4. restlessness,
5. introspection,
6. idealism,
7. enthusiasm, and
8. negative attitudes.

While each of these characteristics is usually recognizable within the framework of the actions of the individual, the comparative importance of each in an individual's development as he or she interacts with the environment comprises the unique nature of that individual. No characteristic can be considered alone; each is related to all other behavioral manifestations.

Tension due to developmental differences

An all-pervasive consideration for middle school theorists is the differences in physical development present during these years. The ages at which individuals achieve puberty along with the emotional and social implications of that phenomenon vary to a great degree not only between males and females but among the individuals within each sex group. Depending on the individual physical development of the youth involved, puberty may be achieved at almost any age between 10 and 20. The emotional impact of an individual's maturing early or late is incalculable. The emotional status of the 13-year-old girl who is two years past puberty is certainly different than that of the 13-year-old girl who has yet to reach this stage. A similar difference exists for males. Most studies indicate that the early-maturing adolescent experiences less suffering as a result of being different from the majority of his or her agemates than the late-maturing adolescent does.

Most psychologists concur with Margaret Mead that "junior high school students are more unlike each other than they have ever been before or ever will be again in the course of their lives."[1] Not only are the differences between individuals most noticeable at this stage but also growth seems most rapid and the evidences of change are most noticeable.[2]

While a majority of pupils are able to go through puberty and emerging adolescence without traumatic emotional effect, various research studies show that an appreciable number of youth do express undue anxiety concerning their physical development. H. E. Jones, in an interview study in 1939, found that more than 30 percent of the boys and more than 40 percent of the girls suffered from varying anxieties associated with physical development. The anxieties centered around such attributes as lack of size, lack of muscular strength, and obesity, and were for the most part concerned with late maturity.[3]

In addition to concerns regarding sexual maturation, many adolescents face problems having to do with developmental differences in other physical characteristics. The awkwardness which occurs with sudden rapid growth of bones and muscles at puberty creates many moments of anxiety for middle school pupils. Stumbling and dropping objects create many embarrassing moments for adolescents. The well-documented developmental characteristics of earlier female maturation is disturbing to boys of a prepubertal stage. The feeling of being immature, physically weaker, and generally inferior to earlier-developing females and to the early-developing males creates problems in the emotional well-being of the individual male, and hinders social relationships as well, particularly between the two sexes.

Ambivalence

A period of transition, regardless of its causes or results, produces a sense of insecurity for the individual. It can be expected that puberty, one of the most critical periods in life, would be filled with such feelings of insecurity to an unusual degree. Emerging adolescents experience wide variations in actions and degrees of maturity, acting like children at one moment and like adults at the next. Their demands upon themselves and their surroundings fluctuate between being unrealistically high to being almost childlike in dependence upon the support and security of adults.

The emotional motivation for this ambivalence is understandable. The emerging adolescent is relinquishing a childhood in which the important people in his or her life are such authority figures as adults, parents, teachers, and ministers. Along with the need to satisfy newfound ideals and selfhood, the adolescent is discovering the peer relationship and the ideas of correctness evidenced by classmates and other young acquaintances. A conflict emerges between depending upon the decisions of adults concerning behavior codes and decisions of his or her own making under the influence of the newly found peer culture.

Because of the social sensitivities newly discovered by the emerging adolescent, and because of an anxiety to secure the friendship and acceptance of peer groups, the adolescent finds that it is nearly impossible to please both the adults and the peer group. Before this problem is resolved, the adolescent will probably go through a period of contrariness during which time the ambivalence will hold sway.[4]

Instability in interests, fluctuations in goals, and ephemeral purposes are characteristic of this period of adolescence. The decisions made today will be changed tomorrow. The overpowering interest in an activity which may consume the emerging adolescent's entire attention may change radically in a remarkably short time. This does not minimize the seriousness with which the particular concern is viewed during its period of high interest.

Sex-role conflicts

The most obvious conflict in the minds of both males and females during the middle school years is that brought about by the differences in the ages at which puberty comes to the two sexes. During childhood the male is, on the whole, stronger and larger than the female. Observation of adults leads them to surmise, correctly, that the adult male is considerably larger and stronger than the adult female. Hence there is complete bewilderment and dismay for the 11 or 12-year-old boy who finds himself weaker and smaller than the 11 or 12-year-old girl. During the early middle school years boys are continually embarrassed because they are shorter, smaller, and weaker than girls, just at a time when they have convinced themselves that they are physically superior. Another complicating factor is that the interests of the two sexes diverge with this uneven development.

> With superior physical development, girls develop more mature interests than boys of their age. No longer are they satisfied with playing with other girls. Now they want more mature forms of recreation, and to be pleasurable these must be shared with boys. But, boys are not yet ready to associate with the girls.[5]

So it is not only boys who are dismayed by the changes—girls are as well. By the sixth or seventh grade this dichotomy of interests becomes very evident as boys avoid girls, while girls, extremely interested in boys, must look to more mature boys for the sharing of this newly developed interest in the opposite sex. Socio-emotional estrangement from agemates caused by uncertainty regarding onset of puberty can create severe problems for late-maturing girls.

Late-maturing boys also face problems which may be even more serious. A late-maturing boy may at first be less concerned with associations with girls, but this can become a major issue if his maturity lags for a considerable time. The late-maturing boy is faced with problems among his male peers. The same ridicule faced by the late-maturing girl becomes a little cruder when aimed at boys. Further, he is at a disadvantage in athletics since he is unable to compete with those of his own age who are maturing earlier. This disadvantage may follow him throughout his school career. Physical education teachers should pay special attention to this problem.

Late-maturing girls are at a disadvantage when other girls around them are more prepared emotionally for associations with boys. Not only is it common for them to be ridiculed by their agemates of both sexes, but they are also likely to feel some degree of insecurity in not being quite sure when this momentous change will occur within them. Tensions thus created vary from individual to individual and range from that which is barely noticeable to that which is almost unbearable for some. The tensions among youngsters of this age seeking to identify with adult sex roles are extremely important factors in emerging adolescent life in the middle school.

Restlessness

The physical changes which take place during the growth spurt and period of puberty seem to have several effects upon the emotional development of the middle school pupil. In addition to the sex-role conflicts noted above, restlessness is common to most emerging adolescents. Restlessness can be attributed to two different causes. First, the physical, hormonal, metabolic development of the human body at emerging adolescence creates a need for movement. Quiescence is an unnatural state. The more natural reaction of a middle school pupil is toward both physical and mental movement.

A second possible cause for natural restlessness is physical exhaustion. With a changing metabolic rate, energy may be diminished to a dangerous degree unnoticed by adults. The emerging adolescent, particularly when especially motivated, is more likely to work from a base of nervous energy. The motivation may be intrinsic or extrinsic, positive or negative. The end result, however, may be unhealthy if the pupil works at a rapid pace and high intensity for prolonged periods.

Hence the restlessness of emerging adolescents may be evidenced in two totally different sets of activities. First, they may be physically inattentive or even disruptive; and second, they may drive toward a goal with an unhealthy amount of intensity.

Introspection

It is during emerging adolescence that the individual first begins to look inward and view the self as an entity. Before that stage of life the child is thought to see everything only as it impinges upon his or her own field of perception. The reasons for the development of introspection are varied. The individual is moving from thinking based on concrete reality toward an ability to conceptualize. A new perception of the individual's developing physical body is taking place. New demands are being placed upon the individual by others. So during this stage of development the individual is reassessing the world and his or her place in it; and reassessment brings both improvement and problems, as does any developmental or transitional stage. Adolescent youngsters who can begin to manipulate ideas and think in terms of relationships come to an awareness of differences between what can or should be and what is. They can now see that the larger society has its foibles and follies, as do those adults whom they have been taught both explicitly and implicitly to respect. They discover that knowledge is not an Aristotelian black and white but is rather some sort of non-Aristotelian gray with wide ranges of contingencies and possibilities. Many adults, upon being questioned by adolescents concerning the reasons for their views and the rightness of these views, find this period of introspection a source of great perplexity and irritation.

This newfound ability to conceptualize leads adolescents to discover an entire range of problems, either unknown or minimized during childhood. They find problems which are actually occurring, and are able to perceive problems that might occur. While this ability leads to an expanded perception of the world, it can create a degree of trauma at its inception as adolescents find the world at large and their personal worlds full of new ideas and complexities with which they are unprepared to deal.

Thus, with the realization that the world is not the ordered universe that it appeared to be to the child, the emerging adolescent must necessarily spend an appreciable amount of time in introspection. A process of re-evaluation of the self and the environment must take place as the adolescent seeks to discover his or her place in a whole new world of perceptions.

Idealism

The newfound ability to conceptualize and idealize leads the individual to focus on the best as being possible in all situations. The fact that this "best" is not always attainable is sometimes difficult for the emerging adolescent to see due to the lack of experience to support this still untutored commitment. The emerging adolescent takes an extremely active interest in the affairs of society and his or her classmates, teachers, neighborhood, and family. This deep desire to help solve problems, combined with the lack of ability to discern whether a given effort is effective makes the idealism expressed by youth a problem for adults as well as for themselves.

Another aspect of the adolescent's bent toward idealism and seeking of solutions to problems is that the plans of emerging adolescents at times do not work out. The result is the experience of failure, as pointed out by Hurlock:

> The idealistic nature of the adolescent predisposes him to disappointments, disillusionments, and cynicism. When he discovers that his efforts to help, to bring about improvements, or to make some contribution to the group are unappreciated or even rebuffed, his attitude toward the group is likely to change to that of cynicism.[6]

The severe discomfiture created by lack of response to an individual's efforts may create a feeling of "sour grapes." A common response is retreat from the situation and return to a visionary world constructed by his or her own idealism.

Another aspect of idealism which should be noted is the "crush" that is experienced by many middle school pupils. It is compounded of idealism, need for direction, and dawning sexual attraction. Of the three elements, sexual attraction is ordinarily the least important even though girls usually form crushes on men, and boys on women. The major source of the attachment arises from the need of the emerging adolescent to view someone as an ideal. The faults of parents are often the first to be noticed, and their weaknesses deprecated by the emerging adolescents who are close to them. Because of these problems parents are for a short time to some extent replaced as models in the minds of their offspring. The youth find some other adult who is temporarily capable of meeting the rigid demands of the idealism characteristic of this stage of development. Most such attachments are relatively short-lived and rather intense, but are not usually expressed overtly in such ways as to become an embarrassment to either the adult or the adolescent.

Enthusiasm

The intense interest and enthusiasm shown by emerging adolescents results from several causative factors. The idealism mentioned above demands that youth move toward a resolution of problems. Inexperience with the real world leads them to expect a solution, which in turn encourages them to continue their quest. Physical restlessness also creates a need for immediate results. These together with a heightened emotionality create a greater than ordinary propulsion toward action and movement for emerging adolescents.

Many adults may be confused in that the enthusiasms of the emerging adolescents, whether overt or covert, are not always focused upon those aspects of development which adults consider most important. Hence the central problem in the education of emerging adolescents is not to develop motivation or enthusiasm in the pupil, but rather to rechannel or refocus the enthusiasm or motivational forces already present but not focused in directions desired by adults responsible for the growth of the individual. This enthusiasm, dynamism, and joy in living tend to make the emerging adolescent both a joy and a continuous challenge for the teacher who is charged with facilitation of healthy developmental growth for emerging adolescents.

Negative attitudes

With the fluctuations and extremes in interest and commitments coupled with attendant disappointments, there will be negative behaviors within the emerging adolescent with which responsible adults will have to deal. This relatively short period immediately precedes puberty and is characterized by feelings of stress and withdrawal of the emerging adolescent from the social group.[7] Further, the reality of the world as it impinges upon the idealism of the emerging adolescent for the first time will cause the appearance of negative behaviors. Such behaviors do not necessarily create serious disciplinary problems, however.

We contend that the emerging adolescent when viewed in a positive light and approached in an effective manner by sensitive adults can be a most delightful pupil. Admittedly, the negative behaviors found among these youngsters arising from their concerns over developmental differences, sex-role conflicts, ambivalence, restlessness, introspection, and such challenge the professional teacher. Yet their enthusiasm, idealism, and desire to mature are all positive aspects which can create a most effective learning atmosphere for teachers who are concerned with the maximum personal development of the pupils who are their responsibility.

SOCIAL PHENOMENA

All individuals are affected emotionally by their perceptions of their physical and social surroundings. Even though each person has a different social milieu, we can identify social needs which are common to emerging adolescents depending upon developmental stages. While the focus of social milieu and associations differs, Hurlock identifies the general areas crucial to the emerging adolescent.

> The young adolescent has three "social worlds," which are of about equal importance to him. The first consists of his family. Many of the social contacts for work and play are with his parents, brothers and sisters, and other relatives. The school provides the second social world for the young adolescent, while the third consists of a small closed world or intimate friendship with one or two individuals of his sex whom he regards as his "best friends" and with whom he associates in many of his activities and with whom he shares his thoughts, hopes, and worries.[8]

The small, third "world" of closed and intimate friendship is the newest area of concern to emerging adolescents. The degree to which an individual is able to accept and integrate this new set of relationships into his or her social milieu determines the future mental health of this individual. In the current American culture close personal friendships are important to all. They are crucial in the socialization process, serving to integrate the expectations and values from the three "worlds," particularly those values attendant to the development of an adolescent subculture. The search for values which can be accepted by emerging adolescents both as individuals and as a group without estranging them entirely from others in the social milieu is characteristic of this period. This particular problem is exacerbated by the plurality of the American value structure. Sebald points out, for example, a wide range of polarities and conflicts in norms and values that the American society has developed in the last few decades: (1) competition versus cooperation; (2) work versus leisure; (3) piety versus free thinking; (4) individualism versus conformity; and (5) sex versus chastity.[9]

It should not be surprising that the idealistic emerging adolescent in a search for "truth" would be confused and vexed by the ambivalent and inconsistent sets of values existent in adult society. As the emerging adolescents are unable to find a rational set of viable responses to these issues in their discussions with adults, they search increasingly among their peers for support and answers. A primary problem created by the so-called answers posed by emerging adolescents is their shallowness and oversimplification, a direct result of the lack of experience of the adolescent subculture. Hopefully this search for "answers" can continue through developmental stages to adulthood.

Four particular characteristics of the socialization process are identifiable with the emerging adolescent stage of development. They are: (1) search for independence from adults, (2) search for peer approval, (3) search for sophistication, and (4) search for correct social behavior.

These social needs of youth should serve as a focus of opportunities provided by the middle school designed to facilitate the social development of emerging adolescents.

Search for independence from adults

The development of the individual from a completely dependent infant to a relatively independent and mature adult moving in the mainstream of our culture consists of an almost continuous struggle for independence against those who, being responsible, strive to assure that he or she perform the "right" actions and remain in a dependent status. Although some parents and teachers are sensitive in the ways they assist youth to achieve independence, much opinion seems to be critical of the struggle for independence. This viewpoint is surprising since this ultimate independence is necessary for the continuance of society.

The unwillingness of adults to grant independence has created a social pressure which facilitates the development of an adolescent subculture. Youth establish not only their independence from the repression of adults, but also a degree of authority over their social inter-relationships with peers.

The social pressures on emerging adolescents considered here are indigenous to the American culture and other technologically based societies. As was noted by Margaret Mead, less technologically advanced societies do not seem to present such a dichotomy in their demands on the individual during this transition period from childhood to adulthood. In some of those societies the reaching of puberty automatically confers adult status and social maturity on the individual. But such is not the case in the United States, where dependent status is often prolonged through the college years and even on into graduate school.

Nevertheless, emerging adolescents are encouraged in an earlier maturing process by the innumerable sources of information and emotional influences daily impinging on them, such as films, television, and travel, which lessen the immediate impact of those adults closest to them. Sebald cited the effects of mobility and travel which have created serious problems and disjunctions in the lives of emerging adolescents.[10]

In order to achieve a healthy emotional and social maturity, the emerging adolescent must establish increasingly more effective levels of independence from adults. The acquisition of this attitude is, however, fraught with great emotional stress. Feelings of guilt along with a tendency to experience violent though suppressed reactions against the important adults in his or her life are present in the emerging adolescent. This need for independence on the part of the emerging adolescent may be the most misunderstood social concern in middle school education. It should not be an issue, since development of independent thought processes is a natural growth concomitant of emerging adolescence. A more appropriate question might concern the degree of independence appropriate to the emotional development of each individual during growth toward maturity.

Search for peer approval

A primary social need for almost all individuals is acceptance and approval by those with whom they associate. As the unabating struggle of adolescents for independence from adults continues, individuals look to other social contacts for the acceptance and support they need. An obvious avenue for such support is the peer culture and agemates. The effects of the interactions of various individuals within the peer group during the middle school years seem to be of utmost importance to the self-perception of the individual emerging adolescent. For school authorities this social phenomenon is not an unmixed blessing. Studies, including Coleman's *The Adolescent Society*, indicate that the primary concerns of emerging adolescents and adolescents are not necessarily congruent with those of the schools which they attend. Pressures such as those relating to college and professional goals seem to evolve primarily from the home, the family, and the school, with little real interest evidenced in them by the peer group.

For emerging adolescents the peer group is a most important source of outside feedback, thus creating a great need for group experience. One's status within the group and its status as a substructure within the larger framework of the school and the entire society make the peer culture one of the more important aspects of middle school education. Any organization, formal or informal, which compels such loyalty from the individual necessarily exerts great influence upon the educational atmosphere of the school within which it operates.

Search for sophistication

A desire for new experiences and a search for knowledge and wisdom in the ways of the world constitute overwhelming social needs for the emerging adolescent. It is heightened by extensive experiences with television, films, and other mass communications. The degree to which emerging adolescents in most middle schools have actually experienced the many phenomena about which they can talk with considerable competence has not as yet been completely established.

The advent of earlier physical development, including puberty, leads toward an increasing sophistication among emerging adolescents. The very nature of the physiological changes occurring within their bodies forces these youths to view their world with a more mature attitude. Earlier sophistication is also encouraged by the increasing ability of the emerging adolescent to conceptualize intellectually. This ability first appears for most individuals at around the period of emerging adolescence, and adds yet another dimension to the ability to relate to the more mature society, even if only by manipulating ideas mentally and visualizing in the imagination.

This fact of earlier sophistication must be recognized by the school so as to accommodate the continuing development of the emerging adolescent. The impact of this sophistication on the middle school is manifest in two relatively different aspects of the social life. First, many emerging adolescents have the impression that schools focus on childish concerns. Second, dating may become a major interest during the middle school years.

There is a dichotomy between the concerns held important by parents, patrons, administration, and faculty of middle schools and those held important by the pupils. Class work and extra-curricular activities which stress academic concerns may be less important to middle school pupils than would be considered ideal by adults. At emerging adolescence the individual begins to experience a society which is not that of the mature world and has its own set of standards, rules, and customs. While this culture is experienced within the school and impinges upon the school policies in some aspects, in other ways it is completely independent of the school goals. In other words, the purposes of the peer culture may be strongly supportive of school functions or antithetical to them.

A second example of earlier sophistication and its impact on middle school life and the development of a separate peer culture is seen in the beginning of dating by emerging adolescents. Coleman points to the recent increase in "going steady" among middle school and high school students. His contention is that this practice is not a move for sexual freedom but is, rather, a form of seeking the psychological security which is needed by adolescents in today's society.[11]

If boy-girl relationships are occurring at an ever lower age, the primary question raised for middle school is what form such activities should take. If dating is considered reprehensible for this age group—which has not been determined—then school officials and faculty should explore other activities which are better adapted to the needs of the emerging adolescent. It is the task of the school to facilitate socialization and minimize the trauma of premature knowledges. Further, the school should assist pupils to acquire the knowledges, skills, and attitudes necessary to the achievement of the sophistication needed by each individual to ensure his or her advance to the next stage of social and emotional development.

Search for correct social behavior

The process of socialization is dynamic and eventful. Both boys and girls seem to be preoccupied with those activities at school which are more social than academic in nature. Selecting their own leaders and organizing their own activities are very important to them. Adult assistance may be seen as interference rather than the well-intentioned efforts of people interested in their growth. The growth sequences between complete dependence upon adults at home or in school and the independence of working within their own peer culture can be difficult.

IMPLICATIONS FOR MIDDLE SCHOOL EDUCATION

Theories concerning the development of emerging adolescence, although numerous, generally agree on the emotional and social characteristics of the youths involved. A primary problem arises from the lack of communication between the psychologists and sociologists who have prepared the various guidelines and the practicing administrators who have instituted the programs for emerging adolescents. Few schoolwide attempts to implement various psychological and sociological guidelines have been highly successful. Those who are most critical of the junior high school have not based their arguments on the efficacy of the principles espoused for the junior high school, but rather have debated the effectiveness of the steps taken to achieve them.

The new middle school will be in no better position to achieve the goals of education with emerging adolescents than is the older junior high school unless more concern is given to implementation of those educational practices built around basic principles. In order to achieve the goals of the middle school arising from the social and emotional needs of the emerging adolescent, the following recommendations are suggested.

Encouragement of differences

Children differ more from each other at middle school ages than at any other time in their lives. Therefore the teachers of this group should have knowledge of these differences and have strategies at their disposal for dealing with a range of needs which spans the psychological aspects of childhood, preadolescence, and emerging adolescence. Consideration must also be given for the earlier maturation of girls which usually occurs during this stage and should include understanding, support, and empathy toward the trauma which is sometimes present.

Specific aspects to be considered by administrators and teachers include concerns such as the following.

1. Nervous energy can indicate at times an approaching physical exhaustion in the emerging adolescent. Therefore close attention should be given to the emotional and physical states of individuals in middle school classrooms.

2. Special attention should be given to the physical differences between boys and girls in the earlier middle school grades. At this time girls are ordinarily stronger and faster than boys, who may be considerably embarrassed to lose various athletic events consistently. Competition between the two sexes in some physical activities may be inappropriate. If present, personal attention should be accorded to the unique problems of boys.

3. Since pupils are at many different stages in their physical development competition between prepubescent and postpubescent boys may also need attention. Special groupings may have practical advantage since the distribution of recognition for general accomplishment might change.

4. Physical education classes should be composed of different groups of students depending upon their purposes. Depending upon the activities, demands, and assignments for the day, integration or segregation of the sexes, special grouping, or random order could be utilized. The requirements of the activity should govern. For example, if square dancing were the assignment, then both boys and girls would be present. The intent here is to avoid com-

petitions and groupings which consistently favor those who mature early at the expense of those who mature later.

Treatment for ambivalence

The sometimes frustrating but always disturbing phenomenon of ambivalence in the emerging adolescent should be treated with considerable caution by middle school personnel. The problem of the emerging adolescent who one minute is a little child seeking the teacher's support and who in the next minute demands treatment as an adult is one which confounds some of the best teachers. A few suggestions for alleviating the situation are included here.

1. The immature clinging child should be continually encouraged to make decisions, to live with those decisions, and to recognize their results in a realistic way. Mere encouragement, however, is not enough. In addition, the teacher will need to move the child systematically along the road toward responsible decision making. This may be an extremely difficult task inasmuch as the immature child may see this as rejection rather than as kindness or responsible action on the part of the teacher.

2. The adult must be able to accept rudeness, or even insults from the emerging adolescent who is struggling for independence. It is not intended that rudeness be condoned by the teacher without comment, nor is docile acceptance recommended. The need is for teachers and staff to see these behaviors for what they are, a striving of the youngster for a meaningful relationship both within himself and with others. Pupils must learn that rudeness is not the correct method of expression, but they will not learn this if they are faced with similarly rude and punitive expressions from teachers and staff. Acceptance of the person and the need for expression without approval of the specific rude behavior is a recommended procedure.

3. The adults working with emerging adolescents need to see themselves as human beings and to recognize their own weaknesses and strengths. When pupils recognize that adults also can be wrong, can admit it, can at times be immature, can at times even be rude, they can then develop an ego based upon a more human and acceptable model.

4. The pupil should have organized opportunities which provide for a wide range of activities, including children's games and just talking, among others, since they will permit the less mature aspects or the remaining childish side of the emerging adolescent to have an approved outlet.

5. The pupil should be allowed the opportunity to make decisions even though they may be incorrect where these are possible without great harm. The complaint of emerging adolescents that they are not allowed to assume a

mature role can be remedied by giving them these opportunities. The responsibility facing the adults working with these pupils is to determine that the decision to be made by the pupils cannot lead to traumatic experiences or be harmful to them or their classmates.

Acceptance of bodily change

The physical development of the child, whether male or female, from the immature to the sexually mature state is a crucial period in the life of everyone. Whether this change is accepted as a natural and wonderful development or as something to be dreaded depends upon many different factors, many of which are not related to the school situation. But school personnel can have a positive effect upon the attitudes of emerging adolescents by exhibiting a view of acceptance concerning the bodily changes of their pupils. Some examples of constructive attitudes which can be assumed by middle school personnel follow.

1. Pupils should come to accept the fact that sexual maturation is a normal phenomenon, one which is not only expected, but anticipated. This attitude can be expressed in many ways, but the pervasive general attitude of any adult working with the pupils is usually more effective than a series of relatively specific comments.

2. Heterosexual activities should be encouraged during this period. Parties where large groups of boys and girls are able to associate without required dating or dancing should be encouraged. Picnics and outdoor activities which not only put boys and girls into the same surroundings, but also present them with opportunities to see many members of the opposite sex fulfilling similar social functions are extremely useful.

3. Opportunities for many organized adolescent activities should be presented in the middle school. This is in addition to the opportunity for childhood activities already mentioned. Mature boys and girls should have the opportunity to begin to experience some degree of informal social activities before the closing of their middle school experiences.

4. Particularly great concern must be given to personalization of education. The degree of maturity of the boy and/or girl should be closely watched in order to aid them in achieving the appropriate degree of maturity in their relationships with the opposite sex. For example, when both boys and girls are prepubescent, childhood activities are appropriate. When girls become pubescent their activities will need to be selected for this new maturity. The fact that fewer boys in middle school will have attained sexual maturity and hence will not be prepared for the more mature activities such as are commonly

found in the high school will create some problems in middle school social activities. Actually, this may be more of a problem for the adults and parents than for the children involved. It may be parents who push for early dating and dancing. Most middle school girls seem to recognize the problems inherent within this situation and either accept them or are able to associate with older, secondary school boys.

In any case it would seem that most of the problems arising from dating and sexual adjustment in the middle school are more worrisome to the faculty of the school than to the pupils involved. This does not minimize the problem, but suggests that alleviation of the problem may best be encompassed by a more measured evaluation of the situation.

Arrangements for physical activity

Provisions should be made for continuing and flexible physical activity. Chairs and tables in flexible settings are required. Pupils should be helped to see the entire school as a setting for learning activities. Halls, laboratories, lawns, cafeterias, and such can all become important in the perception of the pupil. Spaces larger than traditional classrooms need to be arranged if possible.

Within any classroom teachers should organize a variable schedule which will encourage pupils to move actively. Study activities which require of pupils a relatively sedentary position for extended periods of time are out of step with their needs for physical activity and should be abandoned. Since attention spans at this age are short at best, all effort should be given to move rapidly from one activity to another. These different activities should, insofar as possible, be located in various portions of the room, thus permitting pupils to move around.

Emerging adolescents tend to tire easily. Activities should not require such intense physical activity as to exhaust the pupil. It is assumed that the teacher will keep a constant watch over all pupils in the class to determine whether the optimal level of physical activity is being reached. Youth at this stage of development tend to continue physical activity beyond the level of optimum efficiency. Having exhausted their reserve of physical energy, they begin to utilize nervous energy. An excess use of such emotional energy obviously can have bad results on the learning process and should be prevented by the teacher whenever possible. Such prevention presupposes a close, perceptive, and continuous analysis of the physical activities of pupils by the teacher. Physical education teachers have long been aware of this problem, and can serve as a valuable resource to the classroom teacher who asks for

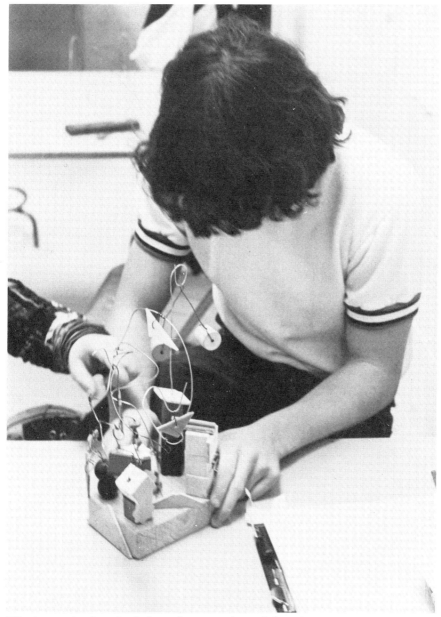

**Effectiveness in education is dependent upon dynamic learning.
Alton Farnsworth Middle School**

(Courtesy of Guilderland, New York, Central Schools)

their help. Here, as in other areas, the importance derives from the consideration of the emotional tone, even though the primary concerns may be physical in nature. The physically exhausted pupil is emotionally incapable not only of learning but of simple emotional reactions and controls which are expected under ordinary circumstances.

Encouragement of pupil independence

If one of the primary emotional and developmental needs of emerging adolescents is independence from adults, one might assume that encouragement of this process would be unnecessary. This is not the case, however. The degree to which independence is achieved, the methods by which it is achieved, the rate at which it is achieved, and the emotional effects of its achievement are all dependent to some extent upon the cooperative efforts of the middle school staff. In reality independence will not be achieved until it is not only permitted by those in authority but actively encouraged by them. The systematic efforts and procedures required in this area make it extremely difficult for the adults involved. The pupils are taught, in effect, to be less dependent and to assume direction of many of their own activities rather than conform to the wishes of those to whom they have customarily given full and immediate obedience. The problem is to make abundantly clear the areas for which the adolescent may assume responsibility.

Teacher-pupil planning and shared decision making with both verbal and nonverbal approval of independence on the part of pupils can be a good start. Because of the nature of the school setting pupils will be in a position to make some decisions for themselves. Teachers should encourage such decision making, not by a permissive attitude in which every pupil decision, no matter what its consequences, is accepted with enthusiasm, but rather where the process is encouraged, and the results are carefully and compassionately evaluated. Where there are few opportunities in any classroom for decision making, classroom-planning procedures should be revised. Decision making will occur only where meaningful decisions are necessary. In other words, the pupil must have something at stake. As previously suggested, even those decisions considered to be "wrong" should be permitted where they do not harm the pupil or the class. Those decisions should be evaluated in such a way that the pupil can learn not only from making decisions and from having responsibility for them but also from experiencing the consequences for them.

One of the major aspects of independence is the ability to see basic problems and the various elements involved in those problems. Pupils should be helped to see these and to analyze the problem with a view to exploring alternative outcomes and solutions which may be sought. Given the idealism and/or cynicism of youngsters at this stage of development, the identification of problems is not difficult. More important, however, is the requirement for pupils to determine which problems are of most importance, which ones are more amenable to solutions, and which ones can be most effectively subdivided and logically analyzed. Pupils are unlikely to identify with and learn from these procedures unless they themselves select the problem areas from their own concerns.

Pupils can gain emotional independence most effectively and rapidly when they believe that their decisions and ideas are of worth, are respected, and will have some effect upon their own future. One of the more effective methods used to develop this attitude among emerging adolescents in the middle school classroom is student involvement in curriculum development. When students have an important voice in the development of an area of study, a course, or even selection of a film to be seen, or a debate topic to be chosen, not only can their interest in the classroom work increase, but they also have the opportunity to develop a sense of responsibility for their own lives.

Two points should be made: (1) pupils will ordinarily make responsible decisions about curriculum if they are assured of the integrity of the offer to allow them to do so, and (2) their curriculum may be more difficult than that which would have been proposed for them by the teacher. In this planning effort, the teacher does not abdicate any responsibility to guide the pupils. If mutual respect prevails, pupils will seek help and advice from the teacher as needed. Also they will usually respect reasons for suggestions where they are given.

On a school-wide level various arrangements for student participation in student government provide other opportunities for the development of independence for middle school pupils. The same conditions pertaining to classroom decisions are pertinent in a student government. Student government will be effective only insofar as the administration permits it genuine responsibility and respect. This does not include the traditional student council, which served little practical function and was permitted participation in only limited ways—popularity contests, the development of school dances, and such. Today if a student council or some other form of student government is to be developed in the middle school it must be capable of dealing with issues and concerns which create an impact upon the lives of the middle school student body in ways which are meaningful to them.

Focusing of pupil enthusiasms

One of the most endearing and yet frustrating aspects of working with middle school pupils is the amount of enthusiasm which they can bring to bear upon those problems which are most important to them. It is endearing when the

**Individual study encourages independence.
Mount Hebron School**

(Courtesy of Montclair, New Jersey, Public Schools)

pupils' interest is engendered in an area toward which the teacher wishes it to be directed. It is frustrating when their enthusiasm is directed toward an aspect of their lives which is separate from or antithetical to the school culture. The middle school teacher's task is different from that of either the elementary or secondary teacher, whose primary task is to encourage enthusiasm (motivation) in their pupils. Even given the variability among emerging adolescents, where some pupils for reasons such as physical exhaustion or emotional pressure may need to be encouraged, the majority of emerging adolescents usually will be "bubbling over" with the enthusiasm which is characteristic of this age.

The primary purpose of the middle school teacher, then, should be either to develop the class lesson from the relatively ephemeral subject about which the pupils are enthusiastic (sometimes possible, sometimes not), or to focus the enthusiasm of the pupils upon the particular topic which is the subject for the day. This focusing or redirecting of enthusiasm is sometimes a difficult process, and the procedures for achieving it vary from day to day according to the topic at hand and the diverse situations which face the class on different days.

Pupil enthusiasm may be focused not only upon individual classroom work, but upon the school as a whole. The term "school spirit" covers a multitude of facets in a school setting. Pride in the school may be expressed by honoring athletes, or musicians, or performers in other special activities. All of these should be encouraged, as well as many other social activities which build pride in the school itself and in the peer culture. Another aspect of the school culture sometimes not stressed to an appropriate degree is the concern for academic excellence and the encouragement of a wide variety of academic activities.

Whether a focusing of pupil enthusiasm upon various aspects of school life, such as student government, academic achievement, athletics, or music, can actually be achieved is perhaps not the major point. Rather, the process of the faculty looking to the students and their needs, interests, and enthusiasms represents a move in the direction of the pupils having an opportunity to achieve and be responsible. Pupil enthusiasm can be encouraged only by the presentation of opportunities for it to thrive.

Appropriate emphasis on academic achievement

Academic achievement is an important part of the schoolwork of emerging adolescents. It is not the only aspect in which they are interested, nor is it necessarily the crucial aspect with which the faculty should be concerned, but the responsibility of the teacher to emphasize academic achievement should not be underestimated. The term "appropriate emphasis" is used in order to differen-

Student enthusiasm should be fostered in many ways.
Alton Farnsworth Middle School

(Courtesy of Guilderland, New York, Central Schools)

tiate degrees of emphasis on academic achievement due to individual preferences among various pupils in the school. Teachers respect intellectual ability. They also know that intellectual ability and academic achievement do not necessarily correlate on a one-to-one basis. Methods of reaching academic achievement vary according to individual students and in individual disciplines.

One of the most effective methods of improving academic achievement among emerging adolescents is reinforcement or reward. Reward may take many forms, but the teacher who accepts pupils, praises their correct answers, and compassionately corrects their incorrect responses, will ordinarily be a most effective teacher. The use of rewards as encouragement does not imply that some forms of punishment necessarily discourage.

Some research studies have indicated that placing appropriate stress upon an individual will sometimes achieve the desired academic results. However, what is stress for one pupil may not be stress for another. Some children react most effectively when placed in a situation which could be classified as stressful to them, while others do not. Both rewards and creation of stress may be utilized in the achievement of academic progress if the teacher recognizes the inherent difficulties in the stressful situation and exercises great care when utilizing stress situations. The emphasis is upon flexibility in instructional techniques which permit a choice of techniques to be utilized in differing situations with different pupils.

Many questions regarding competitive grades in schools in general and middle schools in particular have arisen. The major problem with grades as such is that they are seen by pupils as punitive and repressive. Grading is not an extremely precise operation, and it can be threatening to the ego, negatively affecting self-concept. Grades should represent a relatively imprecise evaluation which would serve as feedback to the pupils in their evaluations of their own progress. Under some circumstances the pupils might have an influential voice in the final grade to be given by the teacher, particularly in some areas of agreement. At any rate, parents, teachers, students, and others must together see evaluation and grading in a more realistic light.

Honor-roll qualifications should not be a univariate type. It is recommended that at least two aspects be considered. First, has the student performed at a level significantly above the academic norm of the group? Second, has the performance been that which could reasonably be expected of a pupil with that inherent ability? A major problem with grades and the honor roll does not seem to be inherent within the process, but rather in the attitudes and opinions which have developed around the uses of honor rolls. If pupil enthusiasm, independence, and other characteristics have been taken into consideration, the so-called problems of grading should be significantly minimized.

An appropriate emphasis on academic achievement will necessitate differing texts, materials, and experiences appropriate for the differing levels of ability found within classes. Such differentiation within the school will permit the teacher to emphasize that level of achievement which is most appropriate for each individual child, rather than expecting some level of achievement which is patently impossible for certain members of the class to achieve and which is far below the capacity of other members of the class.

Encouragement of valuing process

One of the more commonly stated purposes of education has been the development of appropriate sets of values among pupils. Within recent years, however, many dichotomies and inconsistencies in value judgments have become evident in American society. If the American culture continues its trend toward a multi-value system, children will continue to be encouraged to learn how to explore values and the valuing process rather than to accept a given set of values. These two goals are not really in conflict. In any society some values are accepted by all members of that society. These stable values should continue to be taught, possibly not as immutable, but as accepted standards of the present society.

In addition, pupils should be encouraged to explore various value positions and bases for making value judgments. They should be informed of the processes involved in making value judgments. They should learn how to evaluate the effects of such judgments. The ability to make determinations based only upon cognitive development, without having learned to consider affective or emotional aspects of judgments or how to consider value components, would put these children in a most difficult position. It is widely recognized that most decisions are not made according to logic alone, but are also based upon emotional value. Therefore the importance of developing the ability to consider valuing aspects of decisions cannot be overemphasized. The ability of individuals to withhold final judgments and tolerate differences is crucial to this area.

In order to achieve such goals it is insufficient to suggest that teachers should present such valuing opportunities to pupils. A significant part of the formal and informal curriculum must be planned to present opportunities for valuing to pupils. The present curriculum, particularly the academic aspects of it, does not seem to meet these needs to the extent advisable. Therefore the curriculum in all subject matter areas, and particularly in social studies, should be reviewed by teachers, curriculum builders, and administrators with a view toward such revision as necessary to develop a program which would encourage the process of valuing.

Utilization of group dynamics

One of the strongest needs evinced by emerging adolescents is for approval by the peer group. Meeting this need through use of group activities has been suggested as one of the more effective methods of working within a classroom setting. If the teacher can listen to pupils, determine their value systems, and then utilize those systems in both structured and unstructured approaches to the achievement of some of the purposes of the classroom, middle school education should prove more efficacious.

Informal discussions are thought to present pictures of knowledges, values, and attitudes held by pupils more clearly than can be derived from more formal classroom techniques. A teacher who is capable of guiding such discussion may prove to be much more effective with emerging adolescents than one who sets a plan and insists upon following it to the neglect of needs as perceived by class participants at any particular time. Guidance and leadership are still important. There is no place in a middle school classroom for a laissez-faire attitude. The position is rather that a structured approach tends to be dictatorial and not conducive to meeting many different needs of the students. For most pupils to learn most effectively a "give-and-take" atmosphere should pervade the classroom. This does not preclude lectures when they are appropriate, nor any other specific type of classroom teaching technique. Rather, it refers to the general atmosphere of openness and climate in which these techniques must take place.

The material taught by teachers is not necessarily the material learned by pupils. Perceived learnings are the important outcome in any classroom. The problem raised by this observation is that due to the idiosyncratic nature of the individual emerging adolescent, each will perceive the class experience in a slightly different light. For this reason group work becomes extremely important in that it permits pupils to help each other, and permits the teacher to observe which students have learned what aspects of that which is considered important. Without such feedback the teacher must resort to various testing devices with their implicit threat. With the utilization of group processes, however, the perceptive teacher should be in a position to understand the rate and depth of learning achieved by the learners in the class.

The utilization of group dynamics permits and encourages more varied teaching techniques on the part of the teacher. If a particular teaching process is not effective on a certain day, the teacher should be sufficiently flexible to shift technique and reorder objectives in order to achieve the best learning environment for that day. The informality of the group process permits the teacher to obtain reactions from pupils and provides a less structured learning situation.

Encouragement of the development of social activities

"Learning should be fun." This statement has been used many times in many different ways. Learning can be enjoyable for most emerging adolescents. Most of them want to learn. Most of those who feel that school is not enjoyable base their reactions on the formality of the process. Learning can take place in more informal settings and still be effective. It is more difficult for the teacher to achieve systematic progress with an informal class, but many do and report that it is well worth any difficulties experienced.

For children to become mature adults in a social world they must learn how to conduct themselves as emerging adolescents in the social world in which they find themselves, i.e., the middle school. This socialization process can take place in many different ways. Extracurricular and exploratory activities should be encouraged in the middle school, with emphasis placed upon pupil participation, pupil election, and pupil leadership. Adult guidance is ordinarily necessary at this age, but development of social leadership should be a goal for as many emerging adolescents as possible. This can be achieved by clubs, with pupils taking responsibility for their activities to as great a degree as is possible at their age. Although apathy is one of the first signs of problems both to the individual and to the school, participation cannot be forced. With encouragement many pupils will participate in activities programs which are sponsored, supported, and led by members of their peer group.

A number of different types of classroom leadership can be encouraged. Peer teaching is an effective method for students to learn not only cognitive skills, but affective ones as well. A pupil who teaches a fellow pupil must learn the arts of discretion, communication, and probably humaneness. The person receiving assistance must learn to cooperate with others, and will appreciate learning, in ways not evident in other relationships.

Learning can occur in any setting—in the classroom, a school hall, an office, the playground, and the community as a whole. All can be settings for learning. The more socially gregarious the pupil can become, and the more flexible the school can become in arranging learning activities in many and varied environments, the more effective learning will probably prove to be. The degree to which varied learnings in varied settings will be supported or designed will be determined by the success of school officials in recognizing and dealing with the wide variety of learnings which occur throughout the waking hours of the pupils, whether they are inside or outside the school walls.

Utilization of group guidance

Emerging adolescents often need emotional support. They may be quite willing to ask for this help, although other cultural pressures may at times make them unwilling to accept the assistance when it is actually given. The expression of a desire for help should be encouraged at all times even though this is a difficult process. The human reaction may be to reject a second plea for assistance if the first help offered was rejected. The communication line between the emerging adolescent and the middle school staff should remain open regardless of the circumstances. The open communications becomes the responsibility of the teacher, since the emerging adolescent group has not developed to a stage of maturity able to recognize such a necessity.

Middle school pupils are intensely interested in the maturation process. They are inundated with new problems of interpersonal relationships, both within their own sex group and with members of the opposite sex. These problems can be alleviated if group guidance can supplement the important one-to-one relationships between teachers and pupils. The organizational framework for such group guidance may not be as important as the continued presence of such guidance. A homeroom can be effective, as can a special period set aside for this activity. The important justification for group guidance is that it meets the personal emotional and social needs of emerging adolescents as a group.

Individual problems of a more intense emotional or social nature cannot be met through the organization of group-guidance settings. The purpose of group guidance is, rather, to help pupils cope with the pervasive problems which they all perceive in their development as emerging adolescents.

The time set aside for such group guidance can be established on a regular or irregular schedule depending upon the specific needs of the group at any particular time. A general structure may be established over the entire school year based upon known recurring problems of emerging adolescents projected by psychologists and sociologists who have worked with this age group. Any particular structure or schedule should be extremely flexible so that problems perceived by pupils take priority. Only where pupils seem unwilling to present problems for discussion should any particular structure be utilized as an alternative procedure. It is assumed that the more flexible the leadership in the group-guidance situation, the more effective the learning process can be. Responsiveness to perceived needs of emerging adolescents is a requirement for success.

REFERENCES

1. Margaret Mead, "Early Adolescence in the United States," *NASSP Bulletin* 49:300 (April 1965), p. 10.

2. Roland C. Faunce and Morrel J. Clute, *Teaching and Learning in the Junior High School* (Belmont, Calif.: Wadsworth, 1961), p. 30.

3. Harold E. Jones, "The Adolescent Growth Study," *Journal of Consulting Psychology* III (1939): 157–159, 177–180.

4. Elizabeth B. Hurlock, *Adolescent Development*, 2d. ed. (New York: McGraw-Hill, 1955), p. 115.

5. From *Adolescent Development* by Elizabeth Hurlock. Copyright © 1955 by McGraw-Hill, Inc. Used with permission of McGraw-Hill Book Co., p. 59.

6. From *Adolescent Development* by Elizabeth Hurlock. Copyright © 1955 by McGraw-Hill, Inc. Used with permission of McGraw-Hill Book Co., p. 114.

7. Hurlock, *Adolescent Development*, p. 63.

8. From *Adolescent Development* by Elizabeth Hurlock. Copyright © 1955 by McGraw-Hill, Inc. Used with permission of McGraw-Hill Book Co., p. 107.

9. Hans Sebald, *Adolescence: A Sociological Analysis* (New York: Appleton-Century-Crofts, 1968), pp. 145–150.

10. Ibid., pp. 44.

11. James S. Coleman, "Social Change: Impact on the Adolescent," *Bulletin of the National Association of Secondary-School Principals* (April 1965), p. 12.

RELATED READINGS

Cohen, Elizabeth G. "Sociology and the Classroom: Setting the Conditions for Teacher-Student Interaction," *Review of Educational Research*, vol. 42, no. 4, Fall, 1972, pp. 441–452.

Coleman, James S. *The Adolescent Society*. New York: Free Press of Glencoe, 1961.

Coleman, James S. "How Do the Young Become Adults," *RER* vol. 42, no. 4, Fall, 1972, pp. 431–439.

Davitz, Joel R. *The Language of Emotion*. New York: Academic Press, 1969.

DeCocco, John P., comp. *The Regeneration of the School: Readings in Educational Psychology, Sociology, and Politics*. New York: Holt, 1972.

Douvan, Elizabeth A., and Adelson, Joseph. *The Adolescent Experience*. New York: Wiley, 1966.

Erikson, Erik H. *Identity, Youth and Crisis*. New York: Norton, 1968.

Gordon, C. Wayne, ed. "Uses of the Sociology of Education." In *The Seventy-Third Yearbook of the National Society for the Study of Education—Part II*. Chicago: University of Chicago Press, 1974.

Havighurst, Robert J., et al. *Adolescent Character and Personality*. New York: Science Editions, 1963.

Sebald, Hans. *Adolescence: A Sociological Analysis*. New York: Appleton-Century-Crofts, 1968.

Vorrath, Harry H., and Brendtro, Larry K. *Positive Peer Culture*. Chicago: Aldine, 1974.

Wattenberg, William W. *The Adolescent Years*. New York: Harcourt, Brace, 1955.

CHAPTER 4

Intellectual Development in Emerging Adolescence

Although research on intellectual development has not reached the theoretical stages of other areas of study in emerging adolescent development, two major theories which have implications for middle school programs can be delineated. Cognitive-process development as explicated by Piaget will be explored at some length, along with the mental plateau-spurt theory articulated by such theorists as Cornell and Armstrong. While some debate still exists among theorists concerning the correlation between physical and intellectual development, the existing correlation seems to support the need for further study.

Inhelder and Piaget, in *The Growth of Logical Thinking from Childhood to Adolescence,,* set forth a point of view based upon extensive research.

> ...even though the appearance of formal thought is not a direct consequence of puberty, could we not say that it is a manifestation of cerebral transformation due to the maturation of the nervous system and that those changes do have a relation, direct or indirect, with puberty? Given that in our society the 7-8-year-old child (with very rare exceptions) cannot handle the structures which the 14-15-year-old adolescent can handle easily, the reason must be that the child does not possess a certain number of coordinations whose dates of development are determined by stages of maturation....For these reasons, it seems clear that the development of formal structures in adolescence is linked to maturation of cerebral structures.[1]

Specific attention will be given to the period identified by Piaget as operational thought, with particular emphasis upon concrete and abstract formal operations. In the review of the theories of Piaget note will be taken of the affective correlates and the environmental factors which he thought influenced cognitive development. This section will also present data from research studies suggesting the probability of an intellectual plateau just prior to puberty. These data show that a mental spurt correlates with the physical changes at puberty. Implications of these theories and studies will be considered for application in a middle school.

DEVELOPMENTAL COGNITIVE GROWTH

The most thorough and painstaking study of the development of cognitive functions has been conducted at Geneva, Switzerland, under the general supervision of Jean Piaget. The written work of this scholar describes intellectual functions as they develop at various age levels. It uses a clinical approach which focuses on the mental operations that occur as individuals observe a number of phenomena and are asked to account for them. Most of the attention of the research team has been devoted to exploring the questions regarding developmental stages and the capability of children at various ages to deal adequately with common problems. They have studied individuals under close supervision rather than putting tests to large groups of subjects where data are manipulated through statistical treatments of large numbers. The theories of Piaget are based on assumptions and data which seem to run counter to those of many stimulus-response-reinforcement theorists. In the foreword of *Piaget and Knowledge*, Hans Furth presents Piaget's basic assumption.

> Biology imposes profound modifications upon a stimulus-response model, notwithstanding the great number of psychologists who do not see the relevance of these points. In fact, a response is a biological reaction, and contemporary biology has demonstrated that the reaction cannot be determined merely by outside factors but depends on "reaction norms" which are characteristic for each genotype or each genetic pool. This fact implies an indissociable interaction between interior structures and the stimulations of the external environment.[2]

Piaget's training was in biology, and in his studies in development and learning this training is evidenced. Further, his devotion to natural science and scientific method are clear in his laboratory study. Many other researchers have taken Piaget's findings and are testing them in cross-cultural studies, in clinical and laboratory situations, and in classrooms throughout the western world.

Stages of cognitive development

Piaget has developed a theory to encompass stages of development, i.e., periods during which the state of equilibrium of schemata change radically in a short period of time. According to this theory a child functions in equilibrium with a certain set of schemata for a relatively long period of time, and then experiences a shift to a qualitatively different stage of cognitive structuring within a brief period. In his book *The Psychology of Intelligence* (1963) he outlined these stages of cognitive development as follows:

1. The stage of sensori-motor intelligence (0–2 years of age)—During this period behavior is primarily motor with an inability to conceptualize although some intellectual development is observable.
2. The stage of preoperational thought (2–7 years of age)—The development of verbal ability with expanding conceptual ability is characteristic of this period.
3. The stage of concrete operations (7–11 years of age)—The ability to think in a logical way to achieve the solution of problems of a concrete nature first occurs during this period.
4. The stage of formal operations (11–15 years of age)—Logical thought now may be applied to problems. The manipulation of ideas with a variety of projected possibilities beyond observed reality can occur. Maximal qualitative cognitive ability of the individual appears during this period.[3]

In the stage-development theory Piaget does not imply that any particular stage *should* occur at a particular age. He only reports the results of his observations which indicate the ages at which children might most normally be expected to achieve each of the stages. Various factors affect the ages at which different individuals might achieve the passage from one stage to another. The possibilities inherent within the biologically based theories of Piaget are particularly interesting when placed in juxtaposition with other aspects of development. For example, the age of 11 years is approximately the age at which early-maturing girls first begin to reach the stage of puberty with its attendant hormonal and neural changes. The possibility of a causal relationship between these changes and the emergence of the more advanced stages of cognitive functioning is strongly supported.

Factors involved in transition

No stage identified by Piaget can necessarily be equated with specific ages. Certain age ranges, for example, can be identified with sensori-motor opera-

tions, but these ranges are presented as generally possible rather than as absolutes. Flavell emphasizes this point:

> Thus, Piaget readily admits that all manner of variables may affect the
> chronological age at which a given stage of functioning is dominant in a
> given child: intelligence, previous experience, the culture in which the
> child lives, etc. For this reason, he cautions against an overliteral iden-
> tification of *stage* with *age* and asserts that his own findings give rough
> estimates at best of the mean ages at which various stages are achieved in
> the cultural milieu from which his subjects were drawn.[4]

Piaget, writing for the *Journal of Educational Psychology* in 1961, outlined four broad factors related to trans-stage movement in cognitive development: (1) maturation, (2) physical experience, (3) social interaction, and (4) a
general progression of equilibrium.[5] Piaget accounts for maturation as a
growth of brain tissue and a development of the endrocrine system. Although
he minimizes puberty as the causative factor in this development, a correlation
with physical growth, particularly the hormonal-balance aspects, seems to
exist.

A second element in cognitive development listed by Piaget is physical experience in the life of an individual. The tactile operations conducted in regard
to both objects and stimuli in the environment form most important impressions upon the child. As adaptation becomes more sophisticated the child is increasingly able to verbalize and symbolize the environment, replacing the earlier direct manipulation. The basic schemata developed by the child cannot be
expanded nor revised without the physical experience in the environment
which provides for or creates adaptive forces.

A third element in cognitive development is social interaction. This does
not imply socio-emotional values and attitudes, but rather the interactions or
transactions in the environment which impinge upon the cognitive schemata of
the individual. While many objects and concepts can be physically defined and
accounted for, others cannot. Many are dependent upon social meaning, with
the child learning of these through interactions within the culture. Values and
attitudes are not developed nor even created through arbitrary determinations
and indirect means imposed upon the individual by the environment and culture in which he or she is located.

At times physical reality and social demands conflict. In Piaget's construction of critical factors in cognitive development he considers the resolution of such basic conflicts in terms of equilibration. This equilibration is the
unconscious act of the mind in weighing and resolving various conflicts stem-
ming from disequilibrium, searching for a fit within schemata (assimilation),

or developing new schemata (accommodation) all affected by maturation level, physical experience, and social interaction.

Cognitive growth at preadolescence

Ages of pupils attending middle schools may vary from 10 to 15 years. According to the cognitive-development stages of Piaget, the young in such schools would exhibit characteristics of both the latter stages of concrete thought and the earlier stages of abstract thought in their logical thinking processes. Almost all children at the ages of 10 or 11, enrolled in grades 5 and 6, would be functioning at the concrete-level stage of logical operations. Piaget has characterized such operations in the following way: "...concrete logical operations are actions performed on objects to bring them together into classes of various orders or to establish relations between them."[6]

Hence the preadolescent child would be able to classify, thus subsuming various individual objects under various classes. Where an object might not fit into a known, the child could establish a new class or a new relationship between these new objects and the available classes. Logic becomes preeminent at this stage, with the child utilizing this ability rather than the perception depended upon in the preoperational stage of development. Since much cataloging is taking place within the logical mind of the preadolescent child less egocentrism is evidenced here than either earlier or later in the youngster's cognitive development.

During the stage of concrete operations the child is able to establish an elementary type of stable intellectual equilibrium which had not been so much in evidence prior to this time. This level of logical development permits the preadolescent to see situations in life as having antecedents and as results of transformations rather than being static. The preadolescent further is able to understand that the transformations are reversible, and is able to think in terms of extensions from actual toward potential possibilities. He or she is able to arrange a class in such a way that a future object of thought might be subsumed under it.[7]

Another form or style of operation which comes to fruition in the preadolescent period is seriation. The seriation operation can be considered as a complement to classification. Seriation involves the ability to arrange objects logically without actually seeing them. The ability to arrange elements according to larger or smaller size is limited at best during the period of preoperational thought, and develops in a piecemeal manner during the period of concrete operations. Length seems to be a first element considered as amenable to seriation by the child, usually occurring around age 7. Weight usually comes into consideration around age 9 and the concept of volume occurs during the age of preadolescence, approximately around age 12. A child in the pre-concrete stage would actually have to see objects of differing size in order to discriminate differences between them, whereas an emerging adolescent, having passed into the period of concrete operations, can logically hypothesize some of the differences through a mental ordering of elements.

Throughout the attempts of preadolescents to orient themselves cognitively to a new equilibrium are found the efforts to catalogue the world about them in a logical way with symbols rather than through the translation of actual qualities available through an individual's perceptions. Inhelder and Piaget have said:

> . . .at the concrete level, the child does not formulate any hypotheses. He begins by acting; although in the course of his action he tries to coordinate the sequence of recordings of the results he obtains, he structures only the reality on which he acts.[8]

The fundamental logical operations found as youngsters enter the middle school can thus be distinguished as having passed through stages of mental development leading to a period in which they are able to organize their surroundings mentally and logically, independent to some extent of actual sensory perceptions to which they were bound during the earlier elementary years.

Cognitive growth in early adolescence

According to the developmental cognitive theories of Piaget the intellectual capabilities of the individual shift in logical operations from more concrete analyses to abstract analyses. The logical operations which can be conducted by the emerging adolescent passing through the pubertal period are qualitatively different from those of the preadolescent. From the classification activities so characteristic of the later elementary school child and the preadolescent child a shift is found in the sixth or seventh grade of the middle schools to a concern with "as if" thinking, hypothesizing, and consideration of wide ranges of possibilities. Inhelder and Piaget noted this change from concern with reality to the thinking about probability characteristic of abstract thought.

> . . .instead of deriving a rudimentary type of theory from the empirical data as is done in concrete influences, formal thought begins with a

theoretical synthesis implying that certain relations are necessary and thus proceeds in the opposite direction.[9]

Thus a whole new world opens to the mentality of the emerging adolescent who can now extend his or her mental world through projecting possibilities, alternative paths and values, and seeing possible implications deriving from them. This ability is amorphous at the beginning of this stage of abstract thought, leading to a degree of serious questioning on the part of the pupil in both intellectual and socio-emotional fields. Elkind, a student of Piagetian theory, listed three general characteristics of adolescent thought: ability to work in combinatorial logic, ability to work with a set of symbols, and ability to work with contrary-to-fact premises.[10] The ability to conduct combinatorial analysis is a primary property of logical abstract operations in Piaget's theoretical framework. This analysis is characterized by a systematic isolation of all individual variables in a problem, but, in addition, all possible combinations of those variables can be isolated for investigation. This particular ability is one which appears in the thinking of emerging adolescents, but not in the concrete logical operations of the preadolescent child.

The development of this structural framework for hypothetico-deductive operations serves as the culmination of qualitative schemata development. This does not imply that pupils are capable of their best cognitive effort at this age. It does indicate that the structure for thought is considered to be complete as a set of capabilities available for use, with further improvement in intellectual efforts based on additional experience rather than qualitative changes in the cognitive operational abilities themselves.

Affective correlates

Piagetian research and theory considers affective development as a concomitant to the schemata of formal abstract operations discussed in the last section. Piaget includes social development, idealism, and egocentrism as phenomena to be included within the framework of his general theories. He points to emotions as furnishing the energy for behaviors although the structure of those behaviors is seen as a part of the cognitive domain.

Social development is seen as one major factor in the change of formal operations from concrete to abstract. The cause-and-effect relationship is not yet clear. There is some evidence that in more sophisticated societies pupils achieve logical abstract operations at earlier ages than they do in less sophisticated cultures. Whether this is the result of more complex acculturation processes, formal education, or other factors cannot be clearly delineated at this point.

Other questions complicate our further understanding of sources of variability in the thinking operations noted between late preadolescents and early adolescents. Such factors as the complexity of the culture in which the school is located, and differences which may exist between urban-suburban, and/or rural cultures within our society may require considerable study before the source of variance may be clearly identified. International studies of cultural differences may also indicate sources of differences. The degrees of variability in intellectual development found among emerging adolescents may be increased by cultural influences upon middle school pupils. Other factors known to affect the development and effective use of cognitive abilities are the degree to which persons can accept the society in which they find themselves, their perceptions of their roles in that society, and the sophistication with which they view their physical surroundings. These are known to affect their ability to apply their energies and direct their efforts toward success in the intellectual endeavors required in schooling.

Idealism is a second basic concern of the emerging adolescent. Research conducted by Piaget indicates that ideals as such are rarely manifest in elementary school children. The development of formal abstract thought in the emerging adolescent brings the ability to conceptualize possibilities beyond the immediate observed reality, and to visualize alternatives. The emerging adolescent can apply criteria projecting higher degrees of perfection as possibilities. This newfound ability to conceptualize possibilities opens the door to see ideal solutions to problems. No longer limited to a simple cataloging of present solutions, the emerging adolescent experiences a new conscientiousness of social sensibilities and begins to express notions of humanity, social justice, freedom of conscience, civic or intellectual courage, and others.[11]

These expressions of idealism are very strong. If they are met with resistance or lack of understanding a dichotomy may be created for middle school pupils. Where a faculty does not recognize and understand the basis for this idealism and how to utilize its positive aspects, feelings of rejection or cynicism, a polar opposite of idealism, may be engendered.

A third aspect of the adolescent's newly developed ability to cognize on an abstract level is egocentrism. As the emerging adolescent gains in the ability to see possibilities and to generate alternative solutions and future consequences he or she sees these solutions as entirely logical and possible as an almost absolute. In an attempt to reshape reality, any lack of knowledge of the practical obstacles facing such proposals is discounted, even belittled as inconsequential.

This lack of congruence between the thought processes of the emerging adolescent and social realities creates many problems for the youngster. Not one of the least of these is cognitive conceit, a concept articulated by David

Elkind.[12] The emerging adolescent assumes that the solutions to some of the problems faced by society are relatively simple and clearcut. Solutions are equally obvious. Since adults do not solve these problems to which solutions seem so simple the emerging adolescent sees adults and their world as bumbling and devoid of motivations to improve the situation and sees the self as an extremely clever individual who has more ingenuity and who can re-model the world almost single-handedly. While this phase of the emerging adolescent's development does not create a serious imbalance in the emotions or ultimate character of the youngster, it does create problems that subject the adult world in the home, at school, and in the community to a period of in-tense questioning, and for the faculty of the middle school a period of relative lack of respect for their opinions and solutions in many areas.

According to Elkind egocentrism can have both positive and negative connotations.[13] Idealism as a quality is positive. The egocentrism which develops from it is seen as negative in emerging adolescents who are very con-cerned with themselves and their ideas and may tend to exclude the opinions, thoughts, and perceptions of others. The emerging adolescents see themselves at the center of the stage. Many times an individual is reacting not as a member of a class of many individuals but as the "hero" of his or her own drama. Al-though adolescents are often self-critical, they are also self-admiring with much of their intellectual time spent in introspection. Elkind points out that gatherings of young adolescents are unique since each person is acting simul-taneously as an actor in his or her own view, while at the same time being an audience for the rest of the individuals in the group. An adult viewing this situ-ation would probably characterize emerging adolescent reactions as unnatural or overdrawn.

Environmental factors

Three major environmental factors impinge upon the cognitive development of emerging adolescents. These three are the home, the culture of the society, and the school. The interaction of the intellectual demands placed upon the individual by the particular environment determines to a great extent the cog-nitive development of each individual. For example, the cognitive develop-ment of a naive native of Samoa would not be as sophisticated as that of an emerging adolescent in a suburb of a large American city.

Expectations and early perceptual stimulation leading to intellectual de-velopment which are provided in the home have considerable effect upon the level of cognitive development attained by an emerging adolescent. A home where expectations are low or absent and which displays a low level of cog-nitive sophistication creates a background of cognitive simplicity which hampers the pupil in his or her outward movement and perceptions of the world. An emotional appeal for better academic results from a family member may be sufficient to create the internal motivation and provide the intrinsic reward which is implicit and essential for the most effective learning. In addition the family setting may provide additional opportunities for the pupil to utilize his or her newfound cognitive abilities. Where the home values and general intellectual atmosphere are at variance with school goals, the pupil is placed in a position of continuous conflict in the home.

As emerging adolescents move outward toward the peer culture of their classmates both within the school and outside school walls, the demands of that culture upon them expand. A significant portion of the time of middle school pupils is consumed in activities outside the school. These activities will either reinforce, be neutral to, or negate the ideals and goals set by the school culture. The degree to which their peers and others with whom they come in contact outside school hold goals which are in conflict or coincide with the intellectual goals of the school also influences the motivation toward cognitive development of middle school pupils.

The school as a supporting environment and a societal force affects the cognitive development of emerging adolescents. The general atmosphere or climate of the school can either encourage or discourage intellectual effort according to school philosophy. Depending upon the philosophical rationales developed either explicitly or implicitly by the managing establishment, various school districts and different school buildings have varied intellectual emphases. For example, the development of abstract thinking and formal logic is dependent upon organized and systematic efforts. In many schools the major effort of the program and instruction is the accumulation of academic content. The implicit assumption is that such content is the goal of the school. Within the context of the philosophy of the middle school such academic content is seen as the necessary vehicle for the development of the tools of disciplined logical operations with which to achieve the goals of cognitive development.

The importance of the school as an environmental influence upon the development of the intellectual ability can be related to the Piagetian characterization of the child as a cognitive alien. Elkind[14] points out that Piaget sees the child as a person who thinks differently from adults and resembles the person from a foreign country speaking a different language alien to the society. In this respect the child's cognitive processes are alien to the cognitive operations of the adult, and the more mature abilities are achieved by the child only toward the end of the middle school years.

The major concern of a teacher of emerging adolescents might seem to be the determination of an effective language with which to communicate with the youth at this stage of cognitive development. Secondly, the need for flexibility and adaptability to each individual, with the expectation of rapid and sudden changes within and among individuals, is a continuing one. The degree of ambiguity and tolerance for instability and extremes as exhibited in the behavior of emerging adolescents require meticulous care and careful responses to these children, so the positive attributes and characteristics specific to this age can be amplified and encouraged.

FACTORS IN COGNITIVE DEVELOPMENT DURING EMERGING ADOLESCENCE

Controversy has continued for decades over the degree to which physiological and cognitive maturation are correlated. This debate is of particular importance to students of emerging adolescent education. Many developmental psychologists agree that physical and intellectual development seem to unfold in relatively parallel paths except during the age at puberty. Here the debate becomes heated.

Earlier studies and statements dating from 1920 to 1950 generally support the correlation, whereas statements in the 1950s generally oppose such a position. Reports of research from Europe conducted during the 1960s have tended to refocus the issue, showing a strong tendency to support a strong correlation between physiological and intellectual growth. Tanner presented data on both sides of the debate suggesting that in some particular areas a growth spurt might occur at adolescence.[15]

At approximately the same time Heinonen[16] in Scandinavia conducted a research study on the same problem and found the occurrence of a mental spurt, particularly in girls, with the tendency toward a plateau before that sudden growth. He also found the expected difference between the sexes in mental growth and some difference in maturation between differing intellectual functions. Further research published by Ljung in 1965 was summarized.

> Much evidence has been forthcoming in support of the assumption that an adolescent spurt in mental growth occurs in girls. It seems rather uncertain whether such a spurt occurs in boys, but some findings suggest that this is so; in any case, the spurt in boys is much less significant than in girls. . . . The period immediately before the spurt is characterized by comparatively slow growth, and it seems as if a tendency towards the formation of a plateau is present during this phase of development.[17]

An analysis of the Harvard growth data conducted by Cornell and Armstrong in 1955 was concerned with the degree of patterning of mental growth in individuals.[18] They were unable to find any single pattern of mental growth. They did, however, locate what seemed to be a plateau immediately prior to pubescence. Their findings were based upon data compiled from 1922 to 1934 concerning the mental ages from two group I.Q. tests administered each year for 12 consecutive years to 1500 individuals. The purpose of the original study was to afford a basis for the determination of the percentage of development accrued at various ages from six or seven on to maturity. Figures 4-1 and 4-2 show the general results of two mental-growth patterns of the Cornell and Armstrong analysis. There seems to be a period of a mental plateau between the ages of 11 and 13 for girls and 13 and 15 for boys with a subsequent spurt in the next few years with the expected growth spurt occurring two years earlier in females than males.

The combination of the mental plateau-spurt as indicated in several studies combined with prior findings concerning the effect of puberty in intellectual development of children of similar ages would seem to indicate that the original hypothesis of strong correlation between physiological and cognitive development is substantiated by a series of current research studies.

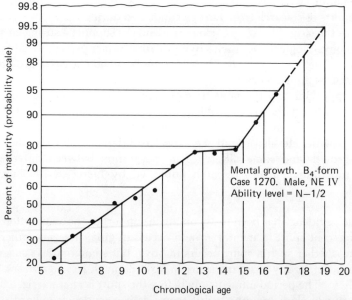

Fig. 4-1. Mental growth plotted as percent of maturity. B_4—form of mental growth pattern. (From Ethel L. Cornell and Charles M. Armstrong, "Forms of Mental Growth Patterns Revealed by Reanalysis of the Harvard Growth Data," *Child Development*, vol. 26, no. 3, Sept. 1955, p. 176, © Society for Research in Child Development, Inc. Used with permission.)

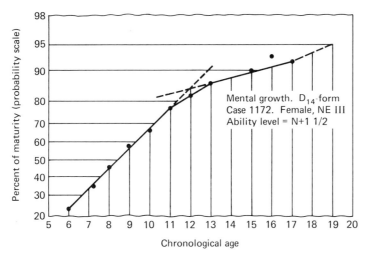

Fig. 4–2. Mental growth plotted as percent of maturity. D_{14}—form of mental growth pattern. (From Ethel L. Cornell and Charles M. Armstrong, "Forms of Mental Growth Patterns Revealed by Reanalysis of the Harvard Growth Data," *Child Development*, vol. 26, no. 3, Sept. 1955, p. 176, © Society for Research in Child Development, Inc. Used with permission.)

Thus, further substantiation may be derived from the findings of both the Ljung and Cornell and Armstrong studies that the mental-growth spurt seems to occur a year earlier for girls than for boys. Present data support the following points:

1. Some degree of correlation between physiological and intellectual development seems present.
2. This correlation is indicated since postmenarcheal girls tend to score higher on group intelligence tests than premenarcheal girls of the same age. The same seems to be true of postpubertal and prepubertal boys.
3. The earlier mental-growth spurt on the part of girls would seem to correlate with their earlier physiological development toward puberty.

Explanations other than the mental plateau-growth spurt theory are, of course, possible. The sampling of the population might be faulty; ineffective statistical devices might have been utilized; evaluating measurements might have been ineffective; various environmental factors may have masked some variables—all are possibilities. If, however, the results of this research are to be applied effectively in middle school education, some of the conclusions reached by Cornell and Armstrong seem appropriate:

*Chronological age is not an adequate basis for assigning the grade level....*If the patterns of mental growth vary as suggested by this analysis of the Harvard growth data, then not only the emotional and physical needs of adolescence need to be provided for at the appropriate time for different individuals, but also *adolescent changes in the pattern of intellectual maturation demand consideration....*The question of *whether the gap between the end of the childhood cycle of mental growth and the adolescent cycle,* marked by a period of no mental growth in early adolescence....*is an inherent phenomenon of certain patterns of mental growth or is the result of the kind of school curriculum provided should also be further explored....*If it is an inherent phenomenon of growth, then those who develop according to patterns of this type must undergo a period of exceptional stress and strain....If it is...the result of certain types of experience, then the school program for at least half of the school population does not provide adequate experience....If early secondary education is intended to meet the needs of young adolescents, *it would seem logical to classify pupils by their growth patterns rather than by chronological age.*[19]

Two different theories have been explicated in this chapter which seem to have little relation to each other. Piaget's work represents an attempt to create a framework to account for cognitive development. The mental plateau-growth spurt theory, on the other hand, is intended to record observations concerning a certain phenomenon, correlation between physiological and intellectual development. If one closely examines the two positions, however, a strong relationship does appear. In Piaget's theory, a period of disequilibrium is evident between the last substage of concrete operational thought and the beginnings of abstract operational thought which seems to occur at or around the age of puberty. During the first stage of abstract operations the pupil is not able to perform operations and comprehend logic which is possible later. This temporary disequilibrium may well relate to the mental-plateau phenomenon observed by many researchers.

IMPLICATIONS FOR MIDDLE SCHOOL EDUCATION

Many implications are inherent in the framework of the present knowledge concerning cognitive development during the period of emerging adolescence. Personalization with emphasis on individual development is particularly appropriate at this stage of development. In considering the developmental theory of Piaget, it should be noted that the middle school would be responsible for a number of aspects in the cognitive growth of individual pupils.

Some pupils are functioning in the later concrete operational stages, others in the earlier abstract operational areas, and still others at various points between. Depending upon specific operations and demands of content areas, some may at times be working in one, at other times working in the other.

Any pupils who may be working at the concrete operational stage should not be asked to conduct logical operations on the abstract level until they have achieved the developmental capability to do so. If placed in a position of expected performance without the prerequisite tools, they are in danger of being labeled as below-average and/or underachievers, when in reality the teacher is expecting from them something which they are as yet physiologically incapable of fulfilling. The obverse of this problem is found in cases where early-maturing sixth-grade pupils may be quite capable of dealing with abstract operations, but can be bored by an intellectual environment pitched primarily at the concrete level.

The *emphasis upon learning skills* is a most important aspect of the program and intellectual environment in the middle school. Since the emerging adolescent's ability to work with logical possibilities reaches its ultimate level toward the end of the emerging adolescent period, the individual needs to develop the ability to utilize those learning operations and, particularly, to develop the capability to perform abstract logical operations. What is needed is instruction which not only focuses on the processes, but also relates appropriate content areas to these operations. Either without the other can make school learning meaningless and limited in use in later life.

The middle school should place an *emphasis upon many modes of learning.* Pupils should learn how to do "either/or" thinking. They should also be required to utilize multi-valued logic, where many alternatives and possibilities must be considered. They should learn not only content but also the skills of using that content. They should learn listening as an aid to learning, but they should also develop the art of discussion. Learning occurs in many ways and in many places. Logical operations may be experienced in many forms and in many discussions of problems in a complex society. The task of the pupils, and thus the task of the teacher in helping the pupils, is to develop many different modes of learning and of communicating that learning.

The *development of a teaching vocabulary appropriate to the learner* is an important part of the task of every faculty member. Elementary school teachers are familiar with this necessity and connect the concept-formation task with the development of appropriate language symbols and syntax for handling concepts. Secondary school teachers are responsible for developing a specialized and subject-centered vocabulary. In the middle school environment the utilization of an adult vocabulary may be inappropriate. Difficulty arises where those pupils who are most advanced in logical abstract operations

Thinking assumes many forms in an effective school setting.
Iroquois Middle School

(Courtesy of Niskayuna, New York, Central School District)

can learn and use a more comprehensive vocabulary than pupils still working
in the concrete realm. Thus the teacher who lectures to a middle school class
using adult language modes to any great extent can bore some significant percentage of the class and yet may, with exactly the same language, bewilder
another significant portion of the class. Not only will the intellectual differences in individuals cause difficulty, but so also will the cognitive developmental differences. The *egocentrism* which causes emerging adolescents to see
themselves as being in the center of the stage, adults as "idols with feet of
clay," and the society as unable to achieve those things which their ideals tell
them are so easy to accomplish, is disturbing to them because they are unable
to understand why matters do not progress as they think they should. The faculty and staff must recognize and empathize with these characteristics in emerging adolescents so as to facilitate their learning and development through the
design of opportunities which do not reflect egocentrism, but rather direct
youngsters' efforts toward desired ends. Recognition and acceptance of the

developmental stages and transitional character of this period permit teachers and pupils to approach both the personal and educational problems of emerging adolescents in a spirit of cooperation and teamwork.

In this effort the middle school teacher should focus on the *development of novel learning situations*. The emerging adolescent who is shifting from concrete to abstract logical operations and can now see many new possibilities, is open and alert to new and innovative ways of doing things. Thus, a novel approach to any problem or learning situation can capitalize on this mental alertness and utilize the more intrinsic motivational drives. The restlessness and energy along with the enthusiasms generally characteristic of emerging adolescents make continuous innovation in the classroom a necessity for middle school pupils. Thus the faculty and staff can utilize overall organizational techniques as well as classroom strategies to provide for a wide variety of new and interesting learning situations.

An *emphasis upon exploratory activities* should assume a most important place in the curriculum of the middle school and in the classroom. Emerging adolescents are able to see combinations of possibilities, and the immediate reality no longer is paramount in their perceptions. They become free to look toward new, strange, and unusual experiences, and they can now perceive them in a more meaningful way. Exploratory activities on the school level and within the classroom permit the pupils to experience these new and interesting activities.

Expectations of the middle school faculty toward achieved levels of performance should vary not only between individual students but between the sexes as well. Research indicates that girls reach puberty and develop intellectual ability earlier than boys. While this difference is not great, the post-pubescent girl in a seventh-grade class can probably be expected to be among the better students, while a prepubescent boy might be expected to be below average in ability to conduct abstract logical operations. These abstract operations may have some influence upon the academic achievement of the pupil. Thus the development of a perception among the faculty concerning the need for adjustments of expectations between pre- and postpubescent boys and girls in light of their abilities to conduct concrete and abstract logical operations is important.

Expectancies should be less stringent toward academic content achievement in the middle school. If greater emphasis is to be placed upon some aspects of learning then some degree of easing becomes necessary in some other aspects of the learning environment. If greater attention is to be given the logical operations then less attention would be given toward the achievement of content objectives alone. It is generally agreed that the average school places considerable stress on content which should be learned. The material that could be presented for children to learn is now excessive. Some systematic selection and limitation must occur to avoid "cognitive stuffing."

Elkind quotes a 1967 Piaget speech:

> It is probably possible to accelerate, but maximal acceleration is not desirable. There seems to be an optimal time. What this optimal time is will surely depend upon each individual and on the subject matter. We still need a great deal of research to know what the optimal time would be.[20]

The time mentioned by Piaget is obviously that time required to learn certain content and thus complete rather arbitrary requirements of a school year or school experience. A search for an optimal educational experience has been taken to indicate more stress upon learning how to learn, and more stress upon exploration, with somewhat less stress upon achievement of specific content objectives, without forfeiting any important conceptual organization in the disciplines and subject areas stressed in school curricula.

Emphasis upon diagnosis and guidance in the learning environment becomes a new essential. Once the progress of each individual rather than a focus on his or her rank in a group-achievement situation becomes the measure, new tasks become a priority of the faculty. The diagnosis of the present intellectual level of each pupil along with direction and guidance toward general development in all areas become the responsibility of adults with whom the pupil works and lives. The school is currently the agent upon whom the major responsibility lies. Teachers are expected to have or to develop the requisite professional capabilities to discharge this responsibility. The assumption implicit in this expectation is that learning is an individual task. The emerging adolescent can become a most effective learner both in middle school and in later life to the extent that he or she develops the skills and tools necessary to conduct abstract operations and to learn the vocabulary-building and concept-formation processes necessary to further learning.

The role of the teacher as a manager of the learning environment and director of learning, while not new as a concept, has been relatively undeveloped. The concept of the teacher as a diagnostician is both relatively new and rarely developed to any extent. The revision of both middle school programs and organizational structure is necessary. So also is professional development of the middle school faculty toward the creation of an intellectual environment in which learning becomes the primary concern and where each individual can assume responsibility for his or her own effective participation in the whole cooperative endeavor. While somewhat visionary, the end is continued learning and more cooperation on the part of all members of a learning community. Boundaries between home and school and community should become blurred, and interaction among and between segments and individuals should be directed toward a more highly developed educational process for all members.

REFERENCES

1. From *The Growth of Logical Thinking from Childhood to Adolescence* by Bärbel Inhelder and Jean Piaget. Translated by Anne Parsons and Stanley Milgram, © 1958 by Basic Books, Inc. Publishers, New York, pp. 336–337. Used with permission.

2. From Jean Piaget, "Foreword" to *Piaget and Knowledge, Theoretical Foundations*, by Hans G. Furth © 1969, p. vi. Reprinted by permission of Prentice-Hall, Inc., Englewood Cliffs, N.J.

3. Jean Piaget, *The Psychology of Intelligence* (Patterson, N.J.: Littlefield, Adams, 1963).

4. From *The Developmental Psychology of Jean Piaget* by John H. Flavell, © 1963 by Litton Educational Publishing, Inc., p. 20. Reprinted by permission of D. Van Nostrand Company.

5. Jean Piaget, "The Genetic Approach to the Psychology of Thought," *Journal of Educational Psychology* 52, 1961, p. 277.

6. From *The Growth of Logical Thinking from Childhood to Adolescence* by Bärbel Inhelder and Jean Piaget. Translated by Anne Parsons and Stanley Milgram, © 1958 by Basic Books, Inc., Publishers, New York, p. 273. Used with permission.

7. Inhelder and Piaget, *Growth of Logical Thinking*, pp. 248–249.

8. From *The Growth of Logical Thinking from Childhood to Adolescence* by Bärbel Inhelder and Jean Piaget. Translated by Anne Parsons and Stanley Milgram, © 1958 by Basic Books, Inc., Publishers, New York, pp. 250–251. Used with permission.

9. From *The Growth of Logical Thinking from Childhood to Adolescence* by Bärbel Inhelder and Jean Piaget. Translated by Anne Parsons and Stanley Milgram, © 1958 by Basic Books, Inc., Publishers, New York, p. 251. Used with permission.

10. David Elkind, *Children and Adolescents, Interpretive Essays on Jean Piaget* (New York: Oxford University Press, 1970), p. 76.

11. Inhelder and Piaget, *Growth of Logical Thinking*, p. 349.

12. Elkind, *Children and Adolescents*, pp. 56–57.

13. Ibid., p. 67.

14. Ibid., pp. 83–85.

15. J.M. Tanner, *Growth at Adolescence*, 2d. ed. (Oxford: Blackwell Scientific Publications, 1962), p. 210.

16. V. Heinonen, "Differentiation of Primary Mental Abilities," *Jyväskylä Studies in Education, Psychology and Social Research* 2, Jyväskylä, pp. 46–54.

17. Bengt-Olov Ljung, *The Adolescent Spurt in Mental Growth* (Stockholm: Almqvist & Wiksell, 1965), p. 255. Used with permission.

18. Ethel L. Cornell and Charles M. Armstrong, "Forms of Mental Growth Patterns Revealed by Reanalysis of the Harvard Growth Data," *Child Development*, vol. 26, no. 3, Sept. 1955, p. 169.

19. From Ethel L. Cornell and Charles M. Armstrong, "Forms of Mental Growth Patterns Revealed by Reanalysis of the Harvard Growth Data," *Child Development*, vol. 26, no. 3, Sept. 1955, pp. 200–204, © Society for Research in Child Development, Inc. Used with permission.

20. From David Elkind, *Children and Adolescents, Interpretive Essays on Jean Piaget* (New York: Oxford University Press, 1970), p. 76. Used with permission.

RELATED READINGS

Ausubel, David P. *Educational Psychology: A Cognitive View*. New York: Holt, 1968.

Cornell, Ethel L., and Armstrong, Charles M. "Forms of Mental Growth Patterns Revealed by Reanalysis of the Harvard Growth Data," *Child Development* vol. 26, no. 3, Sept. 1955.

Elkind, David. *Children and Adolescents, Interpretive Essays on Jean Piaget*. New York: Oxford University Press, 1970.

Flavell, John H. *The Developmental Psychology of Jean Piaget*. New York: Van Nostrand, 1963.

Furth, Hans G. *Piaget and Knowledge, Theoretical Foundations*. Englewood Cliffs, N.J.: Prentice-Hall, 1969.

Gibson, Eleanor J. *Principles of Perceptual Learning and Development*. New York: Appleton-Century-Crofts, 1969.

Guilford, J.P. *The Nature of Human Intelligence*. New York: McGraw-Hill, 1967.

Hilgard, Ernest R., and Bower, Gordon H. *Theories of Learning*. 3d. ed. New York: Appleton-Century-Crofts, 1969.

Inhelder, Bärbel, and Piaget, Jean. *The Growth of Logical Thinking from Childhood to Adolescence*. USA: Basic Books, 1958.

Ljung, Bengt-Olov. *The Adolescent Spurt in Mental Growth*. Stockholm: Almqvist & Wiksell, 1965.

Mueller, Richard J. *Principles of Classroom Learning and Perception: An Introduction to Educational Psychology*. New York: Praeger, 1974.

Piaget, Jean. *The Psychology of Intelligence*. Patterson, N.J.: Littlefield, Adams, 1963.

UNIT II

Sources for Decisions in Emerging Adolescent Education

Public schools are a part of the broad milieu of the society in which they are located. Schools which vary to any significant degree from the norms of the surrounding culture come under pressures by segments of that culture to return to the service of its needs. Hence any change in the philosophy or rationale for the operation of a school system must follow from the dictates of the larger framework of the surrounding environment.

The middle school organization is one response to the larger concerns of the people across the United States. One must look to more important considerations than realignment of grades in order to see the true framework for an evolutionary pattern for change in education in America.

In the broader context of public schools the middle school is an evolutionary growth of the theory for education of emerging adolescents which gained prominence around the beginning of the twentieth century. This theory, in turn, was based upon the liberal tendencies of the society to insist that all children should receive an education through the senior high school years. When general education for all children was extended upward into the senior high school years a transitional school such as the junior high school emerged to bridge the gap between elementary and secondary schools.

This section is intended to portray the middle school as an evolving educational program in a transitional school primarily concerned with variable needs of emerging adolescents. This program is depicted as one which best meets the needs of the culture as it is now perceived by society. The one most impressive aspect of American education in the twentieth century has been its dynamics and change. While the middle school theory in this section may be considered as too traditional within a decade or so, it is the end product of almost eighty years of theorizing and practice. As such it should contain much of interest to those concerned with a rationale for the middle school.

CHAPTER 5

Historical Survey of the Purposes of American Education

Schools are founded to foster the fundamental beliefs and understandings of the society and to develop the necessary skills and abilities to carry them forward. As a society evolves, the school and its relationship to the total system changes. Since social systems rarely remain static, schools can be considered only in relation to a dynamic societal development. In order to trace the more recent development of middle schools in American educational systems, a review of their antecedents in the broader framework of selected historical events will be presented. The development and melding of three differing sets of purposes will be discussed: college preparation and intellectual concerns, purposes which are social in nature, and purposes which focus on the needs of students as individuals.

COLLEGE PREPARATION AND INTELLECTUAL BASE

College preparation and intellectual development were the major purposes of American secondary education in the colonial period. They remained so in varying degrees through the following centuries in spite of variations in societal mores and structural changes within the school organization.

Latin grammar school

The first secondary school formed in the American colonies was the Boston Latin Grammar School. It was established in 1635 to prepare young gentlemen for entrance into Harvard College, which had been established only three years earlier. The curriculum of the Latin Grammar School was classical, stressing such subjects as Latin, Greek, and grammar. Religious concern permeated the secondary schools of New England where the Puritan outlook affected both curriculum and instructional procedures. Instructional procedures and classroom climate were established in accordance with the religious beliefs of the times. The child in school was expected to listen and to learn by rote. Direct methods were used to teach reading and writing, and ciphering when it was added to the curriculum. Since the curriculum of the upper school was primarily classical and oriented toward authority, there was little need for independent or creative thought. Children were expected to be obedient to adult direction.

The schools of that period may be criticized for the limited curricula and restrictive instructional procedures utilized. The tenor of the times, with the heavy emphasis on establishing a fear of the consequences of sin and a focus on keeping God's laws, provided the early schools with their main purpose and source of support. Thus the two primary demands upon the schools were preparation for college and literacy training so that students could read the Bible. This purpose of the secondary school as a preparatory school for college persists to this day.

Academy

The establishment of the Academy is attributed to Benjamin Franklin, who recognized a growing need for including preparation for occupations within secondary education. This need had arisen as life in the colonies became more complex and commercial endeavors developed. The Academy established in 1751 thus had two components, a Latin school and an English school. The struggle to broaden educational opportunities was stimulated by the expansion of the colonial territories, with an attendant need for more capable people to meet the needs of the frontiers. Therefore support for more practical and relevant education continued.

High school

By the middle of the nineteenth century the American culture had evolved to a position where neither the Latin Grammar School nor the Academy had programs adequate to the academic educational needs of the society. Yet another type of school evolved to meet these new needs when the high school was instituted as a liberalizing influence. While the English component of the Academy conceived by Franklin had introduced some degree of general education into the secondary schools, some educators continued to exert a conservative influence on these schools. The rapidly developing American nation required a different education not always available in the Academy. Public support was found for a new conception, the high school. Opportunities for attendance became greater, and girls were admitted. The new high schools were tuition free, whereas many of the academies had charged tuition.

As the high school increased in importance and educational opportunities expanded, the college community became concerned with the unevenness of preparation of their entering students. In the late 1800s President Charles W. Eliot of Harvard College led an attack stressing the need for a more appropriate (i.e., academic) preparation for college in the secondary schools. The National Education Association organized a series of Committees which met between 1880 and 1920; their concern indicated the importance of the relationship between the high school and the college and the importance of both to society as a whole. Their deliberations culminated in the issuance of the Seven Cardinal Principles of Education stressing the importance of the social purposes to be met by the program of the secondary school. Following this statement, the debate favoring the college-preparatory function of the secondary school abated to some degree for a few decades.

The launching of Sputnik in 1957 by the Russians sent shockwaves throughout American society with an attendant reverberation in American education. The confused reaction blunted the societal purposes of the high school, which had remained relatively unchallenged from the time of the statement of the Cardinal Principles of Education. Thus the focus on college preparation received a new impetus as an upsurge of tremendous proportions was again placed upon the development of the intellect, upon learning how to think, and upon the structure of knowledge in the disciplines. This new drive for development of the intellect coincided with the motivation of large numbers of Americans toward increased opportunities offered to college graduates. Increasing numbers of American students selected college-preparation programs in high school, thus reinforcing and strengthening this function.

SOCIAL PURPOSES

Social purposes developed in the secondary schools as a result of the increasing complexity of the new society. In an attempt to prepare children for the culture in which they would live as adults, the goals and curricula beyond primary schools were broadened to include general education and preparation for newly appearing occupations. In some cases these purposes coincided with academic goals and college preparation; in others they did not.

Academy

The Latin Grammar School was intended to qualify students for college in preparation for the professions of ministry and law. As the base of American culture spread both in area and in breadth of economic disparity, the Academy was developed to serve broader goals. Benjamin Franklin recommended a more practical curriculum to prepare young people for serving the newly developing business and industrial needs of the time.

The Academy structure allowed the English School, with its more practical curriculum, to exist side by side with the Latin School, which retained many of the same goals and functions as the Latin Grammar School. Franklin did not originally expect the Academy to solve many of the problems inherent within the structure of the Latin Grammar School. Nevertheless, academies grew, primarily because of their ability to serve a much broader clientele. They increased in numbers, in influence, and in prestige until they reached a peak at approximately the middle of the nineteenth century.

Academies were established with students paying tuition for entrance. This tended to bring the sons and daughters of the wealthier classes into the academies. The practice of a tuition charge was not unusual except in some of the New England states where secondary education had been established through public funds. Many of the academies, in addition to charging tuition, admitted girls. Since the Latin Grammar Schools had primarily served boys, the appearance of the academies gave girls their first opportunity to participate in organized secondary education.

As the frontier continued to move westward and educational opportunities expanded, high schools established in the early 1820s served as a vehicle for even more socially oriented education. With the increase in importance of the high school the influence of the Academy as a major institution in secondary education diminished.

High school

The first high school was founded in Boston in 1821. Originally called an English Classical School, it was soon renamed the English High School. By 1827 Massachusetts required all towns of 500 families or more to maintain public high schools.

Probably the single most important effect of the change from academies to high schools was the levying of public taxes for secondary education of youngsters. This policy was established with the landmark decision in the Kalamazoo case in the Michigan Supreme Court in 1874. The Latin Grammar School with its classical curriculum had been established with public support; the academy with its broader curriculum followed, but charged tuition. The high school with its broadened curriculum and free attendance for all children became the next logical step in the evolution of American secondary education.

When the right of school boards to levy taxes for the secondary education of all children had been sanctioned, the high school as an institution became prevalent. The phenomenal growth in number of high schools coincided with "the closing of the western frontier" in 1890. Prior to that date those dissatisfied with their standing in communities or those who were less educated could move west. After 1890 such opportunities lessened. Gradually the social situation altered until little opportunity existed for those with insufficient education. The trend toward a requirement for more education continues to be critical as society increases in industrialization and technological development.

The Cardinal Principles of Education, as a culmination of the trend toward an emphasis upon the social purposes of education, had many precursors in the sociology, psychology, and philosophy of the time. Pragmatism had just become influential in the educational thought of America. Charles Peirce, one of its earliest proponents, stated that any test of ideas was, in the last analysis, a social test. He held that the true idea is the one that is eventually agreed upon by an infinite community of observers and knowers. Under those circumstances a statement of truth would be a statement of belief that was relatively stable because of the continuing agreement of competent observers.[1]

John Dewey, a prime mover in the progressive educational movement in the early 1900s, noted that the public school was the chief means of social betterment. To Dewey the ideal school was a miniature society with the aim of education being social efficiency.[2] The work of such philosophers as Peirce, Dewey, and William James, along with such others as psychologists G. Stanley Hall and E. L. Thorndyke, who investigated child development and school practices, contributed greatly to the new understanding of educational processes. The studies and the ideas put forth by these scholars supported the fundamental belief in the societal purposes of secondary schools in America. Educators in the 1920s attempted to apply these philosophical theories by deriving the materials for educational experiences from social need rather than from traditional subjects. Central to the work of all these men was the principle that the chief function for education should be to meet the needs of people within the existing society rather than to teach the traditional curriculum of subject matter. This remained the guiding principle for educators until the 1960s, when Sputnik created a temporary insistence upon intellectual purposes.

Those who in the late 1960s espoused a shift from the Sputnik-induced demand for academic excellence and college preparation toward a stronger social orientation based their contention on social unrest, demand of minority groups for equal rights and educational opportunities, and shifting societal goals. A wide variety of pressures have led to the broadening of programs and options in public education. Through federal funding and grants from foundations the interests of segments of the population whose needs had long been ignored were brought into focus. The increased attention given to satisfying the needs of these groups seems to indicate that Americans again consider the social purposes of the schools to be at least as important as the intellectual and college-preparation purposes. Thus the struggle to foster societal goals in the public schools which was initiated by Benjamin Franklin and continued with varying degrees of success through the years seems to be having a resurgence.

Junior high school

Early junior high school educators were concerned with the uneven growth of the public school system in the United States. Schools established in different areas and with different philosophies, practices, and policies developed wide diversities in the education provided to pupils. Elementary schools ranged in length from four to nine or even ten years depending upon district policies. The same variation was found in secondary schools, which might utilize between three and six years according to locality. Not until the early twentieth century did education in public schools come to occupy a more uniform twelve years of the pupil's time. With the upward extension of the elementary school and the lengthening of the high school, the eight-year elementary and four-year secondary (8-4) plan became common.

At this time some of the major concerns of educators revolved around the question of economy of time and the longer retention of children in school. The educational transition from general education in the elementary school to vocational or college-preparatory work in the high school was considered to be an important function of the schools. While not discounting the importance of early adolescence and the facilitation of cultural transition into later adolescence, these were not considered to be as important within the framework of the early junior high school as the more practical questions of grades, content, and educational transition. Not until the 1920s did these socio-emotional factors begin to assume the importance which they exhibit today.

INDIVIDUAL PURPOSES

The stress upon social purposes of education in American public schools which had its inception in the nineteenth century was significantly expanded in the decades following 1920. At that time the concept of education for individual needs and purposes first came to the fore. It was a relatively short transition from the utilization of social purposes as a framework for education to a realization that a focus upon the needs of individuals within society would more effectively achieve these purposes.

One of the most important early proponents of the thesis of individualism was Rousseau. In his book *Emile*[3] Rousseau suggested educational purposes that focused upon the nature of the child rather than societal needs. He emphasized developmental growth, individual uniqueness, native interests, and curiosity as sources of growth. According to Rousseau, education should emancipate the child from the influences of society and preparation for life—the child's nature should be allowed to unfold. Throughout the period from 1920 until the early 1950s professional educators placed strong emphasis upon the individual. During this period the core curriculum emerged as a major curricular approach.

The core movement

One of the most important curriculum developments leading toward the achievement of individual purposes was the growth of the core curriculum concept, its implementation in many schools, and its evaluation in the Eight-Year Study. The core movement was faced with some variations in perception as to the meaning of core, and its place in a school curriculum. Among statements regarding core curriculum which were generally accepted were those made by Faunce and Bossing. According to them:

> It is accepted as a phase of the experience curriculum concept and relates to that part of this curriculum concept that is concerned with the development of those common competencies which it is thought all citizens should have to live successfully within a democratic society.[4]

While this statement is useful in determining the purposes of the movement, it was less useful to the administrator charged with developing the curriculum. To facilitate such development the authors elaborated:

> The core program, then, refers to the total organizational activities of that part of the school curriculum devoted to the determination of the personal and social competencies needed by all, and the procedures, materials, and facilities by which the school assures the adequacy of the learning experiences essential to the development of these competencies.[5]

As the core curriculum concept reached a peak in popularity during the 1930s and 1940s problems concerning definitions continued. In the process of adopting and adapting in each individual school it was inevitable that many variations of core were utilized. Nevertheless, by 1952, when Grace Wright reported the results of a study of core curriculum she had conducted under the auspices of the Office of Education, she found core generally designated in four areas. These were (1) correlated block time, (2) fused block time, (3) preplanned problems, and (4) unplanned problems.[6] Wright's delineations indicate a trend in American education toward increased concern for personalization of education.

A significant question raised as early as 1930, however, was whether education which focused on socio-emotional needs of youngsters could also adequately develop the cognitive abilities necessary to effective education. The Eight-Year Study, initiated to investigate this question, indicated that youngsters in experimental schools which utilized core curriculum approaches had not only achieved as well in academic work as their more traditionally educated paired students, but had also experienced greater success in the socio-emotional areas. Not only this, but the more radical the departure from the traditional college-preparation studies the more the difference was observed to the advantage of the students participating in the experimental program.[7]

Individual needs were paramount in the work of the Progressive Education Association and the Eight-Year Study. Many other researchers and theorists in education were supporting and making pleas for more attention to individual purposes. Havighurst and others published studies regarding the developmental needs of adolescents which emphasized attention to these needs in education. The Educational Policies Commission published several statements pressing for attention to the multi-dimensional and developmental needs of children, which became one of the prime functions of the school.

STRUCTURE OF KNOWLEDGE

Changing societal conditions in the early 1950s caused many educational theorists to question possible overemphasis of the socio-emotional needs approach to education. Following World War II two super-powers emerged upon the world scene, each striving for influence throughout the world. Within this context questions began to arise concerning the function of American education in support of the development of the United States as a world power. The Russian achievement of launching Sputnik in 1957 before America had achieved this goal created immediate concern in all strata of American society. One of the first structures in American culture to be investigated was the school system. While later examination revealed lack of validity in many cases, the immediate criticism created public demand for "better" education by 1960.

National curriculum reform movement

Because of the wave of public criticism, psychologists and scientists associated with various disciplines began to look seriously at the public school curriculum, many for the first time. Criticisms had emanated from some sectors of the education profession even before Sputnik, and significant innovations were soon being suggested by scientists and scholars. The scientific knowledge necessary to the benefit of the American society and the ways in which this knowledge could best be translated into curricula for colleges and high schools drew increasing attention from the academic community.

Curriculum determination by specialists

Curriculum committees and panels supported by newly available funds from federal government and private agencies utilized the services of many different types of specialists. Primary among these were scholars from the particular disciplines being considered. Learning theorists and classroom teachers were included in these groups, but the primary concern was first with the conceptual structure, logic, mode of inquiry, and sequence of major ideas in the discipline.

The assumption was made that if a curriculum were sequential in nature and logical in its presentation, it could be learned by a majority of the pupils in a school. Another assumption was that the methods utilized by scientists in practicing their disciplines could be followed to some extent by the student while still retaining basic concepts.

As early as 1963, however, some concern was being voiced concerning reform through development of a structured curriculum. But in spite of critical reaction on the part of some educators, the movement continued and gained in strength during the 1960s. Educators stressed the logic and sequence of formal knowledge, and reduced emphasis upon the needs of the individual and the societal approaches to education.

RECONSTRUCTIVE PURPOSES

In the 1970s a more introspective mood precipitated a concern for social problems. A reexamination of national goals, conflicting values, and a wide variety of internal problems brought a renewed concern for a more humane life within the United States. While not rejecting the cultivation of the intellect and the disciplines, Americans questioned the social purposes for these processes. The trend toward structure of subject disciplines as a framework for intellectual purposes, leading toward a college degree, was seen to be an important one for some but not necessarily for all. The social propriety of preparing a percentage of youth for professions, while shunting others off to less lucrative and less prestigious positions due to their lack of ability for conceptualization has been seriously questioned.

The predominantly reconstructive purposes of the society during the period between the two world wars seem to be coming again to the fore. Following a period during which societal problems have been mounting, the purposes now seem to lead toward a more constructive improvement of society rather than a passive view of the past or present. Educators aver that improvement of society is needed, rather than a preparation for living within and adapting to a society. This idea was stated in 1932 by George Counts in his monograph, "Dare Schools Build a New Social Order?" Counts proposed that education be seen as preparation for management and control of social change. If social engineering became the purpose, educators could be viewed as statesmen. Under these circumstances education would not only foster changes in society but should lead to change of the very social order of the United States.[8]

These ideas in educational philosophy were revolutionary for their time. But by the 1970s leadership in education took a role in fostering change as new programs were stimulated and funded by the United States Office of Education. With a view to righting previous wrongs in education and abridgement of civil rights and in forcing desegregation of schools, the federal government has clearly established the schools as agents for change in society. Strong efforts have been made throughout the country to upgrade the education of minority-group children and to improve their capabilities for participation in the mainstream of society. These designs to lessen the disadvantages of social class are expected to continue.

While the future is impossible to predict due to rapid and complex changes, the evolving society is attempting to encompass elemental forces working at cross purposes within it. Thus schools will continue to be a focus of the value struggle as the nation seeks more viable alternatives or solutions to these problems. In general, curricular approaches in the early 1970s show more emphasis at all levels upon humanities, language arts, and other subject areas focused on the need for a more humane life.

A continuing problem of education in American society has been the attempt to unify a conglomeration of national and ethnic backgrounds. From the 1870s until recently the theory of the United States as a "melting pot" had been accepted as a basic sociological premise. The mobility of individuals and families during the World War II period, however, exposed great numbers of individuals to other cultures and subcultures both within the United States and elsewhere. Many Americans for the first time were directly exposed to varying life styles and value systems. As a result of this exposure divergent patterns have recently emerged with regard to individuals and their life styles. Value patterns are no longer so uniform nor so commonly held. A group so large as the American society is no longer expected to support so uniform a value system. As the 1970s began, the American culture was in a state of transition with multiple values perceived as possible partial solutions to societal problems. The conflicts among those values held by different interest groups will be the subject of confrontation and compromise in internal affairs for the remainder of the century. A transition from a dominant value system to a multi-valued one is the major challenge of that period.

Another related question arises regarding the advisability of planning for change. Planning for change requires deliberate allocation of resources. Can forces creating change be regulated in a meaningful way, or will no planning take place thus leaving the United States to float with the tides as has been true of many societies in the past? Schools, in addition to other agencies and institutions deriving support from federal and state governments, have been encouraged to take steps toward long-range planning. The implementation of such planning will surely affect our schools. Programs will be affected by the direction in which society moves. The need for improved early-childhood learning experiences, the creation of publicly supported day-care centers, home-start programs, and downward extension of planned education to a period soon after the birth of a child give some credence to the idea of the school as an agent for change.

EMPHASIS UPON INDIVIDUAL PURPOSES

We expect that the idea that each individual has a unique value to society will continue to be accepted in the future. Individuals differ but each has a unique quality, and each is necessary to the well-being and full development of the society as a whole. Thus the mandate for schools in the 1970s is that each individual youth must be educated with a view to his or her own maximum achievement in each of several different development areas. The schools must be able to continue the development of rational powers and knowledge, but must also be concerned with general areas in the social development of the pupils. Four areas of social development which have been accepted as most important in school purposes are:

1. character development,
2. civic responsibility,
3. avocational pursuits, and
4. vocational orientation.

Character development is one of the important purposes of the schools. That the child's character is developed by his or her total environment is undisputed. It is a primary concern, however, whether the school shall continue to strive for character development as an explicit effort. Explicit programs would not necessarily engage in formal religion nor in morality training for youth. Rather, such a curriculum would presuppose that pupils may develop character in part through instructional efforts of the faculty, staff, and administration in the school setting. In the absence of appropriate training in some homes and a lessening of the influence of the church, an emphasis on moral and ethical development becomes an important aspect in the development of each emerging adolescent.

The primary *civic purpose* of the school may be that of developing the means for handling dissent in more constructive ways. Voting as a means of peacefully resolving differences among large groups in our society is considered necessary to the survival of the governmental structure, and some structure is necessary in the transition and development of new societal patterns. Efforts to assist youngsters and adults to develop new approaches to confrontation, dissent, and compromise are necessary if future violence is to be avoided.

The need for *avocational purposes* in schools may be highlighted by the increasing trend toward more leisure time. Increasing uncommitted time makes necessary some preparation in school for means by which each individual can utilize such time constructively and with satisfaction. Some feel that much social unrest has occurred because of a lack of avocational and recreational activities. With many vocations requiring less work time, and with increasing technology and automation, individuals in all walks of life may experience alienation and feelings of aimlessness. A wide variety of activities which require development of alternative talents and abilities are recommended for school curricula in order to lessen these problems.

The purposes of the school in the development of knowledge, attitudes, and skills directed toward a *vocational orientation* for youth include three areas: (1) guidance toward future work, according to the abilities and desires of the pupil; (2) education to equip youth for entrance into a chosen vocation; and (3) the learning clusters of skills which are preparatory for entry into and growth within a specific vocation, as well as ability to add new skills as technological changes occur.

REFERENCES

1. R. Freeman Butts and Lawrence A. Cremin, *A History of Education in American Culture* (New York: Holt, 1953), p. 343.

2. Merritt M. Thompson, *The History of Education*, College Outline Series (New York: Barnes & Noble, 1958), p. 51.

3. Jean Jacques Rousseau, *Emile* (London: Dent, 1911), p. 131.

4. From Roland C. Faunce and Nelson L. Bossing, *Developing the Core Curriculum*, © 1958, p. 56. Reprinted by permission of Prentice-Hall, Inc., Englewood Cliffs, N.J.

5. From Roland C. Faunce and Nelson L. Bossing, *Developing the Core Curriculum*, © 1958, p. 57. Reprinted by permission of Prentice-Hall, Inc., Englewood Cliffs, N.J.

6. Grace S. Wright, *Core Curriculum Development, Problems and Practices, Bulletin—1952, No. 5* (Washington, D. C.: U. S. Government Printing Office, 1952), p. 8.

7. Wilford M. Aikin, *The Story of the Eight-Year Study* (New York: McGraw-Hill, 1942), Vol. IV, *Did They Succeed in College?* chap. X.

8. G. S. Counts, "Dare Schools Build a New Social Order?" no. 11, John Day Pamphlets (John Day, 1932).

RELATED READINGS

Butts, R. Freeman, and Cremin, Lawrence A. *A History of Education in American Culture.* New York: Holt, 1953.

Counts, G. S. "Dare Schools Build a New Social Order?" No. 11, John Day Pamphlets. John Day, 1932.

Cremin, Lawrence A. *The Genius of American Education.* New York: Vintage Books, 1965.

Cremin, Lawrence A. *Transformation of the School; Progressivism in American Education 1876–1957.* New York: Knopf, 1961.

Kettering Foundation. *The Reform of Secondary Education. A Report of the National Commission on the Reform of Secondary Education.* New York: McGraw-Hill, 1973.

Krug, Edward A. *Salient Dates in American Education: 1635–1964.* New York: Harper & Row, 1966.

Morphet, Edgar L., and Jesser, David L., eds. *Designing Education for the Future, No. 4, Cooperative Planning for Education in 1980.* New York: Citation Press, 1968.

CHAPTER 6

Cultural Determinants for Educational Decision Making

One of the primary purposes of the school is to prepare children for the society in which they are presently living and will live as adults. The transitional school between primary and secondary education will be affected by the same cultural forces as the school as a whole. It is influenced by the ways in which life and structure of the society of the United States have evolved. Further, extrapolations for the future are an important consideration since schools are expected to facilitate the purposes of society. Complicating the situation still further is the fact that schools themselves are an influential segment of that society.

Cultural lag, a concept derived from sociologist Ogburn and popularized by Stuart Chase, provides one example of cultural complexity. This term relates to the way new practices or inventions are accepted into society:

> Inventions are usually accepted into culture in two stages. To begin with, people change their day-by-day behavior to accommodate the new device.... Then... people change their institutions and belief systems to allow for the invention.... The time between the first and second stages is known as the cultural lag....[1]

Cultural lag affects both human values and technology itself. Scientific and technological inventions occur in business and industry as a need arises. Human values thus affected are sometimes not carefully studied. Individuals and groups have in the past accommodated to the needs of economic interests. Now, however, attention to human values is becoming an important issue on the social scene. The cultural-lag theory seems to be valid for many areas where current conflicts are taking place. Current societal practices and patterns are not, in some cases, congruent with values and knowledge expressed in the school curriculum, just as they are often out of step with a generally supported system of values and commitments in society.

Issues in technology and cultural transitions over periods of history have been highlighted in terms of resources and power. Mumford divides developments in terms of power stages ranging from wind through water, wood, and coal to electricity by the end of the nineteenth century. The twentieth century brought a biotechnic economy as a dominant pattern.[2] Each stage was accompanied by unique problems caused by its source of power.

Such a major problem faces highly complex industrialized nations today. Atomic energy promises needed new sources of power, but is accompanied by the disadvantage of pollution of the environment. These new sources can be utilized only at a great sacrifice to human values concerning the environment under current circumstances. It is yet uncertain what economic sacrifices may be needed to preserve or maintain an adequate environment.

The ascendancy of humanism in the 1970s exists alongside a stubborn resistance to lowering standards of living or giving up conveniences in human and natural environments. To illustrate the problem posed by competing value perceptions, consider the high priority we Americans place upon self-improvement. Success in the past has been defined in terms of increased size, monetary value, and social advancement in national and individual improvement. Concern, however, has increased regarding the effectiveness of these criteria in relation to our perception of individuals and humanity. These two contradictory tendencies, humanism and improvement of living standards, cause conflict within individuals and among groups in American culture. Inconsistency in action seems to lead to confusion and a lessening of confidence in personal and group affairs. In extreme cases compromise and resolution of societal problems become quite difficult. A determination of new directions and the development of commitment to the new purposes may become as stressful as the existing problems unless sufficient attention is awarded to these concerns in the educational process.

Although attempts to predict the future are often fallacious, trends are an indication of possibilities in general terms. When trends have been observed and checked for accuracy with the passage of time, they may be used to provide indications for the future of American society. Such indications would be invaluable in the formulation of an educational plan most appropriate to that society and to individuals within it. In a summary of the change between sensate and ideational cultures Sorokin stated a drastic remedy: "Our remedy demands a complete change of the contemporary mentality, a fundamental transformation of our system of values, and the profoundest modification of our conduct toward other men, cultural values, and the world at large."[3]

Certain trends are evident. First, the culture of a society is an intensely intricate and complex framework, for which we have not as yet achieved any valid means of prognostication. The general tendency is toward a lessened belief in technology as a primary value and basis for our culture, with a corresponding increase in attention to biological, sociological, and humanistic values. Many forces are reflected as values and revised at a rapid rate focusing upon a need for basic change in the culture. These forces and values may be seen in terms of a number of broad areas including: (1) population explosion, (2) knowledge explosion, (3) human aspirations, and (4) dynamism of the society.

The cultural impact of these developments has implications which will be indicated in terms of their relevance to the education of all, with particular emphasis on the education of the emerging adolescent.

POPULATION EXPLOSION

The population explosion has far-reaching implications for the United States and for the world. The apparent logarithmic increase in population promises to create problems beyond those normally expected, such as the supply of food and resources for higher standards of living.

Shifts in population centers and the clustering of large segments of the world's population in areas of low productivity are problems which will be critical for future generations.

Changes in community structures are reflected in the prediction that 80 percent of the people in the United States will soon be living in communities with populations of 25,000 or more. The changes from a predominantly rural to a predominantly urban society have created dislocations of the customs of the subcultures as well as the larger culture. These dislocations have been complicated and hastened by rapid mass communications, more available transportation, and greater industrialization.

Growth of the urban areas has created an interdependence among people as compared with the individualistic American society of the nineteenth century when those who were displeased with the local community could seek a frontier. Now, in a reverse movement, the United States has rapidly growing urban areas, where many citizens are finding that values concerning independence and self-sufficiency which were important and necessary in a rural culture are no longer appropriate in the urban setting. Large bureaucracies in cities assist in the distribution of goods and services once performed by the family or by rural community groups. Large families, once necessary to provide labor on farms, are now a liability with automation. Changes in family patterns toward fewer members necessitate changes in roles played by those members.

The rural, individualistic culture which existed at the beginning of the twentieth century had shifted by 1970 toward a primarily urban culture with characteristic focus on groups and interdependence. Groups, rather than individuals, exerted influence on public decision-making processes. For example, new power groups emerged during the 1960s as college students, women, and minority groups sought recognition and influence in social decisions. The necessity for individuals to join with others to exert power and preserve rights is a relatively recent phenomenon.

The importance of concerted power has yet to be fully accepted as a means to the exercise of personal rights and power by those who decry the loss of personal influence. The new styles for utilization of power against bureaucracy in the institutional structure are not yet universally adopted. The growth of cities has thus created a social situation in which some individuals feel lost, frustrated, and alienated.

The inability of large cities to cope with the influx of large numbers of poorly educated rural immigrants raises serious questions for the future. One result of this population increase and shift has been the rising need for food, clothing, housing, medical, and other welfare services to persons who are ill equipped to provide for themselves. This dependence upon others to provide basic needs produces serious psychological problems in large segments of the population, and augments feelings of self-denigration and helpless rage as the affluence of other segments of society is witnessed through mass communication and personal observation. These problems are of great importance to education, which has been viewed as the great social equalizer. It seems to be expected that education of the masses can ameliorate these problems.

Education must be considered within the total cultural context; it takes place within the total life situation of the child, not just within the six-hour framework of the traditional school. If new expectations are to be fulfilled, early experiences in the home must reflect these norms. When these expectations are not a part of the home they cannot be so readily absorbed by the child. Recent research has indicated that the achievement of second and third-generation children in urban areas is generally closer to the expected norms of society than the achievement of first-generation children. Perhaps with continued effort and a lessening of the rate of immigration, the urban problem may yield to the educational effort, and inequities may be ameliorated over the next few decades.

The recognition of slum conditions as detrimental to human development is essential. Appropriate steps must be taken to create broadly based programs which deal with all aspects of the lives of persons and families living in substandard conditions. The drain on the available human and material resources of the nation to provide these necessary services is extremely heavy, however. The rate of increase both in numbers and need creates an almost self-defeating situation. How to accomplish the desired purposes is a source of considerable controversy.

Conditions of poverty have become more apparent as a general increase in the level of living standards has occurred among the more affluent and has come to be expected by the majority of American citizens. Perhaps an even greater concern is the loss to the country as benefits and contributions of hundreds of thousands of potentially creative and talented persons go undeveloped through failure and neglect.

Population shift to suburbs

Coinciding with the growth of cities and the rise of slum conditions has been the movement of population away from the central city. A large segment of the population has sought the suburban type of living, differing from city and rural life-styles. There are many evident reasons for the growth of suburbs. Availability of easy transportation has expedited urban sprawl and stimulated growth of outlying areas. Mass media, with instantaneous national and local services available, bring the outside world into the home and ease any need people may have for many services once provided only in the urban centers. Entertainment and cultural advantages are now widely available in suburban areas. Factories, businesses, commercial parks, and shopping centers spring up on rural sites on the fringes of large cities. Necessary services are instituted to meet needs in these new areas. The result is increasingly less dependence on the central city.

The affluence reflected in life in suburbia with its living conditions and advantages of space and fresh air has created certain problems for its families. As individuals and families move to newly created neighborhoods, a sense of commitment to community and concern for welfare of others may be lacking. From a rural nation of independent families at the turn of the century, we have developed into a society characterized by an impersonal interdependence among all persons, whether suburban or city dwellers. Suburban individuals and families who may seem to be independent are in reality both dependent and interdependent according to the phases of life being considered. Widely divergent life-styles exist side by side. Each has its characteristic complexities, and adaptation to one style does not necessarily prepare one to cope with problems of another. Thus the future culture of the United States will depend upon ways in which problems of each life-style can be understood and common needs of all persons met.

KNOWLEDGE EXPLOSION

The knowledge explosion is one aspect of the cultural crisis currently affecting the society of the United States. Among the many manifestations of the expansion of knowledge to be considered are: (1) the development of mass media, (2) the increase in automation, (3) the greater ease and speed of transportation, and (4) the speed of communication.

Radical increases in the amount of knowledge have wrought changes in our society, which have produced accompanying innovations in education. Knowledge expansion has pointed to the importance of education as a continuing activity for all members of society. It has caused a revision in our view of what can be learned, and made it very apparent that knowledge can quickly become obsolete. The importance of learning how to be a continuing learner, how to organize, integrate, and synthesize new knowledge, has also increased. A major problem has developed for education: the necessity for continual deletion or revision of what is taught, and a reevaluation of criteria for selection of what is to be included in the curriculum. The increasing importance of conceptual knowledge as opposed to specific, factual, subject area knowledge is encouraging a new set of processes in curriculum development and instructional strategies.

Mass media

An important impact of mass media upon society has been the effect of creating a more common culture and body of knowledge, regardless of place of residence. Geographic isolation and lack of first-hand life experiences no longer prevent any group from knowing the advantages and corresponding problems faced by other groups of the society.

While acculturation of many subcultures into one general society may be viewed as desirable, some problems are inherent in this development. Dependence upon impersonal authority for selection of what should be communicated is one problem. The decrease in first-hand, direct experience and the increase of reliance upon vicarious experience is another.

The possibility of mind control and indoctrination of various subcultures, almost inevitable for the less educated, is a serious problem for the current society. The effect of the mass media upon national policy and acceptance of that policy has been great. Shaping of public opinion and presenting and deliberately creating images of men and issues via television has been well documented.

The less educated have less opportunity to compare and contrast available views and may be less aware of the need to do so. Children, whose value systems have not been completely set, watch television more hours than adults. Further, children spend more time in front of the television set than they do in the schoolroom.

Given these circumstances, a major problem exists in the relationships between reporting, editorializing, and commentary (all of which have appearances of reporting) in radio and television programs. Many newscasts have been criticized for a tendency toward programming which may border on indoctrination. Rulings by control commissions such as the FCC have been slow in coming. Emphasis upon quality of programming, programs for children, and uses of prime time are a matter for public concern in order to insure adequate protection for young citizens. The schools must cultivate the skills of listening, critical thinking, and assigning values so that individuals may guard against being unduly influenced.

Television has been criticized for not being a sufficiently educative force, and for not presenting more cultural material as a part of regular scheduling. But television is a commercial venture. The viewing audience is in part questioned for preferences by ratings which presumably influence programming. Television executives hold that programming reflects the desires and support of viewing audiences to which programs are aimed. To criticize television

Emerging adolescents meeting demands of advanced technology.
Alton Farnsworth Middle School
(Courtesy of Guilderland, New York, Central Schools)

alone for low-level programming is to ignore a need to revise the taste of viewers through deliberate efforts to cultivate interest and demand for better presentations. Such an educative process is a lengthy one affected by the entire set of influences of both schools and community agencies. The most recent issue considered in the public forum has focused on "violence" in television programs. Conflicting research and opinions exist as to the degree to which viewing violence on television stimulates aggressive tendencies in individuals. A deemphasis on violence in entertainment programs would seem to have relatively small effect where world events shown in both regular and special news programs stress such violence.

Although criticism of the mass media, newspapers, magazines, radio, and television is present, increased communication through these media is credited with raising the national interest in and understanding of internal and world problems as well as generally providing more common knowledge of life in the twentieth century. Thus all become aware of the complexity and conflicting values vying for support that create life as it is currently experienced in American culture.

Automation

Technology and automation represent a second aspect of the knowledge explosion which has created changes and stresses in the American culture.

The development of enormous corporation complexes, large production facilities, and increasing specialization creates social pressures. The first industrial revolution brought a beginning of these pressures reflected in the formation of labor unions to safeguard and protect workers against the abuse of large companies. The average weekly work time of almost 70 hours in 1850 had dropped to an average of 40 hours per week by 1950. The new output per man hour in the same period increased almost sixfold due in part to development of extensions of manual effort by automation. This in part contributes to an almost twenty-five-fold increase in national income. Improvements in production reflected in these three sets of data are expected to continue in the next three or four decades.

Effects of technology and automation have also increased productivity on the farm. Workers have gradually been eliminated as farms become larger and less labor is performed by men. Automation, while eliminating the efforts of large numbers of workers in farms, has nevertheless made possible abundant food supplies for the American people as well as creating surpluses available for export.

Another complicating factor in American life-style arises because much work, due to technology, automation, and assembly lines, does not require great physical energy or strength. This fact, combined with the need for extra labor during World War II, created an acceptance of women in industry, where they were found to perform equally with men.

The shift from the role of wife as homemaker to source of second income became possible as a result of automation and labor-saving devices which make work in the home much less time consuming and laborious. Thus women have more time and can work outside the home, creating another profound change in the American culture.

The scientific advance made possible by computerized services in handling information, guidance systems, and automation is of extreme importance to American society. The wide variety, availability, and use of many inventions in all segments of society have precipitated many changes.

The implications of advances in technology and automation are numerous, and we should consider what educational experiences for preparation for life in the next decades can be cited. For one thing, the shortened work week seems likely, which will make available more leisure time. The creation and development of new interests, avocations, and pursuits for constructive use of time will be needed.

The need for increasing services has created a new vocational area which will require educational changes. New appliances and new vehicles require services. Air conditioning requires trained repairmen, as do airplanes, cars, boats, and snowmobiles. Social services, whether performed by government, churches, or other agencies, require new types of trained personnel. A new emphasis on health services is another example, as is the involvement of increasingly large numbers of persons in all forms of education. These require professional as well as paraprofessional and increased nonspecialized support. Continuing education for adults assumes an ever-greater importance as concerns range from development of initial literacy and basic skills needed by the entire society to the teaching of both vocational and avocational skills. Even recreational pursuits such as golf, bridge, sewing, flower arranging, and other interests are commonly included in special programs around the country.

Transportation

Transportation made easy and available by technology has had a tremendous impact on the evolving American culture. The time needed to transport persons and goods from one place to another has decreased rapidly during this century. Recalling horse-and-carriage travel and trains and boats of the early 1900s as compared to the present day points to radical changes in culture wrought by available transportation. Great distances covered by transport in a short time are now taken for granted and no longer cause the sensation of a few decades ago. Not only are new vistas from almost any location in America or abroad now available on television, but an individual can also be transported there in a very short span of time. Anyone who can afford the expense can travel around the world in a period of time numbered in days.

Paradoxically, ease of transportation has created problems. The suburban communities as cultural institutions are, in part, made possible by the ease with which automobiles can move commuters between suburban homes and urban jobs. But this has created traffic and parking problems. The flying time from New York City to Los Angeles is only a few hours, but it may take almost as many hours to get to and from the airports on each end of the trip. As expressways are planned and constructed to handle automobile and truck traffic more adequately, more cars and trucks become available to clog them almost as soon as they are open to the public. A resistance to more and bigger expressway systems, and more and bigger airplanes may lead to extensive conflicts of interests. Vehicles which allow Americans to move rapidly about the country may be restricted in favor of public mass transit or modes of power less detrimental to the environment.

Communication

Communication as an aspect of the knowledge explosion creates yet another influence upon American culture. As previously cited, television programs relayed through space showing man's first step upon the moon in 1969 graphically illustrated discontinuities in our culture. While television is most often considered an entertainment medium, it is also a communication medium reporting major events and scientific advances, thereby increasing knowledge of all citizens. The development of a visual component added to audio which will make video-telephones generally available is expected by the end of the current century.

The telephone itself has had a tremendous impact upon our society. Instantaneous two-way communications increase effectiveness of personal and professional relations, and expedite business, government, and world affairs. The current quantity of written communications transported through the federal mail system causes problems for the Post Office Department because the organization has not yet accepted the full implications of automation. Initial steps in automating service such as Zip Code and sorting equipment indicate a further need for increasing automation for mail-processing purposes, but hold great hope for the future. With an increase in oral and written communication, growth in knowledge of semantics and skills in linguistics are necessary for precision. Such knowledges and skills will become first priorities in American schools.

HUMAN ASPIRATIONS

One of the more influential factors involved in the current crisis in American society is the rise in human aspirations of a vast majority of the American population. Because of the advantages derived from technological advances and from living in close proximity in the urban situation, many citizens have aspirations higher than those of previous generations. In addition, they aspire even higher for their offspring. Rising aspirations may be a focus for problems as illustrated in a basic tenet of sociology which states that: "Conflict, and especially severe conflict, is more likely when the minority group has secured enough improvement in its situation to appreciate the benefits and want more."[4]

Racial equality

Thus at a time when the quality of human life is at a peak minorities may be found who are bitter concerning their lot within that culture. Paradoxically, it is the high level of the culture which enables lower socio-economic families to own television sets which show how the middle and upper classes live. This does not suggest that there are not reasons for the dissatisfaction displayed by minority groups. Prejudice is one of many difficulties faced by ethnic out-groups. While racial prejudice creates problems for minorities in our society, the resultant complex of problems places the majority under severe stress as well. An emphasis upon the problems of prejudice and discrimination against racial and ethnic groups in our society has caused other interest groups such as women's liberation and youth groups to seek more consideration. All elements of American society are equally concerned in finding a means to end discrimination along with other types of prejudicial treatment.

Aspirations of minority groups are no longer ignored, and a beginning of new achievements in race relations is possible. Public opinion has begun to manifest more and more acceptance of racial equality. Such feelings are deep and change slowly. The shift of large numbers of blacks from the South to the large midwestern and northeastern cities of the United States has created a situation in which problems previously existing primarily in the South have become problems for all.

From a concentration in the rural areas of the South the search for improved opportunities created a movement of blacks to the urban centers of the North where they settled in low-cost housing. Although they seek better opportunities for themselves and their children, they have no patterns for the achievement of this goal. Thus a major problem in inner-city areas is that these groups seeking improved status are purported to have sufficient capabilities, but paradoxically have few supporting attitudes and patterns for achievement. Thus, their goals are more modest than their likely achievements.

While much of the early emphasis on cultural disadvantagement and racial segregation dealt with the Negro in American society, the plight of all racial and ethnic minorities emerges when orientals, Puerto Ricans, Indians, Mexicans, and others seek equal opportunity and consideration. The various radical moves of individuals within all minorities should be accepted as a constructive challenge to a democratic society. Although they may threaten the internal peace and tranquility and force a revision of laws, policies, and traditional values, failure to meet the challenge with equanimity would be disastrous.

Emerging nations

Rising human aspirations seen in individuals and groups within the American culture also exist in newly emerging nations which seek equality with more firmly established nations. With the retreat of colonial powers from southern Asia and Africa, a host of new nations have arisen. Although some of these countries are relatively well established socially and economically, a majority are struggling with crucial problems endemic to their situations.

In addition to struggling for feelings of worth and dignity, the governing groups of these nations are cognizant of common world problems affecting them. The population problem, for example, is common to most of the emerging nations. Industrialization to provide more food, goods, and services and a control of birth rate are required for a solution. Most find it extremely difficult, as yet almost impossible, to achieve these ends without the aid of the white peoples who, because of past history, they detest.

In many ways the plight of the emerging nations can be compared to that of individuals and minority groups in the United States. The same aspirations are present, as are many of the obstacles to their achievement. In each case these groups see the attitudes of the white race as contributing to their problems. The perceptions of these nations, groups, and individuals, regardless of degree of validity, must be recognized and insightfully considered.

Educational aspirations

Education is expected to contribute to the solution of social problems. Those who seek improvements in human relations, generally, and between races and ethnic groups, in particular, can find examples of progress. Those dissatisfied with current gains may, however, substantiate a claim of limited progress in education.

In addition to inequity in educational opportunities, another problem in American society which is reflected in education is the general low status of vocational training. Although large numbers of jobs do not require college-level training, most high schools emphasize programs for general college preparation and have less concern for education for work. Clearly education for work reflects a broader commitment and necessitates changed attitudes on the part of parents in relation to their children. The need to prepare for work generally rather than preparing for a specific occupation should assume a more important place within American schools. The success of these programs will require a basic acceptance by society of the new goals. By attitude, words, and teachings, commitment must be reflected in a demonstrated respect for all levels of work, not only for college-oriented occupations and professions.

Another aspect of educational aspirations is the necessity for a perception of self-worth on the part of individual pupils. Any statement by a teacher concerning educational needs of youth can be effective only if the attitudes expressed, both explicitly and implicitly, indicate approval rather than denigration. Westie points to the transmission of negative attitudes:

> We would hypothesize that children do not learn prejudice as they learn arithmetic, primarily by deliberate and formal instruction, but more as they learn table manners, by the example of and occasional direct statements and object lessons from older people.[5]

Pluralistic society

Many individuals viewing the current American scene maintain that bureaucracy and impersonalization have too much control over individual lives. They are convinced that more importance must be given to the individual as a human being, and to a viable life-style as the most important facet of society. This importance of the individual assumes the rights of minorities as groups of individuals. While some few militants might argue for anarchical rights for each individual, a majority would seem to be stating that the optimal society for all is that society which is best for each individual within a group milieu. Championing the rights of minorities is never a popular pastime in any culture. It is symptomatic of our time that champions of minorities are presently being respected for their views.

The necessity for a pluralistic society in which many views, some conflicting, may be accepted is being investigated in the current cultural framework. Two of the more important problems in such a pluralistic society are the roles of conflict and cooperation. Conflict among various factions of the society must be possible without recourse to violence. The United States has long had a political history of two parties. Within a few years the political system may very well be completely realigned featuring a multi-party system. This is one example of how conflict may be resolved in a pluralistic society. On the other hand, cooperation is essential in a society—without it the society will face great problems in survival. The ways in which cooperation within a pluralistic society will take place can probably be better resolved after the various component power elements have been more clearly defined.

Search for values

The question of the role of conflict and cooperation within the society will be more firmly determined as the search for values within a pluralistic society reaches a more definitive stage.

Youthful idealism, which has created a stir in recent years, seems to be a reaction to the forces of society creating conformity and the emerging values which seem preeminent at this time. Various elements of the society are unsure as to best methods to express discomfiture, but it is still existent.

As might be expected within a pluralistic society, there is a reaction to the various minorities. The pressures of the mass middle class are converging to slow this movement toward pluralism. In the final analysis, the question of whether the American culture will be more singular or more pluralistic is one which will be resolved only with the passage of considerable time. The year 2000 may not see the resolution of the conflict. However, the education of young people in the next 30 years should have considerable impact upon the course of the evolution of the society.

DYNAMISM OF THE AMERICAN SOCIETY

The primary pervasive trend in American society is dynamism—the fluidity, changingness—of the culture. It is not now as it was even three years ago, and will be yet different in another three years. This dynamic quality creates many problems; it has also been responsible for many advantages.

Many changes in our society have taken place. For example, Nimkoff[6] refers to the weakening of family ties and the increasing independence of the female as influences in the development of a changing culture in the United States. Although this development will increase the gross national product and the affluence of the nation, its impact upon the family as a basic social structure in the American culture is crucial. Over several decades the role of the family may change drastically.

There have been significant changes in American life and the process by which socialization of children takes place. The family, once the major institution of socialization, which provided for the physical, socio-emotional, and psychological needs of children, has changed. The mobility of family members weakens relationships which in the past have provided strong influences on children. The social life of Americans no longer commonly centers around family relationships. The church once was a social center where community activities brought family groups into closer contact with each other. A church community was small and the personal lives of individuals were interwoven so that socializing and behavior patterns were affected. The church has recently declined as an institution of personal and social import. It no longer serves as a social center to any great extent, and family groups are no longer brought together in Sunday school activities. A type of surveillance of the lives of children made possible by a continuing social control has largely disappeared from the American scene.

Family groups have changed. An increasing formality and social distance between individuals and groups create a milieu which meets the major social and personal needs of individuals in American life. Secondary relationships in clubs and business and professional organizations furnish some personal satisfaction for adult members but have little effect on children. Adult models and sources of relationships for the child once available within the extended family are no longer provided.

All human beings must struggle together against degrading and corrupting forces before individual welfare and humaneness can become a supreme value. The present respect for knowledge for its own sake can be enhanced when that knowledge is utilized in service to humanity. Thus knowledge which is scholarly will continue, but new knowledges will be gained which are necessary for the improvement of individual members of society. This is not intended to downgrade nor deemphasize the importance of technological, scientific, managerial, or scholarly pursuits. The expected increase in technology will necessitate a corresponding increase in the respect and value to society of those who have knowledge in these areas. However, the increasing importance of services and support occupations should be recognized as vital in the maintenance of society so that individuals who perform in these areas may be accorded an appropriate degree of respect.

New answers for new problems

The most intriguing aspect of American dynamism is the new set of problems faced by each generation. Problems facing the current generation are not those that were important to the previous generation, and there is little certainty

regarding problems which will be facing the children of today when they become adults.

Hence the approach to the next generation could be termed probabilistic.
Rather than attempting to determine answers to problems, a series of alternative solutions may be presented. The current stage in the development of the
culture is such that certain questions seem evident, while clear-cut answers do
not seem so readily available. Proposed solutions can no longer be based on
dichotomous Aristotelian logic. The determination of projected consequences
of each of several selected alternatives would be the important ability for
future generations.

Equally important as the consideration of consequences of alternative answers is the basic problem of whether the right questions have been asked. Unless a problem has been appropriately phrased, data leading to solutions cannot be gathered. This emphasizes the question of priorities as a basis for prob-
lem-approaches to thinking. Hence, due to the changes occasioned both by
dynamics of society and by an extremely amorphous future, the current
younger generation will need to learn procedures for arriving at basic questions and approaches to the solving of those problems. Thus neither the solution nor the problem becomes the basic issue. The important consideration is
the approach to the problem; in other words, how to think on a pragmatic and
yet intellectual base.

IMPLICATIONS FOR EDUCATION

In considering cultural determinants for the curriculum of the middle school,
the point which seems most important is the change in culture, considered
either as transition or crisis. The form and style of education best fitted for
such a period has not been extensively considered since in similar historical
periods universal education did not exist. Hence, this section must, of necessity, be primarily theoretical in nature, since previous experience cannot be
utilized as a checkpoint from which to present conclusions.

General concepts

The first and ultimate consideration to be given to education during the middle
school years must be the *nobility of humankind.* While other creatures must
operate from an instinctual base, human beings have options because of our
abilities of memory, language, and speech. We can use the brain in solving
problems, in theorizing solutions, and above all in hoping and dreaming of
that which is beyond us.

If the middle school, as an institution, can present to pupils a multitude of
new ideas and at their most idealistic stage of development utilize their emo-

tional framework, this concept of ultimate nobility can be achieved. It is during the middle school years that this goal can be achieved most effectively. Consider the growth patterns of emerging adolescents: in later years cynicism may begin to take hold; prior to this period children will accept the dicta of adults with few reservations. So it is during the years of emerging adolescence that youth are most likely to establish the broader framework of concern with themselves as members of the human race.

A second major concern of the middle school must be the *best possible education for all youth* in the American society. If society is to pass through the present cultural transition successfully, it will require the best efforts of a maximally effective populace. Under these circumstances every emerging adolescent should be permitted the opportunity to learn and to develop to the greatest possible degree.

The concept of *personalization*, as a major goal of the middle school, must be emphasized. A maximal education for one young person may not be similar to that for another and different individual. While all will need basic fundamentals and knowledges, the period of personalization should have begun by the middle school years. All pupils must be allowed opportunities to study and have those experiences which will be most effective for their development as individuals. Guidance of a nondirective manner, exploration, and open teacher attitudes are extremely important and must be provided. If the society in which these youth will find themselves as adults is to be the type of society represented above, then each youth should be educated to cope with as yet unidentified problems as well as to develop feelings of self-respect and respect for others.

Since the society of the future will be increasingly service oriented, the *importance of service occupations* must be stressed in the middle school. The attitudes of teachers have great impact upon idealistic emerging adolescents. The attitude that service to others can be of great value must be emphasized. Status and prestige must depend on elements other than accidents of birth or occupation. Stress on academic achievement and college orientation should not be to the exclusion of emphasis on viable alternatives. Guidance and exploration should serve an important function in effecting a personalization of the purposes of each individual.

It is possible that in the future schools may be expected to assume a predominant position, assuming even greater responsibility for socialization of the nation's children. This has already occurred to some extent. Socialization processes must be carried forward. Change will occur in the degree to which the basic family unit is preserved or abandoned. In any event, extreme changes within society are in the making.

Career education aids in individual occupational choices.
John Baker School
(Courtesy of Albuquerque, New Mexico, Public Schools)

Implications of a dynamic society

Viewed in historical perspective the American society of the 1970s is the most affluent one in the history of the world. A greater percentage of its people are better fed, clothed, and housed than in any society in the history of the world. Prospective changes indicate that an even greater percentage will achieve economic subsistence through the concern of influential persons and groups within the society. The first implication of our dynamic society would be freedom from destitution. Thus all can begin to be respected as human beings. The encouragement of each individual or family group to attain economic self-sufficiency through his or her own work has in the past set an economic emphasis upon the value of each individual. In the future value may be placed on individual talent, knowledge, and creativity and not alone on occupational status.

Society and the schools will place much attention on basic and fundamental education. Learning how to cope with personal and family problems and how to develop life-styles which are both personally satisfying and socially constructive will be stressed. Progress has been very difficult in those developmental topics which are common to poverty-stricken and ghetto residents. The elimination of elements which emphasize the hopelessness of being poor are concerns which must be subjected to effective action.

Disciplines to be emphasized in the middle school

Assuming continuity in the social structure and in possible future trends, a reorientation to curriculum balance in the middle schools would seem appropriate. The following suggestions will stress additions and changes in emphases not only to meet present needs for socio-emotional growth but also to prepare emerging adolescents more effectively for the society in which they will live.

Humanities will become of prime importance if nobility of humankind and of the individual are to be stressed. Emerging adolescents must begin to study "what is man?" in addition to those disciplines which are most closely related to the study of humans. Hence an emphasis upon literature, art, music, theater, and such is necessary. The stress in this area must not be upon literature, nor any other discipline as such, but rather upon the human being as exemplified within disciplines. Study in the humanities focusing on self-expression and affective states is most appropriate during the emerging adolescent years.

A second area to be studied in more breadth and depth is that of *sociology*. Again, the *stress is upon the relationship of individual to individual, and people in their environment.* The knowledge which we have gained in technological areas and our control over physical aspects of nature have outstripped our ability to understand societies and cultures. It is now imperative that we learn more about ourselves, as individuals and as members of society. The emphasis should be upon the study of humanity as reflected in the framework of sociological concepts rather than upon a purely academic survey.

A third area demanding attention at the middle school stage is a study of *philosophy* seen as a study of the human's search for meaning and a better way of life. Emerging adolescents should be provided an opportunity to study and compare various ideal solutions to the problems of humanity. In addition, they should be provided ample opportunity to express themselves on issues and problems that they face individually in attempts to develop an ideal concept of society. They should be encouraged to reconcile these ideas with the reality they perceive. Idealism and hope for a better world should be stressed in preference to a pessimistic or cynical view.

One of the major difficulties of the middle school curriculum has been the crowded state of the schedule. Certainly many areas of the curriculum will need to be reviewed for material which is not vital and may be deleted so that the time commitment within the schedule is constructively utilized. Improved methods of learning would also be considered, however, so that there would be a minimal loss of important ideas. The purposes emphasized here do not imply that the modern middle school must necessarily delete material or lessen the influence of certain disciplines, but that they be used more effectively to strengthen certain curricular areas.

Learning attributes

If areas concerned with the human being are to be strengthened without a significant lessening of other disciplines, learning skills and abilities must be taught and efficiently reinforced through appropriate selection of content and teaching methods. The society of the year 2000 will require that the adult of that year be capable of continued learning. Although formal education for pupils of today may end at any time from age 16 through years of advanced education, informal learning should continue for the lifetime of the human being in order that he or she be an effective member of the society.

Use of *rational powers* is necessary to continued learning. The emerging adolescent must develop an ability to think and consider alternatives in a rational way. If the emphasis of curriculum balance is to be shifted toward humanity, it is essential to reduce to a minimum the irrational thoughts and actions of individuals.

Secondly, the emerging adolescent will need to learn to see similarities and differences, to *discriminate between alternatives* and make choices. During elementary years children are accustomed to being told what is *Right* and *Wrong*; later, during the high school years, the older adolescent is expected to know *Right* from *Wrong*. One weakness of the current school system is the lack of effort devoted to teaching the processes of discrimination. In a society where events are evaluated only on a right or wrong bi-values basis, the ability to discriminate is not encouraged. Pupils must learn to attend to all the value positions which will be of importance in a multi-valued society, and which will be crucial in future resolutions of conflicts among values.

Creativity is another area which should be emphasized. The encouragement of creativity (and other learning attributes as well) is not solely the responsibility of the middle school. Yet, due to the plasticity of emerging adolescents, their ability to invent, explore, and try new modes is optimal at this stage. Considerable emphasis in elementary education is placed on acquiring basic skills and learnings where convergence is stressed. In the secondary school students are expected to show evidences of divergence and creativity. Although opinions differ and precise measures of creativity are of limited validity, it is generally agreed that divergence and creativity can be fostered by the formal and informal methods utilized within the learning situation. Children gradually learn to discriminate between fantasy and reality, yet retain their ability to "make believe" and to imagine if encouraged to do so. As children progress from concrete to abstract operational thinking they should be able to continue thinking in creative ways. Hence the school should attempt to foster and encourage creativity in as many areas as possible so that children will retain and develop their imaginations during the middle school years.

Learning attributes which stress a right and wrong, simplistic view of knowledge and thinking are expected to be replaced by a more intricate system of multiple values. The fourth learning attribute to be developed and encouraged is the acceptance of and ability to utilize a *multiple-valued logic* based upon theories of probability. An example of this logic system would state that "if this is true, then there are two (or more) possibilities; however, if the other is true, then there are two (or more) possibilities." Multi-valued logic is an extremely complex discipline which can be approached in the middle school years only in its orientation phase. If emerging adolescents can learn that an open-ended problem is valid, rather than an unanswerable dilemma, they can learn to search for varieties of solutions.

As part of the study of probability as a thought process, pupils may be able to seek partial solutions and progress. This generation has learned that answers with a 100-percent probability level are seldom available. There are an increasing number of problems where probabilities of answers rather than certainties exist. The next generation must be able to work within such a framework. Emerging adolescents can begin to work with the concept of continua to which the concepts of probability apply.

REFERENCES

1. Hornell Hart, "The Hypothesis of Cultural Lag: A Present-Day View," *Technology and Social Change*, Francis R. Allen, et al. (New York: Appleton-Century-Crofts, 1957), pp. 417–418 (with excerpt taken from Stuart Chase, *The Proper Study of Mankind* [New York: Harper, 1956], p. 115).

2. Lewis Mumford, *The Culture of Cities* (New York: Harcourt, Brace, 1938). pp. 495–496.

3. Pitirim A. Sorokin, *The Crisis of Our Age* (New York: Dutton, 1941 [1957]), p. 321.

4. Bernard Berelson and Gary A. Steiner, *Human Behavior, An Inventory of Scientific Findings* (New York: Harcourt, Brace & World, Inc., 1964), p. 515.

5. Frank R. Westie, "Race and Ethnic Relations," *Handbook of Modern Sociology*, ed. Robert E. L. Faris (Chicago: Rand McNally, 1964), p. 603.

6. Meyer F. Nimkoff, "Technology and the Family," *Technology and Social Change*, by Francis R. Allen, et al. (New York: Appleton-Century-Crofts, 1957), p. 307.

RELATED READINGS

Allen, Francis R., et al. *Technology and Social Change*. New York: Appleton-Century-Crofts, 1957.

Barnes, Harry Elmer. *Society in Transition*. New York: Greenwood Press, 1968.

Brameld, Theodore. *Philosophies of Education in Cultural Perspective*. New York: Dryden, 1955.

Della-Dora, Delmo, and House, James E., eds. *Education for an Open Society. 1974 Yearbook*. Washington, D.C.: Association for Supervision and Curriculum Development, 1974.

Mack, Raymond W. *Transforming America*. New York: Random House, 1967.

Mumford, Lewis. *The Culture of Cities*. New York: Harcourt, Brace, 1938.

Reich, Charles A. *The Greening of America*. New York: Random House, 1970.

Sorokin, Pitirim A. *The Crisis of Our Age*. New York: Dutton, 1957.

Toffler, Alvin, *Future Shock*. New York: Random House, 1970.

Toffler, Alvin, ed. *Learning for Tomorrow, The Role of the Future in Education*. New York: Vintage Books, 1974.

CHAPTER 7

Behavioral Science Theories

Theories concerning how learning occurs are of primary importance in the study of education for middle schools. While various psychological schools of thought differ in their interpretations of how learning takes place, all contribute to the knowledge of educators about learning. Thus a review of the formulations of the foremost proponents of the major schools of learning theories, with their implications for emerging adolescent education, seems appropriate.

Consideration will be given to ideas about learning derived from behaviorism, gestalt psychology, cognitive theory, and personality theory, with a statement concerning their common principles for education. A formulation of implications and inferences from those theories for middle school education will be emphasized. The result will be an establishment of a rationale for personalization in the education of emerging adolescents based upon a synthesis of an eclectic learning theory-based rationale.

BEHAVIORISM

Behaviorism, or stimulus-response theory, describes the process of a stimulus being presented to an individual who by responding to it thus creates another stimulus with a continuing series of S-R (stimulus-response) connections being inaugurated.

The person most often credited with being the originator of behaviorist theory is Edward L. Thorndike, with the publication of his book *Animal Intelligence* (1898). Many contemporary S-R theorists operate from the basic premises and principles established at that time. Some of the more important insights attributed to Thorndike in the general area of learning are the following: (1) he saw the differences between bright and dull children as being quantitative in aspect rather than qualitative; (2) he maintained that practice was important because it permitted response to act in creating a connection with the next stimulus; (3) he contended that reward strengthened these connections, although punishment did not seem to have a corresponding weakening effect; (4) forgetting could take place when the stimuli ceased to occur; and (5) transfer would take place only by the principle of analogy with other stimuli and responses.[1]

Behaviorism as a theory of learning was more clearly defined with the publication of Watson's book *Behavior: An Introduction to Comparative Psychology* (1914). Most behaviorists would probably support his assumption that psychology should be based upon overtly observable behavior (i.e., muscular movements and other physical manifestations) rather than upon inferences made with respect to internal nonobservable states or some other source of introspective analysis which cannot be directly studied.

A contemporary disciple of the behavioristic school, B. F. Skinner, has developed a theory known as operant conditioning. The main distinction between Skinner's theory and previous theories is the idea that two types of response can be identified—elicited and emitted. Elicited responses occur in response to a variety of observed stimuli. Emitted responses are operants which are responses to stimuli the sources of which are unknown to the observer. Skinner's theory presents a more lucid explanation to a series of problems not answered by classical S-R theories.

In accord with other behavioristic theories, Skinner found that reward would increase the strength of the operant through reinforcement thus conditioning both types of responses, and that punishment did not have a corresponding weakening influence. He contended that drive levels which were dependent upon the degree of deprivation affected the rate of the responding, but that the inverse was not true. According to Skinner, forgetting occurred as a slow decay rather than as a covering process.[2]

Behaviorism as a basic learning theory for school use has some direct applications but is primarily concerned with stimulus-response-operant-organismic relationships which can be studied directly through the new science of psychology. Its basic tenets in most cases are determined by the study of the responses made in experiments performed under controlled conditions in laboratories using animals, or in the study of human behavior where conditions can be rigorously controlled and stimuli are comparatively unitary. Thus this experimental emphasis in S-R theory can be identified as a molecular theory, i.e., one which focuses upon a minuscule section of a larger problem. Thus, it concerns itself with reaction, with the refinement of the study restricted to as few intervening variables as possible. The purpose of much of the experimentation is to study the basic data on relationships utilizing a high degree of control of variables thus presenting a clear and definitive result from the experiment.

Theories of the behaviorist school are now being studied for applications of findings from the experimental laboratory to practices in the classroom. When appropriately used and properly interpreted, these are expected to increase in importance and use in school situations.

GESTALT PSYCHOLOGY

Gestalt theory differs from behaviorism in that it stresses a molar or holistic viewpoint where a total process of thought is the focus of study. It was developed in Germany with the work of Max Wertheimer in 1912, and was given wider consideration as a theory by Wertheimer and colleagues Köhler and Koffka, who presented this relatively new concept to American psychologists during brief visits to the United States. The primary concern of gestalt psychologists was perception rather than learning itself, and many years elapsed before the impact of gestalt was felt on the field of learning theory. The most visible point of contention was the focus on intelligent learning by the gestaltists as opposed to study of S-R connections and molecular associations by behaviorally oriented psychologists.[3] In his book *Theories of Learning* Hilgard simplified the fundamental theories of gestalt by pointing to the basic organization of gestalt learning. He presented the guiding principle (the Law of Prägnanz) with four laws subsumed under it. Those were: (1) similarity, (2) proximity, (3) closure, and (4) good continuation. The major thesis was that psychological organization tends to move in the general direction of a good gestalt. Basically, Prägnanz can be considered as a state of equilibrium. The first law within the framework of Prägnanz, that of *similarity*, holds that similar pairs are more readily learned than dissimilar ones. The second, the law of *proximity*, states that perceptual groups are recognized according to the proximity of the parts. The third law states that *closed areas* are more readily recognized than unclosed ones, thus aiding in the learning process. The fourth law, *good continuation*, maintains that a straight line will appear to continue as a straight line and a part circle would seem to be a full circle. These principles seem to be aspects of organization which apply to learning as a whole as well as to perception itself.[4]

The major theme or focus in gestalt psychology is upon insightful learning. Hilgard made four statements which characterize insightful learning.

1. A more intelligent organism is more likely to achieve insight, just as it is more likely to be successful at other forms of complex learning. . . .
2. An experienced organism is more likely to achieve insightful solution than a less experienced one. . . .

3. Some experimental arrangements are more favorable than others for the elicitation of insightful solution. . . .
4. Trial-and-error behavior is present in the course of achieving insightful solution. . . .[5]

In considering problems of learning, gestaltists recommend repetitions primarily because they bring to light a set of relationships which can then enter into or facilitate a reorganization into a new structure, thus creating another opportunity to look at the synthesis or new whole. Motivation becomes extremely important with the need of the organism for closure leading toward synthesis and modification of new perception and learning made possible through the achievement of goals. Processes which lead either to success or failure to achieve goals are modified by the result.

Thus it is in the area of understanding that the main debate occurs between gestalt psychologists and behaviorists. The perception of relationships, particularly between the parts and the entirety of the structure, and in the relationships between the processes and the consequences, are of prime importance to gestaltists.[6]

FIELD THEORY

Kurt Lewin also came from Germany to the United States to present yet another focus in the area of perception. His field theory was primarily perceptual, with other educational applications or inferences to be drawn by extrapolation or inference. Lewin characterized the individual human being as traveling through what he classified as a life space.

According to Lewin's theory a person who learns increases in knowledge. This means that the individual moves toward a more complex life space, more clearly dichotomized with more clearly delineated paths. Learning occurs when some unstructured region of life space becomes changed to the extent that one could recognize the new structure and his or her position within it. In these terms learning would be classified as a change in the cognitive structure of the individual.[7] Thus, one of the more important aspects of field-theory psychology is the emphasis upon the surroundings of the learner. This places tremendous emphasis upon the group within which the individual is interacting.

Field theory is particularly appropriate in the basic learning situation of the classroom because of its emphasis upon the differences in individuals. For example, the life space of the adult is more complex than that of the child, just as the cognitive structure of the more-intelligent person is more complex than that of the less-intelligent person. Practice, according to these theorists, is not necessarily a *sine qua non* of learning. Insight seems to have a more important influence. Motivation is of central importance to the learning activities of the individual. Thus, the chief emphasis in field theory is upon a change in cognitive structure, with insightful understanding becoming the prime goal toward this change.[8]

COGNITIVE THEORIES OF LEARNING

Edward C. Tolman has generally been called the first of the cognitive psychologists. In rejecting the molecular ideas of the behaviorists, he developed a theory concerning an area which he classified as purposive behavior. This behavior he saw as being molar (concerned with the whole) rather than molecular in nature.

He identified four descriptive properties in this molar behavior which he considered to be characteristic of behavior as a whole. First, he saw behavior as being *goal directed*, or *purposive*. Second, he saw the individual *using* the environment as a *means* to reach the goal which he felt characterized the behavior as cognitive. Third, he saw the *law of parsimony* in effect, insomuch as the means of least effort was utilized to accomplish the purposes of the individual. Fourth, he saw behavior as being *docile*, that is, *teachable.* He felt that this docility was a mark of purposiveness.[9] Tolman is considered to be favorably disposed toward creative inference and inventive ideation. He regarded a sensible, reasonable adjustment which came from the requirements of the situation to be the most appropriate learning possible. As with other cognitive theorists, he assumed a large measure of transfer.[10]

Since the beginning of the twentieth century and particularly in the last decade, sharp controversy has arisen between the molecular approach of the behaviorist psychologists and the molar theories of growth of the cognitive psychologists. Cognitive psychologists as a group are attempting to describe what happens within the mind of a person as he or she thinks. This organizing process which is so important to them is not of such great concern to behaviorist psychologists.

As soon as the concern of the psychologists is focused on molar categories of behavior or learning, the more general question of perception and its effect upon learning and what is learned is raised. The cognitive structure of the individual is said to be affected more by what meaning he or she attaches to what is perceived in a situation than by the actual features of the situation itself. Thus perception is of vital importance.

One of the more challenging difficulties in studying learning through the cognitive-theory approach is encountered in channeling the molar problems into areas small enough to be studied in meaningful ways. Hence one of the main efforts of the cognitive psychologist must be the focusing of thought. In addition, cognitive psychologists are handicapped by the welter of different stimuli which they must consider in their process of studying the cognitive process outside the laboratory setting.

An even further complicating factor in this problem of the society and its effect upon the cognition of the individual is the fact that different cultures create different cognitive structures.

Cognitive theory, then, emphasizes the organization of knowledge as a molar entity within the framework of the cognitive structure of the learner. Each small step should be understood as an entity before attempting to develop yet more complex entities. The perceptions of the learner become extremely important in this context, since a learning situation must be structured in such a way that the essential features can be understood by the learner. The perceptions of the learner as to his or her purposes become extremely important as motivation for learning. Prior successes and failures determine to a great extent how the learner currently sees the self, and thus how he or she will move in the future toward the objective. Originality is conceived, within the framework of cognitive theory, as being an extremely important aspect of learning. A learner must learn not only the one approved path toward the goal, but also alternative paths suggested by the perceived needs and purposes of the individual learner.

PERSONALITY THEORY

Although current learning theories are usually divided into two general schools, i.e., behaviorism and cognitive theory, the area of personality theory will also be considered because of its importance in learning according to cognitive theorists. In the cognitive framework particular stress is laid upon the social background and perceptions of the learner. The differences between the real world and that perceived by the learner were probably best stated in the work of Snygg and Combs. These scholars contended that learning varies according to the field which the learner perceives, and that the perception is determined, to a great extent, by the circumstances and personality of the learner.[11]

Sigmund Freud was probably the first of the influential psychologists concerned with the effect of cultural environment upon the development of personality and hence learning. While many of his fundamental tenets have been debated by personality theorists, his classic work is still a basic starting point for subsequent studies.

While Freud's theories primarily described the individual as selfish, wishing instinctual gratification, and society as attempting to restrain this process to within reasonable limitations, several contemporary personality theorists maintain a more positive view of the motives and personality of the human. Characteristic of the ideas of some of these theorists are views and dimensions stressed by Carl R. Rogers. For Rogers the chief tendency of an individual is the attempt to actualize the self, i.e., to realize one's inherent potentialities. According to this theory, there is no basic struggle between the individual and the species. The personality has two basic needs; first, a positive regard from other people, and second, a positive self-concept.[12]

Abraham H. Maslow has elaborated upon the same concepts, but has expanded the basic assumptions to include survival tendencies within the human being. According to him the physical and psychological survival needs must be satisfied before the personality can begin the actualization of the potentialities inherent within it. He placed the various needs in hierarchical order:

1. physiological,
2. safety,
3. belongingness and love,
4. esteem,
5. self-actualization, and
6. cognitive understanding.

Each of these needs must be satisfied before the next one becomes important.[13]

Alfred Adler added still another dimension to the preceding theories by maintaining that the personality was always striving toward perfection not only for the person as an individual but also as a member of society. The assumption is that weaknesses within the individual, whether physical, mental, or emotional, are the objects of continual effort in the struggle of a personality for improvement. This does not necessarily imply an insecure person, but rather assumes the creative nature of the individual who could see an ideal above and beyond his or her present status.[14]

Hilgard and Bower[15] in *Theories of Learning* (third edition) have indicated that several principles derived from theories of personality must be considered in educational practice. (1) The learner's abilities and perceptions are important, as are provisions which must be made for differential learning. (2) Prior influences that have shaped the development of the learner are extremely important. (3) The major culture and the subculture to which the individual belongs will probably affect his or her learning. (4) The encouragement to learn may be seen differently by different individual learners according to their anxiety level, so motivation is an individual process, not a group process. (5) The same situation probably will tap entirely different motives from each of the learners. (6) The values held by an individual make the relevance of the subject matter less or more immediate. (7) The group atmosphere of learning (for example, competition versus cooperation) will affect not only the product of the learning but the satisfaction of the youngster in his or her learning.

IMPLICATIONS FOR MIDDLE SCHOOL EDUCATION

Although differences of opinion among learning theorists are obvious there are a number of basic principles upon which there is some agreement. Some of these will be listed and discussed in this section, but a quotation from the article "Personal Thoughts on Teaching and Learning" by Carl Rogers seems best to sum up the primary belief of the authors.

> The only kind of learning which significantly influences behavior is self-discovered or self-appropriated learning—truth that has been personally appropriated and assimilated in experience.[16]

While this idea is certainly neither unique nor new it continues to be a crucial concept in personalization: every learner is an individual and learns as an individual, not as a member of a group.

Many excellent statements have been made about various principles of learning which are acceptable to the various schools of learning theorists, both behaviorists (molecular) and cognitive theorists (molar). One of the best of these is found in Hilgard's *Theories of Learning* (second edition). In this book Hilgard states 14 basic principles which he believes all learning theorists would be willing to accept. These principles are:

1. In deciding who should learn what, the capacities of the learner are very important. Brighter people can learn things less bright ones cannot learn; in general, older children can learn more readily than younger ones; the decline of ability with age, in the adult years, depends upon what it is that is being learned.
2. A motivated learner acquires what he learns more readily than one who is not motivated. The relevant motives include both general and specific ones, for example, desire to learn, need for achievement (general), desire for a certain reward or to avoid a threatened punishment (specific).
3. Motivation that is too intense (especially pain, fear, anxiety) may be

accompanied by distracting emotional states, so that excessive motivation may be less effective than moderate motivation for learning some kinds of tasks, especially those involving difficult discriminations.

4. Learning under the control of reward is usually preferable to learning under the control of punishment. Correspondingly, learning motivated by success is preferable to learning motivated by failure. Even though the theoretical issue is still unresolved, the practical outcome must take into account the social by-products, which tend to be more favorable under reward than under punishment.

5. Learning under intrinsic motivation is preferable to learning under extrinsic motivation.

6. Tolerance for failure is best taught through providing a backlog of success that compensates for experienced failure.

7. Individuals need practice in setting realistic goals for themselves, goals neither so low as to elicit little effort nor so high as to foreordain to failure. Realistic goal-setting leads to more satisfactory improvement than unrealistic goal-setting.

8. The personal history of the individual, for example, his reaction to authority, may hamper or enhance his ability to learn from a given teacher.

9. Active participation by a learner is preferable to passive reception when learning, for example, from a lecture or a motion picture.

10. Meaningful materials and meaningful tasks are learned more readily than nonsense materials and more readily than tasks not understood by the learner.

11. There is no substitute for repetitive practice in the overlearning of skills (for instance, the performance of a concert pianist), or in the memorization of unrelated facts that have to be automatized.

12. Information about the nature of a good performance, knowledge of his own mistakes, and knowledge of successful results, aid learning.

13. Transfer to new tasks will be better if, in learning, the learner can discover relationships for himself, and if he has experience during learning of applying the principles within a variety of tasks.

14. Spaced or distributed recalls are advantageous in fixing material that is to be long retained.[17]

A perusal of these 14 principles reveals that at least nine of them *stress* the importance of the individual learner with his motivations, methods, and capacities for learning (numbers 1, 2, 3, 5, 7, 8, 9, 10, and 13). Given the general acceptance of these statements among psychologists, learning should be considered a unique and personal phenomenon. It should be recognized that school work is molar in nature in the traditional classroom, dealing with many aspects of the entire social, emotional, physical, and intellectual nature of every individual in the class. Even relatively recent attempts to individualize instruction which tend to let the individual work alone seem to lead toward the same problems. Although the pupil is working alone, he or she is progressing toward objectives which have been set up, in most cases, by the demands of the school, class, or teacher, rather than leading from or originating within his or her own personal purposes and goals. Individual learning is enhanced when the purposes and methods are suited to the capacities of the individual pupil rather than externally imposed criteria.

The individual learner in the middle school experiences a number of conflicting influences because of pubertal development, social demands of peers and home, and many other crucial factors arising in his or her life in addition to work in the classroom, or other areas within the school framework. Studies indicate that youngsters spend more time watching TV than they spend in school. Other social agencies or groups such as church, Boy Scouts, etc., create other opportunities for learning for each individual. The wealth or dearth of opportunities for learning within the environment will create differential needs on the part of each individual in the school. The human is a learning organism and, as such, continues to ingest information and develop conceptual structures continuously. All these factors involved in learning make generalizing and predictions regarding learning difficult. Differential life forces act upon or interact with each individual at differing degrees. Even the ecological variables existing within an individual school make teaching generalizations difficult. Homogeneous grouping alone, as opposed to heterogeneous grouping, makes for tremendous variations within the experiences of individuals. Tension caused by varying teacher personalities and methods creates other imbalances. In view of these variables it would seem inappropriate to attempt to translate principles common to most learning theories into teaching practices intended for groups.

The major problem in translating these principles would seem to be that a class as an entity does not learn. A group of individuals learn, each in his or her own unique way, from the various materials which have been presented. The teacher in the traditional classroom who presents the material or content so that the child might learn is working under a severe handicap since, obviously, every student in the class will not learn equally well from one statement, at a particular time, under a particular circumstance. Even the teacher who attempts to individualize learning but who adheres to the basic standards and objectives of the course cannot most effectively aid in the learning of the individual pupil. Only when the teacher discovers the individual purposes, standards, and best methods for achieving them for an individual can he or she most effectively aid in the learning for that individual.

Diagnosis and individual prescription render the task of the teacher complex, and require that teachers develop different attitudes toward learners and toward meeting the needs of students as individuals. No one teacher can accomplish these purposes alone. A school devoted to the pursuit of the goals of the individual could possibly achieve them through pooling resources and talents in a unified effort. In order to accomplish them schools must first obtain a commitment from the staff, faculty, administration, and patrons of the school district; and secondly, employ a systems approach with emphasis placed upon evaluation of the current status of pupils, and provision for alternative paths by which they could move toward satisfaction of their purposes and from their present status toward future goals.

In order to process, retrieve, and store information on student status, utilization of computers and other technological devices will be required. Technology is not a phenomenon to frighten teachers. Rather it should serve as a tool for teachers, counselors, and others to utilize in working with individual learners. The teacher can no longer function as a purveyor of information to passive receptive learners. A teacher working in this framework is in danger of being replaced by sophisticated technology and programs for self-directed learning which can do this task as effectively and reportedly at lesser cost. However, teachers utilizing a systems approach and assisted by technology should be able to achieve the purposes of the middle school through studying the current status of the learner on a wide variety of dimensions. By studying the principles derived from learning theory which could be most effective in facilitating the learning of each particular individual, groups of teachers should be able to help pupils achieve the goals for learning and to have the full advantages to which they are entitled at all levels of education.

While most of the learning theories expressed here are applicable at most ages in the life of the individual, the implications for emerging adolescents in school have been emphasized. The key concept prevalent in all learning theories is that learning is a personal thing, and takes place within individuals, not as a group process. Under these circumstances the emerging adolescent, at the stage of life in which he or she is bursting from one socio-emotional, physical, and intellectual level of development to another, should merit special considerations as suggested within the context of these theories.

REFERENCES

1. E. L. Thorndike, *The Fundamentals of Learning* (New York: Teachers College, 1932).

2. B. F. Skinner, *Science and Human Behavior* (New York: Macmillan, 1953).

3. Ernest R. Hilgard, *Theories of Learning*, 2d. ed. (New York: Appleton-Century-Crofts, 1956), p. 226.

4. Ibid., pp. 227–229.

5. From Ernest R. Hilgard, *Theories of Learning*, 2d. ed. © 1956, pp. 234–235. Reprinted by permission of Prentice-Hall, Inc., Englewood Cliffs, N.J.

6. Hilgard, *Theories of Learning*, pp. 252–253.

7. K. Lewin, "Field Theory and Learning," in *The Psychology of Learning*, National Social Studies Education, 41st Yearbook, Part II, chap. 6, 1942, pp. 215–242.

8. Hilgard, *Theories of Learning*, p. 284.

9. Edward C. Tolman, *Purposive Behavior in Animals and Man* (New York: D. Appleton-Century, 1932).

10. Ibid.

11. Donald Snygg and Arthur W. Combs, *Individual Behavior* (New York: Harper, 1949).

12. Carl R. Rogers, "A Theory of Therapy, Personality, and Interpersonal Relationships, as Developed in the Client-Centered Framework," in *Psychology: a Study of a Science*, ed. S. Koch (New York: McGraw-Hill, 1959), Vol. 3.

13. Abraham H. Maslow, "Some Basic Propositions of a Growth and Self-Actualization Psychology," in *Perceiving, Behaving, Becoming: A New Focus for Education* (Washington, D. C.: Yearbook of the Association for Supervision and Curriculum Development, 1962).

14. Salvatore R. Maddi, *Personality Theories; A Comparative Analysis* (Homewood, Ill.: Dorsey, 1968), p. 493.

15. Ernest R. Hilgard and Gordon H. Bower, *Theories of Learning*, 3d. ed. (New York: Appleton-Century-Crofts, 1969), pp. 562–564.

16. Carl Rogers, "Personal Thoughts on Teaching and Learning," *Improving College and University Teaching*, Vol. 6, No. 1 (Corvallis: Graduate School of Oregon State College, Winter 1958), pp. 4–5.

17. From Ernest R. Hilgard, *Theories of Learning*, 2d. ed. © 1956, pp. 486–487. Reprinted by permission of Prentice-Hall, Inc., Englewood Cliffs, N.J.

RELATED READINGS

Bruner, Jerome S., et al. *Studies in Cognitive Growth.* New York: Wiley, 1966.

Combs, Arthur W. *Perceptual Psychology: A Humanistic Approach to the Study of Persons.* 3d. ed. New York: Harper & Row, 1976.

Hilgard, Ernest R., and Bower, Gordon H. *Theories of Learning.* 3d. ed. New York: Appleton-Century-Crofts, 1969.

Maddi, Salvatore R. *Personality Theories: A Comparative Analysis.* Homewood, Ill.: Dorsey, 1968.

Maslow, Abraham H. *Toward a Psychology of Being.* Princeton, N.J.: Van Nostrand, 1962.

Rogers, Carl R. *Freedom to Learn.* Columbus, Ohio: Merrill, 1969.

Skinner, B. F. *Beyond Freedom and Dignity.* New York: Knopf, 1971.

UNIT III

Curriculum for Emerging Adolescents

Curriculum serves as the basic foundation of school purposes. Relying upon social, psychological, and historical learnings with a profound respect for idiosyncratic development in psychomotor, affective, and cognitive domains, the middle school must systematically strive to enhance the experiences of emerging adolescents in a way to facilitate their growth most effectively. Thus the concepts of the first two units are prerequisite to these chapters.

Four major concerns must be expressed in this unit: curriculum balance and sequence, content acquisition and use, development of learning skills, and individual enrichment. Balance and sequence is primarily concerned with subject matter and its organization, while content acquisition and use is devoted to the means by which such subject matter is utilized in the development of the pupil. The need for a development of specified learning skills and growth in individual enrichment lends an enrichment to the curriculum which is not so readily evident in a more traditional school.

CHAPTER 8

Curriculum Balance and Sequence

Personalization of education is one of the major premises upon which the middle school is based. It requires a great degree of flexibility and variability in the curriculum (i.e., those learning experiences that individuals have within the framework of responsibility of the middle school). Professional personnel responsible for the development of curriculum for the middle school must develop a curriculum that will meet the needs of general education for all pupils, and yet provide for many types of exploration to meet individual purposes. They must be concerned equally with curriculum balance and sequence.

BALANCE

Achieving a *balance between the demands of general education and the function of exploration* for emerging adolescents is an important concern to educators responsible for program development in the middle school. Scheduled learning experiences must be made explicit and available for those general education experiences needed by everyone, while experiences which meet the exploration function must also be scheduled for each individual pupil. Every child must have sufficient time in which to learn what is needed by all, yet must also have time to learn those things needed according to the demands of his or her unique self. Equality of time allocations between these two goals is not necessary (nor sufficient) for curriculum balance. Learning rates differ among children. Some children may need to spend 90 percent of their time in general education; others might need only 50 percent. Rather, the major factor in the development of curriculum is the determination of what goals are needed by all pupils, and what exploration functions should be provided for individuals. A curriculum system must be developed which delineates an allocation of time for each of these.

At all times consideration must be given to the fact that a school program is already in practice, necessitating curriculum revision—i.e., variations on current practices. Time allocations may not only vary between and among individuals from grade to grade, but may also vary from subject to subject. The time to be consumed in general education in the fifth or sixth grades may be more or less than in the eighth or ninth grades. As more independent learning ability develops and more responsibility can be assumed by the emerging adolescent, more time may be given to exploratory functions.

Balance among domains is also a major concern to the educator. Little formal attention seems to have been given to the question of the balance of focus in the curriculum concerning the three domains of knowledge: psychomotor, affective, and cognitive. Textbooks for emerging adolescents may stress the affective domain but sufficient guidance for the teacher in the implementation of objectives in this domain must be presented. Concern for achievement has traditionally focused on the cognitive area. There has been little general attention to sequential development in the psychomotor area except in the traditional physical education activities. An emphasis on psychomotor experiences seems imperative in the middle school so that the program will provide more and deeper experiences.

Affective development requires attention to the emotional experiences most appropriate to emerging adolescents. It is probable that objectives cannot be achieved in any domain without effect on others. Nevertheless, the major focus of experiences must be directly related to the development of specific objectives in the target domain. Even though the domains are interwoven, particular attention should be given to the achievement of affective goals which might be seen as separate and distinct from cognitive or other goals.

Achieving balance in the curriculum among the three domains will require less emphasis on the cognitive domain. Not only will less emphasis upon specific objectives in the cognitive area be recommended, but greater effectiveness and efficiency in their achievement will also be required, thus rendering more class time available for the other domains.

A *balance among disciplines* also concerns educators. Most schools are organized in terms of areas of subject matter. The typical middle school curriculum is ordinarily organized by subjects in nine general areas: language arts, social studies, science, mathematics, physical education, music, art, homemaking, and industrial arts. The four subjects usually classified as academic are language arts, social studies, science, and mathematics, while subjects such as music, art, home economics, and industrial arts have been categorized as exploratory subjects. Physical education is generally required but is accorded less general concern than that accorded to the four academic subjects.

To achieve a balance among disciplines more emphasis may be required for some subjects and less for others. In any case emphasis is directed toward achieving objectives, not necessarily presentation of academic content. If all objectives of a middle school are to be achieved, nonessential objectives, material, and activities will have to be deleted and attention given to greater effectiveness and efficiency in the achievement of necessary objectives. Areas in which more emphasis could be given in a model middle school are the following: physical education, language arts, fine arts, practical arts, and group guidance.

Education has failed in the main in the production of well-developed bodies on the part of high school youth and adults, and in addition has not developed concepts which would lead to a later correction of such problems. One of the most reliable means for insuring a broad range of activities is to allocate facilities, resources, and sufficient time. A minimal allotment of 25 to 30 percent of the school day for the achievement of psychomotor objectives would seem reasonable for the achievement of the broad range of goals in these areas. Activities other than physical education, such as typing, instrument playing, handwriting, industrial arts, and home arts, all of which utilize small motor coordination and skills including affective and cognitive areas, would be stressed. However, continued focus should be placed upon the fundamental purpose of developing a sound physical body.

Language arts should receive considerable attention in the school program. Learning how to be a continuing learner is dependent upon language skills and facility in study skills. Education for the emerging adolescent requires special attention to the four fundamental skills which make up the language arts, i.e., reading, writing, speaking, and listening. These skills are fundamental to learning in other subject areas. While a pupil's basic effectiveness in learning skills should be a concern to the entire faculty, a greater emphasis on language arts development will certainly prove valuable to emerging adolescents as they progress toward the command of learning skills.

The introduction to the fine arts which is characteristic of most programs for adolescents is usually based on the assumption that most children have little experience with the fine arts before middle school and may not have much after. While this may or may not be the case in many school districts, attention to many facets of aesthetic education to a greater depth than mere introduction is recommended. Emerging adolescents should be expected to express aesthetic feeling, and verbalize opinions and ideas in a rational way. All should achieve a degree of skill in various of the fine arts. Emphasis should be given to the performing aspects of these arts since it is in the performance areas that greatest enjoyment and appreciation can occur.

Practical or applied arts should also receive more emphasis in the middle school. Girls should learn some fundamentals in industrial arts and boys some of those in home economics. Curriculum decisions should be made on grounds

Boys gain useful skills in homemaking classes.
Mount Hebron School

(Courtesy of Montclair, New Jersey, Public Schools)

which transcend traditional sex-related roles. All persons should cultivate broad skills in both of those areas. This presupposes careful attention to utilization of additional time given to practical arts in the middle school curriculum.

Another neglected function in middle schools is group guidance, which is not usually considered a part of curriculum. Homeroom could be expanded to some extent to provide a base for group guidance, with school guidance counselors serving in a group situation rather than devoting their entire time to individual counseling. Thirty minutes for group guidance added to a home-room operation would give at least an hour in which affective objectives could be stressed outside the framework of the cognitive domain.

If more time is to be given to learning experiences in physical education, fine arts, practical arts, and group guidance, a careful analysis of priorities in subject matter fields must be made. The basic objectives of science and arithmetic, for example, should not be less rigorous. But a laboratory approach to the study of science and arithmetic problems should provide a base for integration of subject matter in science and arithmetic, with deletion of extraneous content being of major importance. Science and arithmetic as disciplines must still be examined to determine what is necessary for everyone (general education) and what should be provided only for those with special interest. Objectives for this latter group might be allocated to exploratory education pupils to meet individual objectives. Not everyone would need such depth.

Integration of disciplines with attention to objectives in separate but re-lated subject areas is one means of achievement of objectives without an in-crease in school time. For example, a core curriculum provides a mode of meeting the combined objectives of language arts and social studies. Common goals of the two areas can be achieved through only one presentation. Many can be interrelated and integrated with those of other subjects and disciplines so that selection of materials and activities may be made on the basis of their contribution as vehicles for broader understandings. Humanities correlated teaming is a more sophisticated approach to the language arts-social studies team approach with music and art added. The goal for such an approach is to present ideas and materials showing the innate qualities of the human being.

Many different approaches are possible in correlation. Many schools combine science and math in a team approach. Music and art can be jointly considered in an appreciation course, as can practical arts, homemaking, and industrial arts. The development and sequencing of learning experiences for the achievement of basic objectives provide many opportunities for the various subject matters to be seen as related. Educators can find many options for such approaches. Teachers may be reluctant since they may lack informa-tion and experience with the appropriate procedures. In-service activities for teachers are necessary to provide both the knowledge base regarding proce-dures and the new skills and capabilities requisite to correlation of subjects.

Correlation of preplanned and emerging experiences becomes essential as curricular materials and experiences are drawn from more than one discipline and combined for maximum effect. The experience curriculum is composed of all the experiences of emerging adolescents in schools, and all of these experi-ences cannot be planned in detail prior to the launching of the activity. Fundamental aspects should be considered with a variety of alternatives specified in advance. Not all outcomes which occur may have been preplanned; however, both preplanned and unplanned experiences are a part of the curriculum. A good faculty should have a degree of freedom to capitalize upon unanticipated emergent pupil needs and outcomes.

Cooperative planning between and among pupils and teachers is strongly recommended to insure that both formal and informal experiences follow closely those of maximum relevance to both pupil and society as a whole. Cooperative planning may generate a variety of learning experiences which may not occur to teachers who might tend to look toward disciplines as their guide. Cooperative planning is particularly desirable as the informal experiences are introduced into the curriculum. Teachers would be open to suggestions from pupils in developing a range of experiences beyond the preplanned formal curriculum. Experiences, whether formal and carefully planned or less formal and more spontaneously selected, may create many desirable learning situations and environments for pupils. Both should be included because some problems to be considered may not have been recognized when the curriculum was organized. Their very presence may serve as a complicating factor in the development of curriculum. Flexibility and balance between preplanned and emerging experiences is a necessity in education for emerging adolescents.

Balance between needs and desires of pupils should be considered when developing a curriculum for emerging adolescents. Pupil desires are ordinarily honest and meaningful. At times, however, due to lack of experience these desires and interests may be shallow and fleeting; they are also likely to be idiosyncratic. It is thus extremely difficult if not impossible to build a logical curriculum around them.

Emerging adolescents may or may not be able to recognize the real needs that are present in their lives. Their view is likely to be too circumscribed and characterized by shortsightedness. One of the major goals of teachers is to see beyond the desires of emerging adolescents and consider their longer-lasting and deeper needs. This does not presuppose that needs and desires may not be reconciled for the more mature pupil. Responsible adult leadership must be able to observe and assist each emerging adolescent in balancing desires and needs and ascertaining where they are similar and where the differ.

SEQUENCE

Sequence in curriculum development refers to the placement of learning in subject matter and processes in such a way that development can occur in a sensible order. The arrangement of sequences from grade to grade is one of the major tasks of the educator. Much flexibility is demanded in the curriculum and organization of the middle school due to the variability of the student body. Sequence is important both between concepts and related discipline structures and in the development of processes. Pupils will not progress in their command of a subject if they do not possess adequate control over both the fundamental skills of reading, writing, and arithmetic, and learning skills. Sequencing to make these available to all pupils in the appropriate order for mastery becomes all-important.

The development of thinking processes outlined by Piaget implies that during the years of emerging adolescence the pupil moves from reliance on concrete thinking modes to ability to engage in more abstract formal operations. Thus pupils should be able to comprehend and work in more theoretical frameworks by the time they finish middle school years. Each child moves toward formal operations on his or her own unique timetable which is different from all others, thus making planning for curriculum sequence an individual phenomenon. A middle school staff should give adequate attention to basic concrete pupil experiences while moving toward individual conceptual progress.

Curriculum revision must allow for consideration of learning styles. Curriculum is not a simple accumulation of factual material. Learning skills available to each child must be cultivated in relation to sequential growth leading toward the development of more formal operations, yet providing for growth experiences of those pupils who have not yet mastered all the basic skills.

An accentuation of development from dependence to independence is a necessary change for middle school education. All emerging adolescents should be able to work independently at the completion of the middle school years. There will be variability in the achievement of independence, and for some a lesser achievement is to be expected. Nevertheless, the curriculum and its structure must encourage independence and provide decision-making opportunities for all pupils. Structure should be provided for those who are more dependent and unable to achieve a higher degree of independence.

Consideration of sequence of curriculum in combination with personalization necessitates the development of the "open" curriculum. Such a curriculum, most clearly delineated in the work of L. Craig Wilson,[1] has as its primary purpose the establishment of varying experiences for different pupils based upon their needs, purposes, and desires. He has listed three types of knowledge: secure, uncertain, and new. According to this theory, knowledge of secure facts can best be produced by lectures and assigned reading; uncertain knowledge may be best approached by seminars and other such means; and the search for new knowledge is open to research and other exploration.

Such a curriculum presupposes that different individuals will enter the learning experience at differing levels, both in depth and in breadth. Rather than directing a pupil into an ever-narrowing point of study, an open curriculum assumes that, while some pupils with a traditional bent in learning may follow such a path, others may inaugurate learning from a self-directed research learning posture. These individuals may move interchangeably through the three types of knowledge according to their own temporary or lasting purposes.

The curriculum must be an open set of learning experiences in order to permit this type of movement. Systems approaches will be necessary to aid a teacher in better understanding where a pupil is located both in the planned and emergent curriculum, and what next steps may be appropriate in facilitating the advancement of that pupil toward such predetermined goals as have been established. Such an approach does not negate an emergent type of unplanned curriculum, but does emphasize the importance of planning for sequence in any setting.

The development of a curriculum which is balanced and sequenced effectively is not typical of present curriculum practices in many middle schools. The curricula in most middle schools have developed "like Topsy." The situations in which many of the schools have developed have not allowed time and effort for study. However, at the present stage of middle school development it is time to appraise the curriculum and put constructive effort on the development of a curriculum which best meets the needs of emerging adolescents.

REFERENCES

1. L. Craig Wilson, *The Open Access Curriculum* (Boston: Allyn and Bacon, 1971), 304 pp.

RELATED READINGS

Alberty, Harold B., and Alberty, Elsie J. *Reorganizing the High School Curriculum.* 3d. ed. New York: Macmillan, 1962.

Berman, Louise M. *New Priorities in the Curriculum.* Columbus, Ohio: Merrill, 1968.

Broudy, Harry S.; Smith, B. Othanel; and Burnett, Joe R. *Democracy and Excellence in American Secondary Education: A Study in Curriculum Theory.* Chicago: Rand McNally, 1964.

Eisner, Elliot W., ed. *Confronting Curriculum Reform.* Boston: Little, Brown, 1971.

Manning, Duane. *Toward a Humanistic Curriculum.* New York: Harper & Row, 1971.

Saylor, J. Galen, and Alexander, William M. *Curriculum Planning for Modern Schools.* New York: Holt, 1966.

Smith, B. Othanel; Stanley, William O; and Shores, J. Harlan. *Fundamentals of Curriculum Development.* Rev. ed. New York: Harcourt, Brace & World, 1957.

Taba, Hilda. *Curriculum Development: Theory and Practice.* New York: Harcourt, Brace & World, 1962.

Tyler, Ralph W. *Basic Principles of Curriculum Development.* Chicago: University of Chicago Press, 1950.

Van Til, William, ed. *Curriculum: Quest for Relevance.* Boston: Houghton Mifflin, 1971.

CHAPTER 9

Content Acquisition and Use

General education is that education needed by every person in order to live effectively as an individual and participate constructively in the society in which he or she lives. It has two aspects: the cultivation and development of the potential, talents, and abilities of the person as an individual; and the capability and competence necessary to fulfill responsibilities as a member of the society.

The concept of general education includes extension of common learnings and fundamentals begun in elementary school, and the addition of basic conceptual structures which form the core of knowledge and understanding to be enlarged upon in subsequent years. Much of what is taught in the middle school can be considered general education, including not only that which is taught in traditional academic areas, but the arts (both practical and fine arts), physical education, health, and home and family living as well.

General education includes not only the structures of concepts, principles, and generalizations in the subject areas and disciplines, but also the skills and operations necessary for generating meaning and the conceptual structures needed as a foundation for further learning. Learning how to continue to learn, study, and develop an understanding of the processes by which new knowledge is generated in the academic disciplines and in the world of applied arts thus becomes fully as important as conceptual learning. Discovery, inquiry, and information processing are operations expected of students in schools of today.

Within this section a general framework of curriculum for emerging adolescents will be presented. Purposes for knowledge and understanding, and attendant processes which are appropriate for conceptualization and intellectual operations needed by students will be emphasized.

GENERAL EDUCATION IN THE CURRICULUM

Curriculum and instruction are two processes which are so closely related that they can be considered separately only as a matter of convenience. Interpretations of the term curriculum range from the idea that curriculum consists of all the experiences the learner has under the direction of the school to the contention that curriculum is the learning outcomes planned in advance by the educator. Some prefer to separate curriculum planning from instruction so that, for convenience of analysis and evaluation, the two functions can be considered separately. While this approach can be considered logical, it is not the approach used here.

The middle school environment is a situation fraught with complexities, with students as individuals in various stages of development. The variability between and among pupils and even within each child challenges the capability of the staff to deal constructively with the many complicating factors in the learning atmosphere. Thus when we conceive of curriculum as all the experiences which students have in the process of attending the school,[1] we intend to imply and to include in the term *all* the experiences which students have in the process of attending the school—the implicit and hidden as well as the explicit and stated objectives.

With a focus on curriculum, a less formal and more flexible process is recommended where teachers can be called upon daily if necessary to determine concepts and understandings based upon their knowledge of emerging adolescents and the content for which each group of students is ready, or which may only fit the needs of some individual students. The factor of unforeseen environmental stimuli should also be taken into account in prescriptive efforts as teachers and staff determine learning experiences for individuals and groups of students.

To define curriculum in terms of a totality of pupil experiences presupposes a willingness on the part of the staff to consider the experiences of the emerging adolescent in many different categories. The progress of students can thus be assessed within either narrow or broad limits and in terms of a broader perspective than only memory and recall of factual content.

The curriculum should not seem to the student to be a meaningless series of unrelated knowledges and irrelevant data. Broad-based goals along with both general aims and specific objectives and the design of learning activities for achieving them become crucial. Presentation of content and provision for appropriate learning experiences should be based upon student readiness rather than on an inexorable schedule of "covering the material."

Over the years general statements of aims in education have been sparse and conflicting. Goodlad made this point:

The lack of stated aims for education has virtually forced curriculum project groups to turn to school subjects for the determination of their ends and means. As a consequence, ends and means frequently become hopelessly entwined: to learn the subject is the end; learning the subject is the means. There is no external criterion against which to judge the effectiveness of the new or the old.[2]

The philosophy for middle school education expressed in this book places great stress upon the developmental patterns of individuals and the variability of growth rates. Any statement of aims for the education of emerging adolescents should place emphasis upon the unfolding and emerging abilities of these individuals—upon their growth and development. They should be provided with learning environments which facilitate their learning to understand and use their minds, their bodies, and their emotions. Knowledge of subject matter, important as it is to the understanding of a broad range of problems, may not facilitate growth in all areas of development within each individual. The primary question should not be whether middle school students have learned sufficient information, but rather whether they can utilize the abilities and knowledge they possess to cope effectively with situations in which they find themselves.

The need for a more balanced view of school objectives becomes evident in the face of demands from all sides to meet the needs of students who bring with them to school the backgrounds acquired in diverse groups, each with its own cultural values within the broader context of American society. We hold a position similar to that expressed in the Harvard Report, *General Education in a Free Society*,[3] which maintained that schools are attempting to achieve too many objectives. This committee held that when too many tasks are attempted, some even conflicting with others, none of them could be done as well as desired. This contention seems even more valid in the 1970s.

Goodlad noted that in addition to trying to do too many things, schools in many cases vacillate from one extreme to the other. He is critical of this tendency of the school to accommodate fashionable curriculum projects not necessarily appropriate simply because they are currently popular. He recommended more careful consideration of functions to be served by the schools:

> Needed is thorough appraisal of functions thought to be appropriate for each successive phase of schooling, translation of these functions into specific educational objectives, and allocation of human and material resources specifically pertinent to attainment of these objectives.[4]

This statement is particularly appropriate for those concerned with middle school education. While elementary and secondary school goals, processes, and purposes have been relatively stable, somewhat clarified, and applied, the purposes for middle school education have not yet been adequately defined. It is in the realm of clarifying purposes and objectives and in selecting appropriate means for achieving them that middle school educators must work. Identification of both content and processes appropriate in supporting these objectives must receive greater attention. In addition, we need to emphasize processes in all three realms of development, and should not limit our focus to achieving and measuring school objectives only in terms of academic achievement as often occurs.

THE TAXONOMIES OF EDUCATIONAL OBJECTIVES

In order to organize the most effective curriculum for the full development of emerging adolescents, purposes have been considered as they contribute to educational objectives in three areas: psychomotor, affective, and cognitive. A developmental approach to degree of achievement of objectives and criteria for evaluation of them should pervade the curriculum framework. Purposes in terms of the three domains will be couched in relatively general terms with appropriate practices suggested for achieving those purposes. The authors of each of the taxonomies have urged their continual testing and analysis for revision and verification. The necessary research to substantiate all aspects of the hierarchies and suggested sequences has not as yet been completed. Although not isolated from each other, each domain will be presented separately so that a sense of its importance and a suggested organization of educational objectives will be available for reference.

PSYCHOMOTOR DOMAIN

The abilities in *A Taxonomy of the Psychomotor Domain* by Harrow[5] relate to the development of abilities in the psychomotor area, and objectives which may utilize, encourage, and/or develop these inherent abilities. They range in hierarchical manner from simple reflex movements through basic-fundamental movements to perceptual abilities and on to physical abilities, thus to skilled physical movements, and finally to nondiscursive movement communication.

In the realm of psychomotor abilities, the curriculum of the middle school is involved with unique and dynamic growth problems which differ radically from those in the elementary or secondary schools. The physical impact of puberty gives rise to three concerns and requires special consideration in the psychomotor domain for the emerging adolescent: (1) recognition and acceptance of the ramifications of physical growth; (2) recognition and acceptance of an appropriate sex role; and (3) recognition and acceptance of motor-development abilities leading to ultimate acceptance of one's own unique physical capabilities.

The importance of physical condition and motor development to mental development has been emphasized. The contribution of good health to all forms of development is accepted, and it is generally well known and acknowledged that the early years set the pattern for later physical-fitness activities. In addition to these, however, it is the program of activities designed to assist each child toward his or her own maximum development that is emphasized for the middle school. Physical activity is a source of self-expression and pleasure as well as recreation. It is also an inevitable need for the emerging adolescent.

Recognition and acceptance of the ramifications of physical growth

Middle school youngsters usually will require assistance in dealing with the effects of puberty not only as they individually experience them, but as their agemates and peer-group members also are influenced and affected by these changes. The emotional and social ramifications are as critical as the actual physical changes themselves. In considering the needs and developmental tasks of the emerging adolescent, there is a need to provide appropriate focus on the psychological and emotional effects and the interaction between these elements and the cognitive development of the child.

At puberty, physical growth spurts are noted which create problems both in the physical adaptability of the individual and in his or her perceptions of that growth. The entire curriculum of the middle school should be focused to assist the emerging adolescent through this period which will, at best, require considerable understanding and adjustment. If a youngster's unique growth pattern leads to either earlier or later maturation than the norm, the time can be traumatic. The strong desire of youth at this age for peer support and approval and the usually attendant desire to be similar to others is at great variance with the actual state of affairs where pupils find themselves more different from their peers than at any other period in their lives. While all aspects of the educational experiences of the pupil will be affected by this physical variance, one portion of the curriculum directly affected is physical education.

The physical education curriculum must take several areas into consideration if concepts directed toward helping individuals accept and understand their stage of physical growth and status among peers are to be developed. Tanner presents the goal of physical-fitness programs derived from Havighurst, who framed the concepts of growth in terms of developmental tasks. Tanner underscores several concepts which, although not directly related to the psychomotor domain, underlie objectives in this area.

...the goal of physical fitness is organic health, and not merely muscular strength.... Through the physical education program, adolescents can learn to appreciate the normality of variability and, consequently, can learn to accept and use their bodies effectively. Selected coeducational activities can help adolescents in achieving new and more mature relations with age-mates of both sexes, and in achieving a masculine or feminine role. Group activities, including team sports, can be designed and administered to emphasize socially responsible behavior, while contributing to the acquisition of desired values and an ethical system as a guide to behavior. And, if physical education is to be concerned with the integrated human being, it must contribute to the development of intellectual skills and understandings for personal and civic competence.[6]

The American Association for Health, Physical Education, and Recreation in their publication *Fitness for Secondary School Youth* added understandings and outcomes for health and physical fitness in terms of additional specific needs of junior high school youth.

Needs of Junior High-School Youth

Physical fitness needs

1. A balanced and adequate diet for the demands of growth and activity.
2. A safe school, home, and community environment.
3. Sufficient sleep and rest; for some, as much as ten hours daily.
4. Regular dental and health examinations and corrections of remediable defects.
5. Sufficient daily big-muscle activity for normal development; for many, as much as six hours.
6. Experience in an all-round program of health education, physical education, and recreation with enough instruction and experience in skills to be able to participate in a number of socially desirable activities.
7. Participation in selected games and other activities suited to their strengths and appropriate for their developmental needs and adequate guidance.[7]

Therefore each adolescent has several tasks: a realistic appraisal of his or her unique growth patterns, a willingness to accept early or late maturation, a conceptualization of emerging adolescence, and an ability to perceive the self as a small or large physical being.

Recognition and acceptance of an appropriate sex role

This is one of the purposes inherent in the middle school curriculum. During emerging adolescence boys and girls are confronted with changes in sex role. A great deal of interest and concern is generated by physical aspects of sexual development. Social interaction with members of the opposite sex is much desired but is difficult due to changing role and lack of experience. As emergent adolescents begin to mature, their social interest may outreach their social competence. Newly experienced emotions are strong, with new status and values of peers increasingly important. The middle school curriculum and the experiences provided should consider these new characteristics of the emerging adolescent in order to facilitate conceptualizations of new and appropriate sex roles. In addition to conceptualization of roles, goals of sex education in middle school have been proposed as follows:

1. To continue to develop a wholesome and mature attitude toward sex
2. To give students a scientific background and vocabulary for dignified discussion of sex
3. To establish respect for social standards
4. To help students understand the reasons for proper behavior
5. To develop fine family relations
6. To encourage students to talk frankly and to help them find answers to their questions.[8]

Developing an adequate conceptualization of an appropriate sex role without a comprehensive and explicit knowledge of the physical aspects of sex seems rather remote. Conceptualization is multi-faceted, and is affected by emotional and social elements as well as the physical ramifications of sexual development itself. Recognition implies both a cognitive and an affective element, while acceptance is an affective one. Purposes in the curriculum primarily concerned with the psychomotor domain should also comprise a combination of cognitive and affective components in order to be achieved in the curriculum.

Recognition and acceptance of motor-development abilities

Emerging adolescents must come to accept their individual body types, physical abilities, and physical appearances. They should be assisted insofar as possible to accept the responsibility, challenge, and necessity of constructively utilizing their strengths and weaknesses, and to move toward maximum development and utilization of these abilities. The goal of the "sound mind in a sound body" has been expressed many times. Gates, et al., in an educational psychology text say:

> Motor development is a handmaiden of mental development. The child experiments, manipulates, explores, and gratifies much of his intellectual curiosity by way of motor activities. In like manner, motor behavior serves as a vehicle for a large portion of the child's social contacts and his learning of ways of cooperating with others. Similarly, motor development also has an important bearing on a child's emotional behavior, since a child's strength, speed, coordination, and skill very often determine whether a child will experience success or failure, and whether he will be thwarted and angry or threatened and afraid.[9]

The structure of concepts in kinesiology stresses the study of human movement. Mackenzie has suggested seven major classifications:

1. movement forms (descriptions of sports and dances, strategies of competition, instruments and surroundings)
2. mechanical principles of movement (isometric and isotonic contractions; gravity, inertia, force, and leverage; positioning and movement for specific tasks)
3. structure and function of the moving human organism (anatomy, physiology, environmental conditions)
4. movement and the person (personality, group dynamics, aesthetics, nonverbal communication)
5. learning how to move (motor learning)
6. movement and health
7. movement and meaning (interpretations of movement)[10]

These classifications provide a basis for individual conceptualizations and understandings beyond motor development itself. The necessity for personalization of curriculum to provide for progressive achievement in each of the areas of development becomes paramount with physical education assuming a more individualized and rigorous approach much beyond the usual organized activities, sports, and games.

AFFECTIVE DOMAIN

The taxonomy of the affective domain compiled by Krathwohl, Bloom, and Masia[11] presents a hierarchical listing of emotional outcomes which are considered desirable in an ideal curriculum. These include receiving, responding, valuing, organization, and lastly characterization by a value or value complex.

The affective goals appropriate to the middle school curriculum can be categorized in four general areas. These are: (1) development of emotional health; (2) ethical growth and moral development; (3) aesthetic appreciation; and (4) socialization.

Development of emotional health

This concept is based upon the theory that the human being is inherently good, and that adequate and appropriate developmental experiences for training in emotional expression will create potentially well-balanced and emotionally healthy adults. Given these assumptions, affective goals require the design of a learning environment and experiences expressly intended to cultivate the humane qualities of the individual and to facilitate the development of the natural potentialities of each student as a human being.

Research indicates that education becomes meaningful to individuals when they are able to relate that learning to themselves and reality as they are experiencing it in their lives.[12] The task of the middle school faculty is to work toward the creation of a situation where children are challenged. The curriculum will focus on concepts, particular knowledges, and processes that adult society considers important, but, in addition, the adults must discover and make clear the relevance of the content and its relationship to the needs and interests of individual learners. It is through the process of individual learner perceptions in the assigning of personal meanings that what is learned is made available for the learner's use. In the A.S.C.D. 1970 Yearbook, *To Nurture Humaneness*, psychologist Arthur Combs suggested seven changes needed to create a more appropriate environment for humaneness which would afford students more personal meaning in their experiences with the curriculum.

1. Deemphasizing information and objectivity....
2. Valuing meaning....
3. Developing sensitivity to student meanings....
4. Accepting students....
5. Encouraging personal exploration....
6. Testing, evaluating, and rewarding meaning....
7. Teachers, too, must be evaluated and rewarded for humanism....[13]

The depth of emotional balance and health which can be effected by school experiences cannot be fully assessed until stronger emphases are placed upon higher level cognitive development. There is difficulty in evaluating higher-level thought processes and the emotional development of human beings in areas where feelings, beliefs, aptitudes, and values are factors which influence the acceptance or rejection of new and contradictory evidence.

A common misconception is that humanism is less than intellectually rigorous. The error of this notion will be shown when it becomes clear that the overall development of human quality requires a curriculum which synchronizes and coordinates development of all domains, allows many alternatives, and is indeed much more demanding and rigorous than a curriculum which focuses on any one alone, or which fails to provide for broad development. William James characterized human problems as constituting the "strenuous mood" rather than the "easygoing way" of life.[14]

Hence the development of a curriculum based upon humanistic concepts, including the development of emotional health, does not stress freedom of choice, student responsibility, student initiative, development of commitment, and such as a means to a weakened or "watered-down" curriculum. We intend a rigorous concept-based curriculum, but one predicated upon the needs, purposes, and desires of the pupils who must be *involved* for the learning process to be activated toward maximum development.

This requirement would bring about a change in the structuring of the learning experiences. In order to maximize meaningfulness and relevance, knowledge would need to be related and integrated across disciplines. Knowledge would be utilized as a base only when it was necessary to answer the problems which human beings confront at certain stages of their emotional development. The faculty, with the aims and goals well internalized, would become masters at recognizing "the teachable moment." "When the body is ripe, and society requires, and the self is ready to achieve a certain task, the teachable moment has come."[15]

Ethical and moral development

Ethical and moral development might be assumed as subsets of the development of emotional health. A sense of ethics and sets of functional moral concepts can be developed only within the framework of a healthy emotional growth where the teacher provides freedom to explore a wide range of alternatives in human behavior and dilemmas of individuals where choices are difficult. Bossing differentiated between authoritarianism and democracy in the classroom by the degree to which the individual pupil felt free to articulate differences in opinion.[16] There is a close relationship between the development of healthy emotional expression and interaction of the individual with others. The process of moral development and ethical growth requires not only that the individual cognitively understand the prevalent values and ethics in the subcultures of the society, but that he or she also be able to process this information in stages from awareness to commitment and emotional acceptance of a set of values.

Study of moral values has, until recently, entailed inculcation of traditional values, with the individual having very little experience in overtly examining moral judgments and their bases. Renewed attention to affective education and the increasingly pluralistic society require that more attention be given to studying inevitable conflicts and concerns in the larger society, particularly those which the individual is likely to experience in the multivalued culture where individual value structures come into conflict with each other, necessitating the development of an accepted set of criteria for moral choice-making.

Aesthetic appreciation

Aesthetic awareness should be stressed to a greater extent than it is in most schools today. An understanding and cherishing of beauty in whatever form it is found should be fostered. Whether auditory, as in music; visual, as in art; or intellectual, as in the elegance of logical development in mathematics: all share in the quality of experience and the beauty afforded.

To know that a form is called beautiful is not enough. One may know the intricacies of any field of interest without having been awakened to the intrinsic beauty of that field. While it is more difficult to appreciate an art form or elegance without understanding, it is possible. But for best results appreciation should constitute an intellectual understanding as well as an emotional expression and pleasurable sensation. Perception is the primary basis for a determination of aesthetic worth. The more perceptive the individual and the more rigorous the application, the more likely that a strong base will be present for varied and deeply based perceptions inherent in the experience. The deepening of the bases for aesthetic appreciation is through a "strenuous mood" generated through guidance and knowledge of the form being considered, and usually not through a relatively unguided experiential base.

Socialization

With its base in societal values, socialization may seem anomalous in a curriculum stressing personalization. On the contrary, just as moral development and ethical growth are constituted by the interrelationship between the values of the individual and those of the people around, socialization is the gradual process both deliberate and structured whereby the values of the society are developed within each unique individual. Those attitudes and values which are reflected in the society are those which will encourage in the individual the greatest possible emotional health within the framework of that society. Persons must be able to cope with the problems and values as well as with the changes they will experience. This process is becoming more complex as the subcultures and alternatives increase the range of values and choices open to each individual.

Individuals live with a multitude of others and each needs to learn about himself or herself and others as beings who are valuing and judging worth and making individual commitments. Socialization is that process by which the predominant values of the society are learned. The understanding and appreciation of the purpose of values should make social interaction with other members of the society less constrained. An ideal program should provide a number of experiences to facilitate the development of skills in adapting and adjusting in relation to expectations of peers and others. The following goals of a social program are listed by Faunce and Clute.

1. The social program should provide a wide variety of activities appropriate to various stages of maturity.
2. Help should be given new students in orienting them to their new school, and to all students to help them overcome their timidity and self-consciousness.
3. Students should participate in planning, carrying out, and evaluating social experiences.
4. The building and the schedule should facilitate social life.
5. Adults should guide, but not control or dominate.
6. There should be many opportunities to help less fortunate individuals.
7. Relationships between and among peers should be strengthened and extended.
8. Teachers should seek to promote wholesome social relationships, not only in student activities, but also in the classrooms.[17]

Socialization is an important function of school and should not be on the periphery of the curriculum in the middle school. Rather, through carefully developed curriculum organization, structured learning experiences covering a wide variety of values and attitudes necessary to the individual in living in society may be provided. It is through deliberately planned and organized programs developed in each of the affective areas that the efforts of teachers and individual students to achieve these purposes can be effective. The affective domain must be considered equally as important as the intellectual demands of the cognitive domain which tend to focus school efforts on academic achievement.

COGNITIVE DOMAIN

A similar taxonomy of educational objectives in the cognitive domain has been prepared by a team with Bloom[18] editing. The suggested hierarchical order of objectives of these abilities assumes a movement in cognitive capability toward utilization of these abilities, each of which encompasses or depends upon the one before it. They range in the domain of knowledge from comprehension, application, analysis, and synthesis to evaluation.

Certain specific purposes are inherent in the recommended practices designed to enhance the intellectual education of emerging adolescents. These are: (1) development of self-evaluative processes; (2) transition in learning modality; (3) acquisition of relevant knowledge; and (4) integration of knowledge.

Self-evaluation

Self-evaluation is a concomitant of self-determination in learning. If emerging adolescents are to learn how to learn, they must learn to make their own decisions. It follows that they must judge the effectiveness of their own efforts. Freedom of choice based in part on needs, purposes, and desires requires that the faculty of the middle school develop a series of procedures and processes by which each pupil may make successively more comprehensive and important decisions. At each stage each pupil will learn to evaluate the degree to which self-selected goals have been met. Each may elect a goal set by the teacher, but select his or her own means of reaching the intended learning outcome.

One of the goals for students and staff alike is to transfer responsibility for learning from staff to pupil. Responsibility for individual development is enhanced when the goals sought are the pupil's or when the means utilized are selected either by the student alone or in joint session with the teacher. Only through experiences developed in appropriate sequence from limited decisions and consequences to more comprehensive ones can this responsibility be acquired.

In order to determine their progress in the realm of self-determination pupils must learn the process of decision making and how to evaluate their success. Then they can progress to the achievement of the goals they have each set for themselves. One of the first things the student must learn is self-discipline. Faculty members must be willing to guide pupils in the development of necessary abilities. They must become more explicit about criteria and must be prepared to allow pupils to assume the responsibility for evaluating their own progress. Cooperatively setting criteria with students will be more time consuming, but if pupils are to learn to be responsible and to accept consequences, responsibility for evaluating progress must be shared.

A major rethinking of the evaluation process and appropriate techniques will have to occur if this program is to be a success. The tendency of emerging adolescents to be overly self-critical will need to be understood, with the staff being supportive of the efforts of the student, yet resistant to negatively expressed criticisms. The task of the teacher where emerging adolescents are indeed given responsibility in their own evaluations is to assist them in a realistic appraisal of their own efforts rather than to support them in a rejecting or negative viewpoint. In practical terms, this means that the teacher may find it possible to evaluate the students more highly than they might evaluate themselves, or choose to overlook some aspects of the pupil performance. No attempt is made here to minimize, to weaken, or to withhold judgment. Rather, a full set of criteria can be developed but only successively applied as students build toward more complete repertoires of behavior.

Evaluation will thus assume new dimensions in the framework of the middle school. Both the teacher and the pupils will possess the information and criteria necessary for evaluation. The teacher's task will then require considerable insight into the thoughts and values of individuals as these are reflected in each pupil's determination of goals, and in the way all of his or her efforts affect his or her feeling about self-worth. If a particular pupil has an extremely strong or weak (whether deserved or not) self-concept, the task of the teacher is to assist the pupil in becoming more realistic in his or her self-assessment. The teacher's role should not be that of dispenser of grades. Rather, he or she should be a helping person, a guide in the ultimate development of competence in the self-evaluation process for emerging adolescents.

Learning modality transition

Although personalization is one of the fundamental purposes of the middle school, this does not obviate the necessity for each person to acquire basic knowledges, skills, and attitudes. The responsibility of the school to provide general education demands an assessment of the presence of knowledges needed by each individual and persistence until they are adequately developed. It is in this framework that transition from elementary to secondary content becomes important, and in which the middle school becomes a unique

**Coeducational opportunities in physical education.
Algonquin Middle School**
(Courtesy of Averill Park, New York, Central School District)

entity. Much of elementary education is intended to serve the general educative function so that a substantial portion of the essential knowledge and skills needed by individuals in our current society may be acquired by the time of entrance into the middle school.

The middle school serves a transitional function between the skill-development and general education purposes of the elementary school and the specialized educational functions of the secondary school. Recent cognitive psychology has focused on Piagetian research into intellectual operations which seem to develop in stages along a continuum from concrete to formal operations with the major change found to occur at approximately the middle school ages. Thus the treatment of content and processes as the student moves from elementary to secondary school must take into consideration this change in ability toward more formal reasoning.

The middle school student should be rapidly moving toward reading more theoretical and sophisticated materials. Introduction and exposure to many types of materials is one of the purposes of middle school curriculum, whereas studying for more careful analysis might be expected in secondary schools. The transition in cognitive functioning toward more complexity may be expected in all content areas included within the general educational field. At the same time, personalization and analysis of developmental levels or stages of thinking should be assessed. Even in the general education area it is of prime importance that each individual's ability to utilize formal thinking, reached at a different age for each individual, be included as a guiding factor in curriculum development in the middle school.

Relevance

Relevance to the needs, purposes, desires, and perceptions of pupils involved in the learning process is of utmost importance in the formulation of a curriculum pattern for the middle school. Research in personality and perception theory has indicated that pupils learn as individuals, not as a group. Content, no matter what its importance to society, will not be assimilated unless it is perceived by the learners as relevant to their needs and desires and subsumed under structures they have formulated for themselves.

Relevance may vary because of the dual purposes of the school. Some content may be relevant to the needs of society and not relevant to the perceptions of the student; other content may be relevant to the perceptions of the student and not relevant to the needs of society. Some content may be relevant in both contexts. This dilemma accentuates the importance of the teacher as a guide to the learning of the pupil. If material is relevant to the needs of society, it behooves the teacher to motivate the pupil toward consideration of these materials so they can be perceived as needed by all. On the other hand, if material seems relevant to the pupil but not to the needs of society, it becomes the task of the teacher to determine first, whether the material is in fact relevant, and second, how to enable the pupil to learn the material without disturbing other necessary work or the work of classmates. The teacher should be reluctant to refuse time or opportunity to study material which the pupil perceives as relevant.

Integration of knowledge

One telling criticism of school curricula has been the crowding of subject after subject into the school day. Consideration must be given to alternative procedures so that less time is consumed in general education without sacrificing the structure or function of crucial knowledge. One means of conserving time is the integration or correlation of various disciplines. It is fallacious to assume that the content and methods of each discipline must be taught within the framework of a 40 or 50-minute block of time segregated from other subjects. The experiences of block-time and core teachers have shown that disciplines can be taught in either correlated or fused block-time approaches with great effectiveness.

The content of the middle school curriculum in math and science, with the learning modalities involved in these areas, can be related and presented by one teacher or by a team of teachers in a meaningful way, as can the language arts and social studies. More recently, organized humanities courses have shown the efficacy of such an approach by including not only language arts and social studies but art and music as well. The fine arts have also been correlated with the practical arts in some middle schools.

Support for correlation of subjects is two-fold. First, the knowledges and learning techniques are both related and similar in the subject areas to be correlated, and thus tend to reinforce each other by being presented together. Second, time can be saved if the related content can be considered once by either teacher or team rather than separately as two different and unrelated subjects.

PRACTICES IN THE CURRICULUM

In order to develop an adequate curriculum whereby stated purposes of the middle school may be achieved, certain basic questions must be considered. Many of these questions have been considered within content areas and have dealt largely with scope, sequence, and balance between and among disciplines. Structure and organization of the disciplines as an approach to curriculum development became particularly popular during the 1960s. This emphasis contributed to clarification of the relationship between concepts and processes and to the importance of the development of both conceptual structure and processes in the curriculum. However, the logic which has been so carefully developed for content organization should not necessarily be assumed to be related to the psychological processes by which learning takes place with individual learners. These structures and guides which should be used by teachers should not be followed without due regard to the logic, stage of knowledge development, and fundamental understandings being built by each student.

Content restructuring

Restructuring of the various disciplines is a recent development resulting from studies in curriculum stimulated by Sputnik. Modern math in its various forms, new means of looking at science as a process rather than as content, and new efforts in social sciences and language arts to develop a meaningful structure for the discipline have been most helpful in the educative process in the last decade. The fundamental premise of such structural devices has been the establishment of basic concepts and procedures which authorities in the discipline felt were the fundamental framework for that discipline. According to this theory the emphasis on the mastery of details in the content would be lessened and a corresponding amount of time could be devoted to the learning of the basic concepts and syntax of the discipline. Here again, two differing purposes can be seen: one, a more effective presentation of general education; and two, a method of conserving time by the elimination of unnecessary details.

Many educators in the late 1950s and through the 1960s felt that students should learn to develop a conceptual framework with data in more elemental states and draw inferences for themselves. This would lead to generalizations, thus to principles, and then to laws, establishing the conceptual structure. Thus much of the curriculum development which took place was organized around the primary structural elements of the major disciplines. The development of concepts, generalizations, principles, and modes of inquiry was assumed to enable the student to develop an intellectual ability to approach unfamiliar problems and relate them to previously experienced problems much as experienced scholars might.

Such curriculum development efforts led to a series of conferences and projects in which similar sets of logical structures were developed for most of the disciplines found in school subjects. Most of these structures were based upon four aspects of the disciplines: the content, the practices, their modes of inquiry, and their outcomes. Since pupils were expected to act as inquirers utilizing the logic of the structure as seen by authorities in the discipline, it was soon realized that one of the more important and more desirable objectives of such a curriculum was the development of higher-level intellectual abilities.

Focus on inquiry and learning skills is central to the four mandates listed by Parker and Rubin for the achievement of the new combination of curriculum content and intellectual goals.

1. Subjects of the curriculum and their content must be reconstructed so that they deal with the truly important, and so that they in total yield a quality education;
2. Subject matter, from kindergarten to the graduate school, must be organized so that minimum waste motion occurs and so that content which offers multiple benefits is utilized and exploited;
3. Methods must be devised for teaching subject matter which makes for serious intellectual pursuit, which has its roots in a sensible respect for the way humans learn which exploits the total range of the individual's capacity for assimilating knowledge, and which tests itself against high standards of excellence;
4. Provisions must be made for the enormous spectrum of individual differences, both in ability and in ways of learning, in the school population.[19]

The emphasis upon quality of experience, focus on basic elements in fields of knowledge, assimilation of knowledge, maintenance of high standards of excellence, and development of ways of learning stressed in this excerpt indicate the intellectual requirements of such a curriculum. An emphasis on intellectual growth should begin even before middle school, and by then should certainly be available for all students, with particular attention given to those who need or desire such intellectual stimulation.

Among problems which arose with the development of the structure of disciplines theory were overgeneralized use and misinterpretation on the part of those who were unfamiliar with its basic premises and tenets, and the overly enthusiastic manner in which it was introduced and recommended by some of its proponents.

Despite some shortcomings, the structure of disciplines theory has made a constructive contribution to the development of curriculum. Much inconsequential factual information has been deleted from curricula due to a more critical examination of concepts and processes of inquiry recommended by scholars and content specialists.

**Boys and girls participating together in school activities.
Algonquin Middle School**

(Courtesy of Averill Park, New York, Central School District)

The advantages of a curriculum based upon structure of disciplines were presented by Bruner who suggested four general advantages of learning in this manner: first, "that understanding fundamentals makes a subject more comprehensible"; second, "unless detail is placed into a structured pattern, it is rapidly forgotten"; third, "an understanding of fundamental principles and ideas...appears to be the main road to adequate 'transfer of training'"; fourth, "by constantly reexamining material taught in elementary and secondary schools for its fundamental character, one is able to narrow the gap between 'advanced' knowledge and 'elementary' knowledge."[20]

Structures of discipline can be utilized in middle schools most effectively when teachers and curriculum builders see them as guiding principles for conceptual development which should be utilized in their relation to the needs, purposes, and desires of emerging adolescents. When seen as a primary influence the structure may tend to block some of the learning paths which might be most effective for individual youngsters. This was not the original intent of the theory, and should not be so misinterpreted at this stage of its development. We would do well to retain the best features of these projects in relation to the developmental needs of emerging adolescents, and thus relate the content to relevant concepts and processes for education of those enrolled in middle schools.

Inter-relationships between disciplines

The attitude of middle school educators toward sources for curriculum development should be eclectic in nature. In addition to giving attention to the logic of the structure of disciplines, one should also be concerned with the logic of inter-relationships between subjects. Such relationships have existed throughout the history of education. The courses of study currently conceived are not similar to those perceived in the middle nineteenth century nor at other times in the past. Writing may be seen as a separate skill or as part of a language arts program, as part of the social studies program, or as part of a dramatics class if such exists. It may be perceived as a skill if one is concerned with grammar, spelling, or penmanship. It may be perceived as conceptual in nature if the focus is on style or on ideas expressed. In other areas there are several interpretations open as to purpose and content. Comparisons between the "scientific method," Dewey's logical methods of inquiry, and any number of suggested approaches to problem solving are impressive because of similarity rather than difference.

The acquisition of concepts occurs differently in individuals because individuals have different educational experiences and develop different thought patterns and processes of thinking. The role of the middle school teacher should be to assist the pupil in concept acquisitions without regard to the individual discipline from which that information may be derived. Since some teachers may be more familiar than others with some concepts and structures, the most effective process is to utilize them in teams and across disciplines. Even though the teacher's knowledge may be somewhat limited in related areas, the conceptualizations that middle school pupils acquire are also usually less complex and at the beginning stages. Teachers should be able to assist in developing more complex concepts or to locate appropriate resource persons within the community if necessary.

Concepts and structures which cannot serve to meet the developmental purposes of the emerging adolescent should be considered for deletion. Curricular relevance connotes a purpose, in this case the meeting of the developmental needs of the individual emerging adolescent. That content which would further development of conceptualizations is a necessary part of general education. Factual information which is irrelevant, trivial, or nonessential, and conceptual acquisition as an end in itself not related to general educational needs should be set as supplemental, or appropriate only for some.

When deletion of irrelevant material is recommended, it is posited that many concepts and/or facts currently being presented at the middle school level are not appropriate or do not satisfy the requirement of general education (i.e., that education needed by all emerging adolescents). A most rigorous pruning of this segment of middle school education should occur with an eye to delimiting the content to be learned by all middle school pupils. All pupils should be expected to learn only those concepts and/or facts which are needed by all, rather than the usual practice of having all pupils attempt to learn that which is needed only by some. For example, the idea that all pupils should learn the same mathematics through the eighth grade, or that all pupils should study a foreign language through the eighth grade should be reviewed carefully. The contention here is not that some students may not need these subject matter concepts, but rather that *all may not need them*. The fundamental issues facing curriculum developers at the middle school level are: (1) what content is actually needed by all pupils; (2) what learning processes are in fact needed by all pupils; and (3) what enriching experiences should be made available to pupils on an individualized or personalized basis.

The development of interdisciplinary learning experiences seems to be one of the more effective means by which curriculum might be developed. Such experiences are expected to better serve the expressed needs, purposes, and desires of the clientele which are in many cases more global in nature than those which can be met if learning is that strictly related to individual disciplines.

REFERENCES

1. Robert W. Frederick, *The Third Curriculum* (New York: Appleton-Century-Crofts, 1959), pp. 3–5.

2. John I. Goodlad, with Renata Von Stoephasius and M. Frances Klein, *The Changing School Curriculum* (New York: The Fund for the Advancement of Education, 1966), p. 94. Reprinted with permission.

3. *General Education in a Free Society: Report of the Harvard Committee* (Cambridge, Mass.: Harvard University Press, 1945).

4. John I. Goodlad, "Direction and Redirection for Curriculum Change," *Curriculum Change: Direction and Process*, ed. Robert R. Leeper (Washington, D.C.: Association for Supervision and Curriculum Development, N.E.A., 1966), p. 8.

5. Anita J. Harrow, *A Taxonomy of the Psychomotor Domain—A Guide for Developing Behavioral Objectives* (New York: McKay, 1972), pp. 1–2.

6. Daniel Tanner, *Secondary Curriculum—Theory and Development* (New York: Macmillan, 1971), p. 344. Reprinted with permission.

7. Karl W. Bookwalter and Carolyn W. Bookwalter, eds., for the American Association for Health, Physical Education and Recreation, National Education Association, *Fitness for Secondary School Youth* (Washington: The Association, 1956), pp. 25–26. Reprinted with permission.

8. Helen Manley, "Sex Education, Where, When, and How Should It Be Taught?" *Journal of Health, Physical Education, Recreation*, March 1964, 21–24, vol. 35. Reprinted with permission.

9. Arthur I. Gates, et al., *Educational Psychology* (New York: Macmillan, 1948), p. 61. Reprinted with permission.

10. From *Toward a New Curriculum in Physical Education* by Marlin M. Mackenzie. Copyright © 1969 by McGraw-Hill, Inc. Used with permission of McGraw-Hill Book Company.

11. David R. Krathwohl, Benjamin S. Bloom, and Bertram B. Masia, *Taxonomy of Educational Objectives, The Classification of Educational Goals, Handbook II: Affective Domain* (New York: McKay, 1964).

12. Carl R. Rogers, *Freedom to Learn* (Columbus, Ohio: Merrill, 1969), p. 120.

13. Arthur W. Combs, "An Educational Imperative: The Humane Dimension," *To Nurture Humaneness: Commitment for the '70's*, ed. Mary-Margaret Scobey and Grace Graham (Washington: A.S.C.D., N.E.A., 1970), pp. 177–178.

14. William James, "The Moral Philosopher and the Moral Life," *Pragmatism and Other Essays*, ed. J.L. Blau (New York: Washington Square Press, 1963), pp. 214–235.

15. Robert J. Havighurst, *Developmental Tasks and Education*, 3d. ed., newly revised (New York: McKay, 1972), p. 7.

16. Nelson L. Bossing, *Principles of Secondary Education* (New York: Prentice-Hall, 1949), p. 218.

17. From *Teaching and Learning in the Junior High School* by Roland C. Faunce and Morrel J. Clute. © 1961 by Wadsworth Publishing Company, Inc., Belmont, Calif. Reprinted by permission of the publisher.

18. Benjamin S. Bloom, ed. *Taxonomy of Educational Objectives, The Classification of Educational Goals, Handbook I: Cognitive Domain* (New York: McKay, 1966).

19. J. Cecil Parker and Louis J. Rubin, *Process as Content: Curriculum Design and the Application of Knowledge*, Rand McNally Curriculum Series, ed. J. Cecil Parker (Chicago: Rand McNally, 1966), pp. 28–29. Reprinted with permission.

20. Jerome S. Bruner, *The Process of Education* (Cambridge: Harvard University Press, 1960), pp. 23–26.

RELATED READINGS

Bloom, Benjamin S., ed. *Taxonomy of Educational Objectives, The Classification of Educational Goals, Handbook I: Cognitive Domain.* New York: McKay, 1966.

Bookwalter, Karl W., and Bookwalter, Carolyn W., eds. *Fitness for Secondary School Youth.* Washington: American Association for Health, Physical Education and Recreation, NEA, 1956.

Frederick, Robert W. *The Third Curriculum.* New York: Appleton-Century-Crofts, 1959.

Goodlad, John I., with Von Stoephasius, Renata; and Klein, M. Frances. *The Changing School Curriculum.* New York: The Fund for the Advancement of Education, 1966.

Harrow, Anita J. *A Taxonomy of the Psychomotor Domain: A Guide for Developing Behavioral Objectives.* New York: McKay, 1972.

Joyce, Bruce R. *New Strategies for Social Education.* Chicago: Science Research Associates, 1972.

Krathwohl, David R.; Bloom, Benjamin S.; and Masia, Bertram B. *Taxonomy of Educational Objectives: The Classification of Educational Goals, Handbook II: Affective Domain.* New York: McKay, 1964.

Tanner, Daniel. *Secondary Curriculum: Theory and Development.* New York: Macmillan, 1971.

Taylor, Peter A., and Cowley, Doris M. *Readings in Curriculum Evaluation.* Dubuque, Iowa: William C. Brown, 1972.

CHAPTER 10

Development of Learning Skills

The general education needed by all emerging adolescents includes both conceptual structures and processes by which these structures can be maintained and enhanced. Skills are required by pupils in the middle school years for continued development, and are built upon those previously acquired in the elementary schools. Thus the middle school could be conceptualized as an immediate post-elementary school. During the elementary years emphasis is placed primarily upon basic skills in language arts and mathematics and development of study skills in these areas. The child must make the transition from learning to read, write, and do basic arithmetic to using these processes and skills in successively more demanding and sophisticated ways. At the conclusion of middle school the child is expected to be able to utilize them readily and effectively while building more complex structures in the disciplines included in high school and post-high school curricula. Thus, development and mastery of the basic skills and their applications need to be insured through practice. The application of these skills should be further developed to include exploration activities both in and outside of school during the middle school years.

We consider the development and cultivation of the basic skills, the study skills, and higher level thinking as processes—the full range of intellective capabilities. The treatment of processes separately from concepts is done for the sake of clarity. Both aspects of learning are basic to the organization and manipulation of ideas in abstract thought and in the search for solutions to problems encountered both in school and in life outside the school setting. The separation of conceptualization of specific sets of ideas from processes is necessary in order that processes may become the focus of study. Of course, processes are utilized only in relationship to some type of substantive knowledge, i.e., just as learning to set the table is ultimately useless unless one sits to eat. This section will focus on techniques and skills of the learning processes intended to enhance and facilitate learning of many types and in different areas of study.

PSYCHOMOTOR DOMAIN

Equal emphasis in emerging adolescent education should be placed upon the achievement of purposes in each of the three domains: psychomotor, affective, and cognitive. A balanced middle school curriculum organized to enhance the fullest development of the emerging adolescent should include major goals in three aspects of the psychomotor domain: physical development, motor development, and physical fitness.

Physical development refers to large-muscle development, which is so important to a viable self-image of the individual emerging adolescent, and to small-muscle development as it emerges. The development of a physique which enables every pupil to engage with some degree of success in one or more sports is considered essential. Every pupil should be required to participate in a physical development program appropriate to his or her needs, purposes, and desires. Emphasis in such a program should be placed upon the idiosyncratic needs of each individual. A pupil should know the rules and the fundamentals of many games, should be reasonably proficient in some, and hopefully, quite proficient in one or more. The purposes of such activities, however, relate to the development of the physical attributes of the individual, not the mere playing of a game. Games which focus on teams and which are subject to exploitation of students for competition should be controlled by administrative policy to eliminate possible ill effects in the developing adolescent.

Concern with *motor development* allows attention to special abilities, particularly in activities which require small muscles and hand coordination. Curricular focus should be placed on physical activities involved in typing, playing a musical instrument, sewing, and such, which require dexterity and flexibility rather than great strength. Finger exercises demonstrating control and independence of movement are but one example. Teachers in the middle school should be aware of activities utilizing motor development and cultivation of motor skills evident in every classroom as well as those usually associated with the department of physical education.

Physical fitness usually includes aspects of health and development of emerging adolescents, such as posture, alertness, general physical tone, blood circulation, breath control, and support, which together optimize body functions and generate possible energy. Efficiency and control of body movements is yet another concern in general physical fitness. While these concerns may be considered within the jurisdiction of the physical education program, none should be ignored by staff in any classroom or area of study.

All teachers should be aware of alertness or lack of it. Alertness comes from a physically healthy body and is necessary for intellectual functioning and motivation. Bad posture can be just as evident to a classroom teacher as to a band director or a physical education teacher. Difficulty in breathing, awkwardness, and other inefficiencies in body movement are readily evident. Means should be provided to sensitize each student to his or her own needs in these areas.

PHYSICAL PROCESS DEVELOPMENT

Processes which utilize the physical attributes of the emerging adolescent and which tend to make them more effective have received less proportionate specific attention in schools than processes concerned with cognitive and affective objectives. In many cases this is due to tradition and lack of experience among teachers. Efforts in the following areas should be encouraged within the curriculum of the middle school as a means of developing psychomotor processes: (1) physical education experiences, (2) handwriting, (3) typing, (4) utilization of machinery, and (5) playing musical instruments. This listing can be suggestive of other physical processes which should be considered by all teachers.

Physical education experiences

Physical education courses have been considered as an allocation of time for exercises and sports from which emerging adolescents have been expected to achieve physical fitness and efficiency. Physical education to be most effective should include not only an extended period each day, but should also be integrated into the activities of the other part of the school day. Such integration could elevate the importance of physical objectives and enhance the possibility of their being achieved.

In order to achieve skill in the various physical processes certain activities should be a part of the physical education experience. Fundamental body movements can be achieved through the practice of calisthenics. Various drills used during the calisthenics period may be conducive to the achievement of those types of physical skills which should become automatic.

Another portion of the physical education period should be devoted to the needs of each individual within the class. If the purpose of the activity is to teach the skills and procedures of a certain game, the instructor should ascertain in advance which pupils are more and which less familiar with the activity. Peer teaching, permitting the most knowledgeable pupils to serve as officials, and separating to some degree according to talent might prove useful to individuals. The skills of the sport, to be learned most effectively, should be taught on an individual basis rather than on a "hit and miss" game procedure where some will learn much and others little.

While placing an emphasis on individual skills both in developing muscles and dexterity the physical education teacher should also strongly emphasize the peer relationships which occur in team sports. Due to the need for peer approval, and because of the changing physical nature of the emerging adolescent body the pupil should be made to feel adequate to the demands of the situation. Thus an emphasis upon team sports and group activities should be maintained, with the effort of the teacher being concentrated upon the improvement of the individual in developing the skills necessary to such activities.

Sports and activities with carry-over value should be stressed. Individual sports such as archery, swimming, bowling, and golf should receive more organized attention, with an effort on the part of the instructor to keep the activities based upon small-group interaction in addition to individual skills. Such instruction cannot be limited to the confines of the classroom, gymnasium, or field. Arrangements could be made with bowling alleys, golf clubs, etc., to permit pupils to utilize community resources. Camping and the development of survival skills should become a basic part of the middle school curriculum, thus making possible a further integration of subjects, with the physical education teacher, homemaking teacher, social studies teacher (ecology), and science teacher working together to indicate the integration of various disciplines.

Handwriting

Handwriting is one psychomotor skill to which every classroom teacher can contribute. Legible handwriting is essential in most jobs and in handling the many forms and applications which are a part of personal and business affairs. The physical process of handwriting begins to deteriorate as soon as specific instruction in its use ceases, which is ordinarily before the middle school years. Handwriting skills should be stressed in the middle school since this is the time of physical growth when bones in the hands of emerging adolescents create a new set of physical problems. As the hand and finger bones lengthen during adolescence the motions which once achieved a set of patterns for the child now achieve totally different results. New bone structure and lengthened muscles must be retrained. In order to insure handwriting skill emphasizing careful and legible styles, specific instruction should continue throughout the middle school years.

Typing

The ability to use a typewriter in a reasonably competent manner should be both a right and a requirement for every pupil in the middle school. While competency in this case does not necessarily presuppose a set speed and accuracy standard, each child should reach a competency equal to that which he or she can attain in handwriting. Such a goal is advisable since typed material can be read so much more easily than handwriting. Further, given a reasonable degree of competency, work can be finished in a shorter time. In a technological society typing is used in a wide variety of ways, one of which is for dialogue with computers. Thus we hold that typing should be required as a skill for all pupils, not merely allowed for some few.

Utilization of machinery

Middle school pupils should be instructed in the combination of physical, cognitive, and affective processes necessary to understand and operate basic machines with which they will come in contact during their school experiences, as well as, to some extent, those which they may be expected to operate as a routine part of their futures. In school the manipulation of science laboratory equipment, practical arts tools, lathes, saws, and other machines requiring manual dexterity should be added to the emerging adolescent's skills.

The purposes for these experiences are four: first, the pupils learn to deal with objects in the physical world; second, they develop motor skills and processes necessary to manipulate physical objects; third, hopefully, they will be able to transfer both the actual processes and the knowledge that objects are constructed on certain basic principles to the physical world in which they live; fourth, they will be able to operate and repair simple equipment both at home and outside. In short, emerging adolescents need to prepare themselves to some extent for common tasks in the technological society.

Playing musical instruments

The physical dexterity necessary to play a violin, clarinet, trombone, or piano varies considerably. Learning to combine cognitive, affective, and psychomotor domains effectively is imperative in the production of music. The physical skill to coordinate muscles and control fingers is especially important. Each

Pupils develop psychomotor skills through instrument playing.
Linton High School
(Courtesy of Schenectady, New York, Public Schools)

instrument has its specific demands on the body mechanism. For example, playing wind instruments requires excellent physical body tone, with special demands made on mouth and jaw muscles which must be particularly developed. The importance of body tone is also seen in the case of vocal music, since the body becomes the primary instrument, demanding breath control, support, and correct tone placement—skills and abilities which should normally be evidenced in a typical emerging adolescent.

AFFECTIVE DOMAIN

Processes which involve emotions and their interactions with and effect upon the cognitive and psychomotor domains are difficult to describe in brief and simple terms because they are intensely personal and are accessible only through introspection and self-examination. The mechanisms which are triggered in emotional responses to stimuli are so complex that even to the individual they are not readily accessible for analysis or review. But emotionality is recognized as one aspect of human nature. Understanding and cultivation of capacities for enjoyment and creativity present opportunities for the middle school pupil to appreciate the generative power of emotion and to cope constructively with this energy source.

The school staff has a contribution to make to help each individual keep all aspects of his or her nature developing and growing toward maximum self-realization. Teachers need to be aware that emotions affect and shape cognitive input, and that conditions under which school learning occur are important factors in the way in which that learning is remembered and re-called.

The following seven processes in the affective domain are examples which should indicate directions in which faculties might move in developing affective process objectives:

1. development of viable self-image,
2. development of social skills,
3. inculcation of sportsmanship,
4. encouragement of creativity,
5. development of leadership capabilities,
6. engagement in the valuing process, and
7. cultivation of aesthetic skills.

The *self-image* that individual students possess and the image they think others have of them create a tremendous emotional impact. It influences their perceptions of others in their peer group as well as perceptions of adults as they experience associations both in school and out. Acceptance by their peers is one of the strongest personal needs of emerging adolescents.

The development of *social skills* in relating to the peer culture and adults involves such areas as etiquette, courtesy, grooming, and general communication skills to be used in personal interactions with others. If these skills can be developed among all individuals in the school, including adults, the school atmosphere can be supportive of efforts to achieve individual and group goals such as respect for others and concern for the rights and responsibilities both of self and others.

Closely allied to social skills is *sportsmanship*. Many of the skills included in the general socialization process are involved here, with the distinction that the situations involved are usually more emotionally charged and stressful. A complicating factor arises when recipients of the negative aspects of this trait are not personally known to the pupils. Thus they tend to discount effects of their attitudes in terms of later consequences (e.g., pupils from other schools who are unknown to individual pupils might be treated differently than close or casual friends or acquaintances). Sportsmanship, a refined version of the broader social skills, demands special attention to personal attitudes, public morality, and school morale.

Creativity, as a form of thinking, is more fully developed in the section on cognitive processes. In order to be able to think creatively, however, a certain emotional context is necessary. The creative individual must be flexible, risk-prone, and imaginative. These emotional sets are developed only through their specific encouragement, hence the practice of creativity should be considered within the framework of emotional processes and a psychologically supportive accepting environment, and not alone as an isolated cognitive process.

Leadership is a function of the situation. The leader in a classroom setting may not be a leader in a sports setting, who in turn may not be a leader in a homeroom setting, and so on. Leadership is primarily based upon the singular abilities of the individual and the advantages that those abilities confer within the context of a particular situation. In addition, cooperation is a vital element, requiring the development of group-interaction skills. Each leader must realize that the ability to lead presupposes the ability to follow. Individuals need to learn a wide variety of skills so that the individual who is a leader in one activity may develop leadership skills appropriate to a variety of situations. Leadership also requires full recognition of the abilities of others and a willingness to utilize each person's best efforts in each situation to the advantage of the total group.

Valuing as a process of clarification, as presented by Raths, Harmin, and Simon,[1] is worthy of considerable effort. In the past a fundamental function of the school as a primary agent for socialization was the inculcation of a common set of values. From the early years of the industrial revolution, when large numbers of immigrants came to the United States, the "melting-pot" concept was prevalent. With the more recent acceptance of the importance of preserving cultural pluralism, however, staffs are urged to provide opportunities and learning experiences which encourage pupils to examine the many sets of values expressed in current society. Pupils need to have experience with conscious engagement in the processes of valuing so that they may learn to consider values and dilemmas created by conflicting or inconsistent beliefs. The value structure of each individual is continuously changing and is shaped by experiences and pressures in both the home and small groups.

The ramifications of such a move are not yet known. It is hoped that the detrimental effects which accrue from denigrating any subculture will be alleviated as the society comes to appreciate the richness created by a variety of subcultures. We hope that examination of both values and situational contexts of those values will lead to increased understanding of the reordering or restructuring of values.

Aesthetic consciousness should be cultivated in every individual as a continuation of the valuing process. Instead of resting primarily on personal belief systems and social skills, it has as its focus the awareness of beauty and the satisfactions to be realized in the expressive arts and in those feelings which arise from the emotional content of many different kinds of experiences.

The curriculum should provide many opportunities for self-expression through participation in the physical process of playing, writing, painting, theater, puppetry, and such. Also the cognitive side of aesthetic appreciation can be developed through observing, listening, reading, and studying works of art, which can include one's own responses to aesthetic works.

DEVELOPMENT OF PROCESSES IN THE AFFECTIVE DOMAIN

The purposes for development of processes in the affective domain have received less attention and are less understood than those in the psychomotor and/or cognitive domain. Processes are dynamic actions which may or may not produce a measurable product at a given point. Emotional development as a desired goal for each individual is less amenable to measurement and evaluation than cognitive or psychomotor development. Lack of criteria for measuring outcomes and general difficulty in assessing emotional development should not cause an exclusion of appropriate experiences, however. Many results in our current curricula are not measurable at this time. Test makers have only recently been asked to develop instruments in these areas. Improved psychometrics will follow only as the demand for attention to this area continues. Aesthetic appreciations and awareness of emotional responses are important factors in our quality of life and should be included in a human-development curriculum in the middle school.

Experiences in the following school areas should be encouraged in order to facilitate affective process objectives: (1) homeroom, (2) assemblies, (3) athletic participation and observation, (4) classroom creativity, (5) valuing exercises, and (6) aesthetic experiences. These areas are intended to be suggestive, and may be utilized for an expansion to a larger list of such activities in a middle school curriculum.

Homeroom

In the structure of the middle school there are a wide variety of opportunities for the development of processes in the emotional domain. In a homeroom situation it is possible for pupils to practice continuously the accepted procedures they learn, such as personal and group etiquette and courtesy. They can consider the impression they make upon their peers through grooming and in their face-to-face interaction. Both leadership and followership can assume an important role in the homeroom. The homeroom teacher can be a great influence on students in the development of these processes. In order to teach respect for other persons by example, the teacher must show respect for pupils as individuals. In teaching consideration and concern for others, the teacher needs to show these characteristics in relationships with emerging adolescents. At this stage of their development the pupils are beginning to be more aware of themselves and others. They can consider how things might be. Their idealism leads them to expect all adults, and especially the teacher, to practice those characteristics which society seems to require.

Assemblies

While congregations of the entire or some large part of the student body may achieve purposes on the intellectual level, many social and emotional purposes may also be achieved concurrently. The assembly can present opportunities to learn how to behave with peers in large groups. Need for order, procedures, and organization can be discussed and observed. Again, etiquette and courtesy are important behaviors to be practiced during such educative functions. At the same time aesthetic values may be inculcated when the performances include various art forms of a level understood and appreciated by the middle school pupil.

Award assemblies can provide valuable experiences. The process of accepting honors, or having them denied when they may be thought to have been deserved, provides an important emotional experience at this stage when youth begin to try to realize dreams. They begin to recognize that the likelihood of success can be problematical—a most important educational experience for emerging adolescents. On the school's part great caution and discretion must be exercised to ascertain that enough awards are given, and across broad levels and ranges of achievement so that many if not most pupils can at some time in their educational experience achieve some sort of valued award.

Athletic participation and observation

Athletic participation and observation present many opportunities for the consideration of emotional processes. The phrases "good winning" and "poor losing" represent only the sportsmanship involved in such activities. Athletics also provide socially acceptable channels for aggressions experienced by all, yet without the harmful side effects which can occur if these aggressions are not sublimated in some manner. One of the most difficult problems faced by a school staff as well as physical education instructors is the question of appropriate degree of emphasis to be placed upon winning, school spirit, pride, and other manifestations of emotional behavior. If insufficient emphasis is placed upon the importance of winning, whether the activity be intramural or varsity, the fullest emotional impact of the physical experience cannot be achieved. At the same time, an overemphasis upon winning, probably more common, can create ill effects.

Sportsmanship is an abstract concept which can be easily understood at a cognitive level, but when coupled with activities which generate emotional impact, is most difficult to reach in real life. It becomes even more difficult if the activity or athletic program is staged in a circus atmosphere with an emphasis upon winning and school pride. A preplanned program setting rules for courtesy suggests that the visiting team be treated as guests of the host school. A program of welcoming events and a postactivity social event can be planned. Spectators should be able to enjoy the activity or game and show a natural desire to cheer for their school without resorting to discourteous acts. Such an atmosphere can be present in middle schools where sportsmanlike attitudes are fostered.

Classroom creativity

Creativity can be defined in different ways, but here it refers to the seeking of divergent solutions to an identified problem. Traditional education as experienced by most individuals tends to focus on one accepted answer, rather than encouraging diverse or alternative directions leading to several possible solutions. A sophisticated culture requires an emotional set in which emerging adolescents are able to accept the reality of alternative approaches to problems which once might have been seen as having a single solution.

This emotional process requires a degree of nonconformity, a willingness to tolerate ambiguity, and a sense of humor. The intellectual process of creativity will be considered at another point, but certainly such an intellectual operation cannot be consummated without the emotional processes originally having been present. An open learning situation is required where teachers deliberately foster the appropriate emotional attitudes and processes.

Valuing exercises

A growing concern for peer approval and idealistic approaches characteristic at emerging adolescence lend importance to the valuing process during middle school years. Values may be attained through the relatively passive action of absorbing values presented by others in an uncritical cognitive operation. Such values may remain shallow or unexamined unless emphasis is placed upon them. In contrast, where pupils learn the active process of valuing and value clarification through systematically examining values and contextual relationships, they can become proficient at carrying on this process for themselves. They can develop an inquiring, open attitude regarding situations in which they may find themselves, and thus develop values which are appropriate to the total circumstances.

Aesthetic experiences

Opportunities for aesthetic appreciation should be provided in the design of the middle school. Classrooms should be attractive, halls should be decorated, and school landscaping should be aesthetically pleasing. Emerging adolescents should be encouraged first to appreciate this beauty, then they should be assisted in development of an ability to create beauty to the extent of their abilities. Continued exposure to works of expressive arts and the opportunity to produce aesthetic works aid in the cultivation of the emotional processes involved in aesthetic appreciation. The emerging adolescent's ability to visualize alternative art forms and interpret abstractions can, with continued encouragement, culminate in actively developing works of art pleasing to others as well as to the self.

COGNITIVE DOMAIN

Cognitive learning processes are those which require the application of basic processes (i.e., reading, arithmetic, composition, and speech) in the achievement of higher cognitive processes necessary for continued learning and participation in our complex technological society. Some of the purposes for the development of these processes are to:

1. acquire learning skills,
2. develop basic skills,
3. apply basic skills,
4. investigate areas of personal interest,
5. develop future capabilities in learning skills, and
6. acquire an independence in learning.

The primary purpose for development of any process is the acquisition of that process. In the case of *learning skills*, efficiency in learning assumes greater importance as the complexity of life in our society is considered. Amassing detailed knowledge is no longer adequate, especially with no recognition of relationships or organizing principles. Thus the school student is expected to learn those processes which will develop throughout life.

Current data indicate that *basic skills* are not being adequately developed by the end of the elementary school years. For example, normal distribution of sixth-grade students on achievement and skill-development evaluation reveals that some pupils' skill development is at what is considered third-grade level. Therefore, the next school level must provide continued attention to the development of those skills. This policy is now mandated in some states—students who have not yet acquired command of basic skills to the requisite levels may not be placed in regular classes of the next level.

Even where student test scores are adequate, the emerging adolescent needs to be able to *apply basic skills* and processes to learn in various areas. From learning to read, the emerging adolescent must progress to reading to learn in a variety of subject areas and for many different purposes. Basic processes form the groundwork for middle school education, and students are expected to learn their application.

A major purpose for full development of basic skills is to enable each individual pupil to *investigate areas of personal interest* and to have the capability to explore new areas. Since personalization of purposes and goals is a primary commitment for a middle school program, achieving basic learning processes which enable each pupil to go beyond the common general education curriculum should receive the required support of faculty.

Learning how to *develop future capabilities in learning skills* is a central focus of schooling at all levels and is of particular importance in emerging adolescence. To *acquire an independence in learning*, to be able to learn independently, to exercise habits of self-discipline, and to be willing to assume initiative and responsibility for learning should be stressed. Middle school teachers must move to encourage students to pursue learning goals on their own and to reward them for doing so. Although content and acquisition of structures and processes are requisite in the middle school, *at least equal attention* must be given to the attitudes and instrumental processes entailed in that learning. Mastery of study habits should enable the pupil to master content more readily and thus make learning a more satisfying experience.

COGNITIVE PROCESSES

A shift from concrete to formal intellectual operations will occur, for most individuals, during the middle school years. These formal processes are basic intellectual operations performed by everyone and entail the ability to do "as if" thinking, to think in more abstract realms, and to use more abstract ideas. Also, greater understanding and use of formal logic and processes become a more prevalent mode. These, of course, depend upon past learning experience, encouragement, and opportunities as well as innate capacity. Prior to the middle school years many of these operations have not been developed to any great extent. The Piagetian theory of development holds that the formal-thinking achievement is to some extent based upon maturity and age or stage and sequence of development. Thus in the middle school years most formal processes first reach a viable stage of development. Many facets of the learning processes delineated here cannot occur unless or until the emerging adolescent is able to move from concrete to formal thought operations. Some of the more important cognitive processes are discussed utilizing commonly accepted terms. While recognizing conflicting definitions of some of these terms, it is contended that middle school faculties should be aware of and concerned with these crucial elements of emerging adolescent education: (1) rational thought, (2) analytical thought, (3) critical thought, (4) synthesis of thought, (5) inquiry, (6) multi-faceted logic, and (7) creativity.

Through these modes of thought and their use in problem solving the pupil will be able to develop and utilize specific learning and decision-making processes which apply previously learned basic skills and newly acquired rules and process skills to new subject matter. Pupils should thereby be able to advance to more sophisticated levels of intellective operation and inquiry in various areas of knowledge necessary for informed understanding and constructive participation in an increasingly complex society.

The development of mastery of levels of abstraction for emerging adolescents appears to require a systematic effort. For example, research indicates that pupils can learn to generate ideas of high quality, ask more relevant questions, be more sensitive to crucial clues, make use of information, and achieve solutions to problems.[2]

Development of such higher thought processes is dependent upon a solid grasp of more fundamental processes which must first be achieved. The learner then needs extensive practice in utilization of learning skills so that he or she can step from the mastery of study habits and effective thinking to the application of these abilities to further learning.

Rational thought

Persons who engage in rational thought are able to look for reasons beyond their own particular mind set, their unexamined beliefs, and their prejudices to facts or data, to evidence which exists or can be presented to substantiate a position or a proposed solution. The question of reasonableness is resolved by the credibility of the evidence presented. What would a reasonable person accept? What are the criteria for acceptability of evidence? By what warrant does a fact become a fact? All of these questions have to do with the utilization of objective, external data, rather than a reliance upon internally conceived, subjective data.

The mental processes entailed in rational thought do not come about naturally. Habit patterns in the emerging adolescent which require disciplined activities may be difficult to achieve. The idealism and newly emerging self-consciousness of the young adolescent run contrary to the requirements of greater objectivity and suspended judgment in rational thought.

One of the recognized approaches to achieving a more rational thought process is the utilization of Dewey's five steps in problem solving. These are:

1. recognition of a problem,
2. analysis of the problem,
3. suggestion of possible solutions,
4. testing of the consequences, and
5. judgment of the chosen solution.[3]

Utilizing these procedures will permit the pupil to approach the problem from as objective a stance as possible. Such a posture will strongly enhance the ability of the individual to pursue rational thought.

The pupil must learn how to study without being biased by emotions. One example of a way to sensitize students to a variety of uses of language is to study propaganda, its uses and abuses, and in this way the student learns the problems involved using language in ways to persuade rather than to inform.

Study of semantics increases the range of understanding. Skill in rational thought should be developed by all teachers, regardless of subject matter area. It should not be considered just as an aspect of philosophy, semantics, or logic.

Analytical thought

Analytic processes may be treated as discrete skills required in breaking a communication into parts in order better to understand the whole. The Taxonomy of Educational Objectives in the Cognitive Domain[4] divides analysis into three types or levels. At one level students are expected to break down the material into its constituent parts, to identify or classify the *elements* of the communication. At a second level they are required to make explicit the *relationships* among the elements, to determine their connections and interactions. A third level involves the *organizational principles*, the arrangement and structure which hold the passage or communication together as a whole.

Analysis as a thought process can be an extremely sophisticated level of thought. One purpose of a middle school experience is to *initiate* analytical thought processes, applying the basic skills which have been mastered in order to permit further advancement in the subject being studied. An analysis of a single statement would permit a pupil to ascertain whether a statement is a fact, amenable to verification, or whether it is an unverified assertion. Attention to the objective and subjective aspects of a statement should enable the student to see semantic problems involved, analyze the bias of an author, and think carefully concerning written, spoken, or implied statements. With such ability he or she could move toward a more sophisticated frame of reference in various academic fields.

Critical thought

The chief function of this mode of thought is to determine how and why particular thought processes are occurring. Emerging adolescents would consider why certain statements create certain impressions. They would learn to express themselves in ways which would precisely convey their intended position. Verbal and written style would be practiced and carefully studied and amended where necessary to achieve the purposes of the writer, utilizing criteria and skills learned through critical review of the writings of others. Skill in criticism of one's own work and the work of others and the ability to understand how certain thoughts follow from certain stimuli are significant features of cognitive development.

Synthesis of thought

One of the major problems in American education is the inability of the school structure to encourage the development of knowledges, processes, and attitudes of the various subjects. The ability to synthesize, i.e., to take many seemingly disparate ideas and form them into a whole which is something a little more than the separate parts, is most important to an individual pupil.

It is difficult to ascertain how disparate bodies of knowledge, cross-disciplinary approaches to inquiry as well as modes of inquiry within each discipline, can be attained while working to establish relevance to the learner. Nevertheless, unless the middle school staff makes a concerted effort there seems to be less possibility that individual staff members can assist the middle school pupil in this synthesis and interrelatedness.

Inquiry

One of the first phases of the inquiry process is the development of an ability to ask direct questions. These questions should be relatively simple in the beginning in order for the pupil to analyze the process of inquiry. Learning by inquiry is predicated upon skills of asking questions and probing data which will lead to some end or solution. Skill in the utilization of thought processes should not be confused with mastering content; however, mastery of content and skills of learning cannot be separated. In order to inquire, think on a subject effectively, or form a hypothesis, some knowledge of content is necessary. Also, learning skills and the ability to think, ask questions, develop concepts, and note implications are necessary in order to learn content most effectively. If middle school pupils are trained in the asking of significant questions they will soon develop the ability to arrive at answers which relate to the appropriate data, relations, and logic. They can then move to the next higher level question, and so on.

Inquiry places pupils in a position where they must ask questions in order to learn answers. The ability to ask appropriate questions is strengthened by prior monitored practice. A teacher's task is to present data that are in apparent conflict, thus encouraging the pupils to ask questions. The next steps are to guide them in their search for possible additional data, to raise next questions and so on until they have come to the next level of understanding.

Multi-faceted logic

For centuries logic has been presented and studied as a bi-valued, right-wrong process. The student was expected to move from the general to the specific or from specifics to the general. When the logic of proof and valid or invalid reasoning is discussed the usual reference is to formal processes. Problems in the present more complex society require much more use of the concept of probabilities where there are many contingencies and few if any absolutes. The teachers and staff of all schools have a greater need to become more skilled at dealing with possibilities and differing sets of assumptions when dealing with either a specific problem or more general problems. Pupils will need to learn both deductive and inductive logic, and also learn to accept and live with greater ambiguity and an increasing absence of single definite answers.

The study of psychology, sociology, and cultural anthropology as well as current affairs are recommended for the middle school. All provide examples of the type of problems and approaches where probability in establishing parameters is stressed. Pupils must not only learn to accept ambiguities, but must also develop the comprehension skills to recognize and deal with them. They must also continue to cultivate the thought processes required to consider the ramifications and consequences.

Creativity

Creativity as a human capability has many meanings and entails many different processes. Within the framework of this text it is considered as something which is new to the pupil, is true, and is generalizable. As a process, the discovery or creation of something unique or new to a child is accepted as creative. The arriving at new or different ideas for that child qualifies as a creative thought, even though the idea has long been known to a society. Creativity, then, is the ability to think in divergent ways. This capability is accepted as a developed one. Within adolescents it should be cultivated lest they come to accept the already-present ideas, processes, or products as the only possible ones. Such acceptance generally has the tendency to stifle creative thinking.

Creativity is important in a changing society. Gold has stated that the releasing of an individual's potential to design the new is more important than merely learning to apply the old knowledge. Such learning might permit rapid leaps forward or the movement in new directions rather than the slow progress of extrapolation.[5]

It is assumed that creativity is a set of attributes which is more abundantly present within those youth who are observed to be artistically creative and in those who are scientifically creative. A study by Lowenfeld[6] indicates that those who are creative in art are relatively similar in thought production to those who are creative in the sciences. It is our position that all individuals can be more creative if the situation and environment provide appropriate stimulation of the interest and motivation as well as the processes through which these abilities are known to be amplified.

The development of creative abilities seems to require a supportive, encouraging climate as well as focus upon the ability to think and produce divergent ideas and/or products. Dealing with problems in new ways is a process which, due to the sometimes conflicting need for approval on the part of the emerging adolescent, must be stressed continuously.

REFERENCES

1. Louis E. Raths, Merrill Harmin, and Sidney B. Simon, *Values and Teaching* (Columbus, Ohio: Merrill, 1966), 275 pp.

2. Robert M. Olton and Richard S. Crutchfield, "Developing the Skills of Productive Thinking," from *Trends and Issues in Developmental Psychology*, ed. Paul Mussen, et al. (New York: Holt, 1969).

3. John Dewey, *How We Think* (Boston: Heath, 1933).

4. Benjamin S. Bloom, ed., *Taxonomy of Educational Objectives, The Classification of Educational Goals, Handbook I: Cognitive Domain* (New York: McKay, 1966), pp. 144–161.

5. Milton J. Gold, *Education of the Intellectually Gifted* (Columbus, Ohio: Merrill, 1965), p. 102.

6. Viktor Lowenfeld, "Current Research on Creativity," *N.E.A. Journal* 47 (November 1958), pp. 538–540.

RELATED READINGS

Block, James H., ed. *Mastery Learning: Theory and Practice.* New York: Holt, 1971.

Brammer, Lawrence M. *The Helping Relationship: Process and Skills.* Englewood Cliffs, N.J.: Prentice-Hall, 1973.

Flapan, Dorothy, *Children's Understanding of Social Interaction.* New York: Teachers College Press, 1968.

Parker, J. Cecil, and Rubin, Louis J. *Process as Content: Curriculum Design and the Application of Knowledge.* Chicago: Rand McNally, 1966.

Robinson, Francis P. *Effective Study.* 4th ed. New York: Harper & Row, 1970.

Robinson, H. Alan. *Teaching Reading and Study Strategies: The Content Areas.* Rockleigh, N.J.: Allyn and Bacon, 1975.

Romey, William D. *Inquiry Techniques for Teaching Science.* Englewood Cliffs, N.J.: Prentice-Hall, 1968.

Torrance, E. Paul. *Encouraging Creativity in the Classroom.* Dubuque, Iowa: William C. Brown, 1970.

CHAPTER 11

Individual Enrichment

Exploration takes place when the pupil exercises initiative in seeking experiences which arise from his or her interest and his or her own unique personal needs, desires, or purposes. Since each individual is a unique entity, self-motivated learning is considered an essential element of the curriculum for every middle school. A significant portion of in-school time should be available to meet the exploratory function. Within this time pupils should be allowed to pursue as much independent study as they are capable of and willing to undertake. As the learning skills are mastered they should each be able to assume responsibility for a much larger portion of their own learning. It is assumed that as much as 20 to 40 percent of the emerging adolescent's time depending upon maturity can be set aside for self-initiated efforts.

PURPOSES

In order to justify such a large proportion of time in personalized study, the objectives of such effort must be carefully considered. A major function of the middle school is to provide for transition, a shifting in emphasis from self-contained elementary classrooms to departmentalized secondary approaches in education. This requires a period during which each pupil can develop from being a dependent to a more independent learner based upon his or her individual internal cognitive capacity. Independent learning composed of self-instituted and directed pursuits occurs only when strong individual motivation exists. Emerging adolescents have a strong idealistic bent and need to be placed in an academic atmosphere in which to take fullest advantage of such motivation. This can be accomplished when teachers assist pupils in needs seen as vital by the pupil.

Personalized purposes can be achieved when the following aspects of the individual and learning are considered: (1) individual interests, (2) individual values, (3) individual needs, (4) individual purposes, (5) individual standards, and (6) individual modes of learning.

Individual interests

Since intrinsic motivation is the primary determinant of pupil learning in schools, it seems reasonable to consider the interests of the individual pupil in the development of the curriculum. Increasing attention has been given by patrons, teachers, administrators, and pupils to an appropriate allocation of time for pupils to explore their individual interests as well as those of the society. Relevance, as beauty, is in the eye of the beholder and, as such, is a valid concept only when applied to an individual.

It might be that individual pupil interests are evanescent in nature, and may have little impact upon the formal curriculum. However, the recommended time allotment for exploration has been limited to approximately one-third of the school day. The recommendation is not to establish an entire new curriculum around the framework of individual interests, but rather to provide appropriate experiences to give time for consideration of these interests. In a curriculum development program in which a wide range of experiences is possible, time must be allocated to exploration, which is determined to a great extent by pupils.

Individual values

The development of personal values for individuals is an accepted major purpose of the middle school. The traditional program does not tend to teach such values because of an emphasis upon knowledge and structure in the classroom. If emerging adolescents are to develop sets of values, both those important to society and unique to themselves, a considerable effort must be made by the school. Effort must be made in two directions: first, to help the pupil to develop a sense of the range of values acceptable in the society in which he or she will live; and second, to assist the pupil in the development and clarification of the values which he or she presently holds. Within the emerging adolescent a continuous struggle ensues as sets of values which he or she can accept establish a dichotomy between the personal and public realms. A program of value clarification must not be presented in too authoritarian a manner. Those values which are self-imposed and self-regulated will be of continuing significance. Those values which are forced upon one from the outside are usually seen to have a less lasting effect.

Individual needs

Emerging adolescents may have many needs which, although visible to others, may not be visible to them. One of the purposes of exploration is to provide an opportunity for others to assist pupils in meeting their *individual* needs. The implication that the topic selection for the exploration phase of learning is influenced by staff should be avoided. Rather, the teacher should have a close enough relationship with each youngster so that while individual perceived needs of a particular pupil are primary, remedial or developmental tasks could be developed within the exploratory framework which would help to meet those idiosyncratic needs which are not noticed by the pupil.

Individual purposes

It is during the emerging adolescent stage of development that individuals begin to look toward purposes as being determinants within their frameworks of decision making. These purposes might be short lived, such as passing a course in order to play football, or of long duration, such as a future life vocation or avocation. Exploration of such interests should assist emerging adolescents to consider possible futures for themselves. Individuals concerned with looking to what the future might hold can consider what their purposes in life might be, and how best to operate within current educational frameworks to move toward particular goals. Here we are not considering such courses as traditional industrial arts or home economics (which we place in general education because it is our position that everyone should have these experiences as background) but rather the purposes of the individual, both vocational and avocational. The technological society provides more leisure time, and purposes considered here might be more focused upon avocational pursuits in addition to those of vocational orientation.

Individual standards

Individual standards must be considered when planning exploration in the psychomotor, cognitive, and affective domains. Each individual is capable of different levels of development and expression in each of these three areas due to prior experience, interest, and ability. Thus, standards of appraisal based on group norms should not be applied to individual endeavors. The gifted emerging adolescent in any of these areas should study at a different content and skill level than one who is less gifted. Since much work in exploration is based upon an emphasis for gifted and average pupils, a greater concern for less gifted pupils is recommended. All pupils must be granted equal educational opportunities to explore, and standards must be appropriate to the selected work. Advantages to be derived from individual exploration are that students with special abilities may utilize them while slow pupils are usually capable of doing at least some one thing well. All may achieve far beyond the expectations of their teachers in their areas of individual interest.

Various means of personalized study meet individual purposes.
John Baker School
(Courtesy of Albuquerque, New Mexico, Public Schools)

Just as it is possible to set levels of expectation too high, it is also a grave error to set standards too low. Spurred on by individual interests and values, and with individual purposes made evident, most children perform much above the expectations of their teachers. Standards which are set should be flexible, and vary for each pupil according to his or her interests, values, needs, and purposes. They might even vary from day to day. Possibly expectations might be a better word than standards. Certain results may be expected without demanding them. An undemanding atmosphere full of expectation should allow for more educational gain than the traditional grading system.

Individual modes of learning

Different students learn in different ways. Some pupils will do well in highly structured sequences, while others prefer less structured approaches. Many of these differences are attributable to differences in the way these individuals have learned to think. Preferred styles of learning, interaction, structure, or organization lead teachers to consider learning modalities of individuals in guiding learning experiences, particularly during exploration. For the primary expectations of exploration, students should be encouraged to learn that which uniquely interests them, by whatever mode of learning in which they are most competent, while not abandoning other modes. Learning skills are important, but emphasis on the purposes of exploration should be primary in this context. Later time should be set aside for the mastery of learning skills in which a student is deficient.

EXPLORATION AREAS

In order to achieve the personalized learning appropriate to each individual in the middle school, exploration should be possible in all areas of the curriculum. The areas we will consider include: (1) exploratory learnings in the classroom, (2) innovative courses, (3) extra-class activities, (4) media, and (5) homeroom.

Exploratory learning in the classroom

Exploratory learning in the classroom should, in an ideal setting, be able to satisfy many of the interests expressed by emerging adolescents. The teacher, concerned with individual interests of his or her pupils, can work to assist pupils in this direction. This section will be concerned only with those types of exploration which can be accomplished within the classroom environment: enrichment, acceleration, classroom leadership, and unit approach.

Many of these experiences can be provided under the direction of each individual teacher and need no administrative support or action. These differ from other aspects of the exploratory experience which require more general faculty and administrative planning and support to develop a necessary curriculum framework. Exploration in the traditional classroom is of crucial importance since the attitudes of the pupil, teacher, and principal are shaped by these experiences in such a way that further expansion of exploratory experiences might be possible. The primary prerequisite of exploratory experiences in the classroom is an inquiring and flexible mind on the part of all three.

Enrichment. Provisions for individual exploration within the classroom are generally structured in one of two ways: first, enrichment experiences, in which the individual is able to fill gaps in his or her learning along the same general level of cognitive difficulty; and second, acceleration, in which the pupil remains within the general framework of the subject matter structure and moves at a faster tempo. Enrichment is based on the assumption that study areas in the middle school (i.e., social studies, language arts, arithmetic, and science) may be too narrowly structured to provide the general education which should be available to all.

The classroom teacher's task in enrichment is to free the pupil for some set period of time to study in areas which are not group assignments for the entire class. These studies, which are of great interest to a particular individual, should arise from motivation and initiative of each student, encouraged by the teacher. For example, many emerging adolescents are interested in probability as one aspect of arithmetic. Those interested in this field would find some aspects of it no more difficult than some aspects of the traditional arithmetic content in the sixth, seventh, or eighth grades.

Acceleration. Acceleration is based on one concept of individual differences—rate of learning. In current educational thinking certain pupils may develop a basic structure in a subject field (i.e., social studies, language arts, arithmetic, or science) and develop it with supportive facts and understandings at a faster rate than others. For the individual pupil concerned with exploration of his or her own unique concerns, exponents of this theory would suggest allowing the pupil to move at a more rapid pace. For example, the pupil in sixth-grade arithmetic with sufficient background and interest may study algebra even though it is usually a ninth-grade study. Acceleration would thus enable the pupil to complete that education needed by all youngsters at an earlier age, and would permit exploration at a more sophisticated level at an earlier age. There is some debate between those who favor enrichment and those who favor acceleration. Neither of these methods of exploration should be rejected in favor of the other. Some aspects of both are to be encouraged within the framework of the middle school. Particularly, individual needs and purposes are to be considered as different individuals with a common set of learnings might explore in either of these two directions because of their own unique situations.

Classroom leadership. One product of exploration is the development among pupils of the ability to assume responsibility for their own learning activities. Leadership will take place only as the teacher indicates that such leadership is a desired attribute. This is accomplished by putting children into positions where leadership will be fostered. Exploration demands responsibility on the part of individual learners. Those who are slower in assuming this responsibility should be encouraged to look to their fellow pupils as well as to teachers for such leadership in the learning activity as may be available. The development of classroom leadership is valuable in two ways. It is valuable to those exercising it among the group since the attribute is worthwhile within itself, and also is valuable in its effect upon other pupils who are able to learn more effectively due to peer support.

Unit approach. The unit approach to learning is one means of implementing individual exploration within the classroom. A topic is selected either by the students or the teacher, or is perhaps designated in the course of study. Possible approaches to the study of this topic are considered and measures for achieving the objectives of the unit are developed by the group. As a focus for study, the unit is particularly effective because it usually can be related in a context that has some relevance to the learning of individuals within the class. Within this framework it is relatively easy to arrange for personalized objectives for individual youngsters.

In conclusion, it is possible for a teacher in a traditional setting, by utilizing the resources available from the library and media centers, by stressing unit topical studies, and particularly by conceptualizing and implementing the purposes of exploration, to achieve some degree of exploration within the classroom. While other approaches to exploration, which are usually arranged by administrators, may be effective, the teacher must at times assume individual responsibility for this most important goal of education.

Innovative courses

Two categories of innovative courses may be found in the middle school. The first is those courses which are derived from one of the basic seven areas of study in the middle school curriculum: language arts, social studies, science, arithmetic, fine arts, practical arts, and physical education. The second is the areas which are outside the framework of general course offerings or which might correlate two of the subject areas.

The primary exploratory purpose for the individual in innovative courses within one of the subject areas would be to develop deeper knowledges within the area or to examine the area for new knowledges. Most courses which have been conceived within the various subjects have generated from a more traditional approach to subject matter. As one example, many language arts courses have units on speech. Perhaps an individual wishes to spend his or her independent time learning voice inflection and other aspects of public speech necessary to become a more effective speaker. The utilization of tape recorders, video tapes, or motion-picture cameras would permit the pupil the greatest possible lattitude in an independent study of his or her own ability. The teacher role is to assist the student in utilizing resources and developing skills, knowledges, and insights which lead to better speech habits.

An examination of areas different from those ordinarily included within a specific discipline is a valid purpose for individual learners. Some pupils would be interested in such studies as Far-Eastern history or religions of the world. While history of the world might touch upon Far-Eastern history in a peripheral way, the individual pupil whose curiosity has been piqued by this exposure might want to continue this particular area in an independent mode.

New courses need not be tied to standard time sequences. They can range from one week to as much as one year depending upon motivation and resources. The length of the course should be determined by the needs and purposes and *interests* of the individual pupil. A few subjects within each of the major subject areas are listed below for illustration.

1. Language Arts

   a. Journalism
   b. Speech
   c. Debate
   d. Drama
   e. Creative writing

2. Social Studies

   a. History of certain areas, e.g., Far East
   b. History of certain eras, e.g., twentieth century
   c. Sociology
   d. Economics
   e. Government

3. Science

   a. Botany
   b. Zoology
   c. Astronomy

4. Arithmetic

   a. Probability
   b. Statistics
   c. Computer science
   d. Computer language
   e. Boolean algebra

5. Fine Arts

   a. Ceramics
   b. Painting
   c. Sculpture
   d. Music composition
   e. Music conducting
   f. Foreign cultures

6. Practical Arts

   a. Sewing
   b. Cooking
   c. Child care
   d. Plumbing
   e. Electrical wiring

7. Physical Education

   a. Sports officiating
   b. Coaching
   c. Golf (any sport not ordinarily in the physical education curriculum)
   d. Weight lifting
   e. Karate
   f. Kinesiology

New courses may be found outside the framework of the seven subject areas or may be correlations of them. These courses need not be limited to a certain time or specific schedule. Rather, they should be based upon the needs of the pupils and the demands of the study. What is important is that pupils be able to explore new areas within the framework of their own concerns. Such subjects might not fit within any of the areas in the regular structure of the school day. They would assist the pupil to recognize interrelationships between the disciplines, thus correlating knowledge into some sort of meaningful synthesis.

A small list is included for illustration.

1. Courses stressing subjects other than traditional disciplines

    a. Foreign languages
    b. Mythology
    c. Psychology
    d. Philosophy
    e. Logic
    f. Meteorology
    g. Ecology
    h. Stock market
    i. Radio-TV repair
    j. Auto repair
    k. Computer technician

2. Courses stressing interrelationships between disciplines

    a. Radio-TV production (combines drama-speech-production techniques)
    b. Anthropology (combines sociology-history)
    c. Economic geography (combines economics-geography)
    d. Humanities (combines literature-history-art-music)
    e. Marine biology (combines ecology-biology)
    f. Bio-chemistry (combines biology-chemistry)
    g. Symbolic logic (combines arithmetic-semantics-logic)
    h. Ballet production (combines dance-set design-music)
    i. Operetta production (combines dramatics-dance-music-scene designing)
    j. Camping (combines home economics-industrial arts-physical education-social studies-science)

Courses organized for exploratory purposes of the emerging adolescent should be those which are appealing, yet which are purposive, recognizing particular strengths and limitations of individuals involved, and responsive to the values, needs, and modes of learning of the emerging adolescent.

Extra-class activities

Many middle schools have effective extra-class activity programs which stress the exploratory needs of their clientele. Pupils participating in extra-class activities ordinarily do so for one or more of four reasons. These motives are:

1. to indulge unique individual interests,
2. to establish meaningful interpersonal relationships,
3. to achieve specific objectives in the affective and psychomotor domains in addition to the cognitive, and
4. to develop a sense of contribution to pride in their school.

Each emerging adolescent has a unique field of reference in his or her relationships with peers and the school. His or her particular set of interests and needs has been developed during childhood, and is being modified by experiences in the middle school. Each pupil is different, so each will select extra-class activities for different reasons. Some may show little interest in such activities and participate in very few; some may find that participation in such activities may be their primary reason for attending middle school. Extra-class activities must be varied enough to meet these different needs and sometimes conflicting purposes of emerging adolescence.

As emerging adolescents participate in various extra-class activities, they are striving to achieve a relationship with their peers and with adults different from that experienced in elementary school. During the middle school years they are concerned with developing relationships with their peers. Peers become more meaningful to the emerging adolescent as he or she seeks to establish a newly independent stance toward the world which until this time has been determined largely by adults. Hence the emerging adolescent is struggling to achieve independence; to react to new feelings as well as new dimensions of knowledge, and a developing physical maturity.

Emerging adolescents recognize the importance of the socio-emotional, the physical, and the intellectual realms. The broad interests of emerging adolescents are exhibited by their extensive participation in extra-class activities which may stress affective activities, psychomotor skills, and cognitive understandings. Participation in extra-class activities has led to the development of talented musical groups, outstanding athletic organizations, and other programs which indicate that pupils can utilize these activities to express themselves. Motivation and intrinsic purpose are most often revealed through voluntary participation.

Extra-class activities vary so widely that no attempt will be made to give a comprehensive list. Types of activities identified by Robert W. Frederick in *The Third Curriculum* are listed below.

A.   The Semi-Curricular Activities
B.   The Large Technical Activities
C.   Co-operatively Sponsored Activities
D.   Fairs, Pageants, and Carnivals
E.   Camping and Outdoor Activities
F.   Religious and Welfare Activities
G.   Scholarship Activities
H.   Social Activities
I.   Subject Related Activities
J.   Trips and Excursions
K.   School Service Organizations and Activities
L.   Youth Centers
M. Fraternities
N.   Special Senior Activities
O.   Special Interest Clubs[1]

Extra-class activities may diminish in both numbers and importance if other areas, such as independent study, assume a larger role in public school education. If pupils are allowed to spend the recommended 20 to 40 percent of the school day in activities of their own choosing the need for extra-class activities may be lessened in the future.

Principles for extra-class activities have been developed and tested in many schools which operate according to the assumption that personalization should play a prominent part in the curriculum of the middle school. The principles enumerated below are suggested for such schools.

Extra-class activities must:

1.   have clear and accepted educational objectives,
2.   provide a wide variety of activities,
3.   have sponsorship as a regular part of the faculty teaching load,
4.   take place during school time under school jurisdiction,
5.   encourage participation for every child in some activity,
6.   avoid exclusion of any child because of expense,
7.   offer acceptance regardless of specific student achievement or conduct, and
8.   have periodic evaluation of all facets of the program to determine their viability as a continuing activity.

An activity should be included in a school program only when the objectives and rationale for its inclusion are clear. These objectives and the means of their achievement should be evaluated within the framework of the total educational experiences of the middle school. Objectives should be primarily aimed toward the personalization process in the elective aspects of the extra-class activity program.

Sufficient variety, including both scope and sequence within activities, is essential to the program since the needs, purposes, and desires of individual emerging adolescents range over such a wide field of concerns. This variety should elicit the best effort and commitment of staff equivalent to that given to an academic class. Teachers should not, however, be expected by the administration or school board to accept sponsorship of an extra-class activity on an added basis. The time and personal commitment necessary are equivalent to that required for a class and should receive equal credit in the teaching load.

Extra-class activities should take place during school hours and on school grounds where possible. Exceptions might include those which require extended time such as camping, long field trips and such, or special location requirements such as golf or bowling. The fundamental issue is the importance of these activities in the hierarchy of educational objectives deserving the use of school staff and facilities.

Every pupil should be strongly encouraged to participate in some activity within the program. The fundamental premise of personalized exploration requires participation for each pupil. Given a sufficient variety of activities, all should find an area which would promote their growth and interests. Pupils are usually highly motivated and knowledgeable about activities in which they have primary responsibility and which they have selected.

Expense of some activities may be a barrier to some students. Theoretically, no student should be excluded from suitable activities because of undue expense. Students themselves should consider the availability of financing as they assist in planning the activities. Whenever possible, the school should absorb the legitimate expenses of the extra-class program. When this is impossible, the activity should be carefully reviewed with a particularly careful analysis of those goals which require money of the individual child above and beyond what might be considered a minimal amount.

Participation in extra-class activities should not be withheld from a student on the basis of his or her achievement or conduct in the classroom. The right of emerging adolescents to participate in extra-class activities should be as inviolate as their basic right of attendance in the middle school. Lack of motivation and/or ability in the regular school program should be dealt with in that context, and should not be used as a basis for depriving the individual of the right to participate in other activities. It is not usual, for example, to deprive a child of instruction in social studies because he or she achieves poorly in mathematics. The same reasoning should apply to other program areas, one of which is extra-class activities. The fundamental educational goal is to provide each emerging adolescent with opportunities for growth and development in all possible areas.

An evaluation of extra-class activities should take place at periodic intervals during the year, and certainly at the year's beginning and end. It should be based upon stated educational objectives and their achievement. The achievement of previously unplanned objectives should also be noted. New activities probably should be added to the activities program, while others may be temporarily or permanently discontinued if a loss of interest is evident. The extra-class program when examined at any one point should consist of those activities which have accepted educational objectives, are reaching them, and are of continued current interest to the student body.

Media

In order to achieve the personalization essential to exploration the individual pupil must be accorded some period for independent study. The quantity and quality of media available to an individual will to some extent determine the effectiveness of the learning accomplished. Pupils cannot reasonably explore toward many ends if sufficient materials of a high caliber are not available and easily accessible.

A learning-resources center for the middle school where appropriate numbers of pupils can work on an independent basis free from classrooms where they might ordinarily be located becomes necessary. There should be comfortable facilities adequate in size for a significant percentage of the student body to have easy access when they so desire. This size center would still be operated under the assumption that some pupils could be studying independently in their classrooms, in other parts of the building, or even in the community.

Beyond the ordinary utilization of media in the exploration of individual interests in a middle school, wider use of media provides at least three other aspects in the program:

1. motivation-novelty-etc.,
2. increased understanding of technology as a tool for learning, and
3. discovery of technology as a means of enhancing life.

The importance of technology in the future life of the emerging adolescent requires that some attention be given by the middle school to the processes involved in the use of media.

The utilization of media may provide a motivating factor in the learning of emerging adolescents. The use of a variety of media relieves both teachers and pupils from the limitations of lecture and discussion as singular methods of teaching. Individuals and groups develop greater interest as they become more actively involved in the learning process. In addition, media utilize more sense modalities and give pupils opportunities to experience new fields for exploration that may not arise in the course of the normal approach. Each new experience should lead to related experiences. Selection of media may provide more satisfaction, intrinsic motivation, and focus on learning for the sake of learning rather than learning primarily to meet the demands of a teacher. Students may come to relate individual efforts and rewards in the acquisition of understandings, skills, and attitudes to be gained from learning.

Technology as a phenomenon in our society and the place of media as a mode of communication for the general population represent an important aspect of the life of the emerging adolescent. The utilization of the instructional-resources center can contribute to a respect for technology and its impact on life. The utilization of technology requires that the individual learn to operate and care for machinery, and know how and when to utilize each element. An important by-product in the use of technological devices is the exploration of the machinery located in the learning-resources center. Above and beyond the learning which takes place through the media, the knowledge of the operation of that media and the actual practice in its operation are important to the development of the middle school pupil.

Education may be envisioned as having sustained two major breakthroughs in presentation. The first of these resulted from the invention of movable type. After books could be presented to the student the teacher was no longer the sole repository of knowledge. The second breakthrough in the classroom is the recent introduction of media where students may not only listen to the teacher and read books, but also see and hear other sources of learning. The degree to which media are utilized in educational programs may in part determine the effectiveness of the learning which takes place.

The following media devices are included among those which have created an impact upon learning in the middle school:

1. programmed machine,
2. programmed text material,
3. computer-assisted instruction,
4. tape recorder,
5. video-tape recorder,
6. record player,

7. television,
8. film projector and camera,
9. photograph projector and camera,
10. film-strip projector, and
11. overhead projector.

Each of the devices listed has unique capabilities and characteristics which must be related appropriately to educational outcomes. The staff should explore the purposes and methods of each type of media device and utilize each appropriately to exploit maximum effect on learning. Pupils in addition to teachers need to relate their expectations from the utilization of media in the implementation of learning. Appropriate guidance of the teacher is required in this process.

Homeroom

If individual study should be concerned with all developmental areas of the emerging adolescent, the socio-emotional needs of the emerging adolescent must be met. The homeroom is the place where all aspects of exploration can be brought into focus. More attention can be given to affective learnings in that period than when teachers are focusing on subject processes and learning outcomes related to subject matter. Emphasis on learning and expressing values and attitudes can occur in a well-organized homeroom program. As an administrative device the homeroom is concerned with such matters as roll-taking and announcements. But its major function should be to focus on the concerns of emerging adolescents. Six major functions for the homeroom in a model middle school are:

1. counseling,
2. evaluation and representation to parents,
3. facilitation of interpersonal relationships,
4. personalization of administration,
5. development of self-government, and
6. organization for extra-class activities.

An effective homeroom program should be preplanned and operated co-operatively by pupils and teacher. The counseling role of the teacher should be exercised in a relatively informal manner and should be based on expressed attitudes and values of the group. A formal counseling program is present to prevent the homeroom period from becoming a series of "buzz" sessions in which evanescent perceptions lead only to discussions of the irrelevant and unimportant.

One function of the homeroom teacher is that of compiling pupil evaluations as garnered from classroom teachers. The homeroom teacher prepares the overall evaluation and is responsible for its presentation to the pupils and parents. Face-to-face, joint, and relatively structured conferences are being utilized with increasing frequency in order to achieve the most interaction. The pupil, being better equipped than anyone else to assess his or her own progress and interests, should be present. The question of grades should not be the focus of the conference except as they are indicative of achievement of the jointly shared purposes of the pupil, teacher, and parents, all of whom should be primarily interested in the emerging adolescent. Emphasis would be upon the purposes of the individual and how these are being achieved. The format of the report can be dependent upon the decisions of the particular community. If the role of the teacher is to guide learning in the affective as well as the psychomotor and cognitive areas, then his or her function should be to know the phases of individual development of each emerging adolescent as thoroughly as possible in order to function in the role of facilitator. The development of a middle school devoted to the personalization of instruction can be successful only if some one individual, probably a homeroom teacher, can be responsible for knowing the total development of the individual.

In order to evaluate the work of the pupil and interpret that progress to parents the homeroom teacher should have the appropriate records of the pupil's past progress conveniently available. The following nine points have been considered necessary as a basis for effective advisor-pupil relations:

1. intelligence test results,
2. past and present achievement in school,
3. participation and extraclass activities,
4. vocational, avocational, and educational interests,
5. physical and mental health,
6. home and family backgrounds,
7. character and personality qualities,
8. citizenship qualities, and
9. vacation and part-time employment.[2]

With this information the homeroom teacher might be able to serve the role of diagnostic advisor to the academic classroom teachers. In addition, he or she would be able to serve the pupil as an advisor in terms of expectations. The idealistic emerging adolescent has a tendency to establish some unrealistic goals, and sensitive recommendations made by a faculty member who is aware of the pupil's unique learning situation and emotional and physical needs should be in the best position to render the appropriate guidance.

The homeroom should serve as a "home away from home." In this room each child can feel an attachment to the teacher and to other members of the group. Relationships between individuals within the group and between an individual and the group as a whole should be a primary concern to the homeroom teacher. Emerging adolescents develop ideals through modeling, examination, and practice, not through the "preaching" process. Opportunity would be given children to discuss and consider together with their peers those values, characteristics, and capabilities appropriate to the school environment which also satisfy the purposes of society. A selection of case studies, critical incidents, and current problems and issues within the school may serve as a basis from which to give the greatest possible development in the socio-emotional areas for emerging adolescents.

While striving for personalization, the homeroom teacher is the individual to whom the pupil may react concerning various rules and regulations of the middle school. Every social organization requires rules and regulations to provide structure and order to its operation. An intermediary who can personalize those rules to suit the needs of the pupils in the school is needed, however. Regulations, by their very nature, should be observed by all unless there are some extenuating circumstances. A homeroom teacher, however, may be able to serve as the intermediate counselor-administrator who would be able to speak to the developmental needs of the pupil in relationship to the requirements of the school.

Since the developmental growth of the emerging adolescent is a major purpose of the middle school, and since the individual pupil is the prime referent in this learning process, it follows that the individual must be in a position to judge how much and how well he or she has learned. This postulate makes a student government an important facet of the middle school. Student government should not only be organized to give experience to pupils, but should also be an organization which expresses the purposes and needs of individuals within the student body. There is an assumption of homeroom representation in this process, with homeroom teachers acting as guides in assisting the pupils to reach mature decisions.

The homeroom can have relative freedom of schedule and organization, and can serve as a base for extra-class activities such as intramural athletic programs, social activities, parties, picnics, and trips. The number and types of activities which can be included in the homeroom program are almost infinite. A representative list includes:

1. development of programs for special days,
2. introduction to hobbies,
3. orientation to the school,
4. assistance in planning the school experiences,
5. development of specific process abilities,
6. inculcation of courtesy,
7. election of student council members and other student functionaries,
8. preparation of school policies,
9. election of homeroom officers,
10. preparation of social activities in the homeroom,
11. study of parliamentary procedure, and
12. organization of service and charity activities.

Personalization of education requires that some aspect of the program be devoted to evaluating the needs, purposes, and desires of each individual emerging adolescent. At this juncture the homeroom would seem to be the most effective administration procedure for achieving that purpose.

The purpose of the recommended homeroom program places important demands on the teacher who assumes the responsibility for the homeroom. A much longer period of time for the homeroom period becomes necessary, plus a correspondingly longer time for the teacher to spend in preparation for the meeting. The homeroom period is probably the one most important period in the school day. The teacher responsible for this homeroom period should be given commensurate time, salary, and prestige, as befits the most crucial aspect of middle school education. If these changes take place the homeroom can assume its place as the formal aspect of the middle school schedule in which affective education is most strongly stressed.

IMPLICATIONS FOR TEACHERS

Certain issues involved with curriculum development have such crucial importance to teachers that special attention must be given to them. These issues seem to be divided into four major areas, among others: (1) interdomain objectives and activities, (2) affective goals and experiences, (3) deletion of activities, and (4) homogeneous-heterogeneous activities.

Members of a middle school faculty must be prepared to respond to these issues singly, in small-group teams, and as a total faculty in order to achieve the most effective education for emerging adolescents. Confrontation and possible solution of problems in these areas depend upon individual initiative and creativity plus a strong devotion to group consensus as a means of problem solution.

Interdomain objectives and activities

Middle schools boasting the most effective programs for emerging adolescents have placed strong stress upon cooperative faculty and student body discussion, and determination of objectives and learning activities based upon domains rather than subject matter areas. Concerns for goals and objectives in the psychomotor, affective, and cognitive domains and the interrelationships among them remain a primary topic in many in-service workshops. Thus thorough knowledge of the three taxonomies and their interrelationships becomes a necessity for faculty members. In considering the interaction and interrelationships among the three domains teachers become concerned with three specific types of problems: (1) interdisciplinary objectives, (2) restructuring subjects, and (3) results of the restructuring process.

Interdisciplinary objectives. In developing objectives which are not related to individual disciplines faculty members must determine what steps need to be taken to be most effective in an interdisciplinary framework. Having previously determined a series of goals relating to interdomain relationships, small groups of teachers organized on an interdisciplinary basis begin the procedure of determining how each teacher's individual discipline contributes to these goals. The first step is to interrelate the established goals of a course, with which a teacher might be familiar, with those already established on the schoolwide interdomain basis. After this interrelationship has been determined, course objectives, if not already established, must be developed in order to contribute the best knowledges of each separate discipline to the overarching goals. In this way knowledge derived from structure of disciplines is related to overarching societal goals which have been related to the basic domains.

Such a series of predetermined goals and objectives, while combining the best efforts of the community, faculty, and student body, cannot be most effective unless couched in more specific terms which can be rendered measurable. Thus a teacher will find it necessary to consider each goal separately and divide it into measurable objectives. These objectives by their nature are of a much more specific order than course or unit objectives and are amenable to a measurement process which can assess both pupil learning and the worth of learning activities.

Learning activities must then be developed which will enable pupils to achieve the measurable objectives determined by common agreement. They will be divided into total-group, small-group, and individual learning activities. They will also be subsumed under activities for every member of a class, for gifted members, and for slow members. They can be still further subdivided into activities for those particularly talented in the cognitive, and/or psychomotor, and/or affective domains.

Finally, assessment procedures must be developed on a cooperative basis between faculty and students to determine the level at which individual pupils have achieved the predetermined measurable objectives and whether the unit and/or course has been successful in aiding pupils in the achievement of the interdisciplinary objectives which were the purpose of the entire procedure. In cases where assessment indicates that measurable objectives were not achieved to a desired extent it becomes the task of faculty and students to determine the underlying cause for such failure, whether it be lack of student motivation, weakness of learning activities, irrelevance, or poor selection of experiences.

The development of interdomain goals and interdisciplinary objectives is necessary if interdisciplinary team teaching is to take place and if structuring of the curriculum for emerging adolescents is to occur. While structure of the discipline, as evidenced in departmentalized classrooms, may be appropriate for high school education, serious question must be raised concerning its appropriateness for middle school pupils. Emerging adolescents, by their very nature, tend to seek and in some cases perceive interrelationships more readily than youth at an earlier or later school stage.

Restructuring subjects. Another difficult task for the middle school teacher is that of restructuring subject matter for most efficient and greatest impact upon the lives of emerging adolescents. In addition to development of goals and experiences which cross disciplinary lines, the teacher must conduct other developmental curricular processes. For example, a rigorous examination of goals and learning experiences of middle school pupils must be conducted in a search for those which are and those which are not necessarily required for all members. A significant segment of the middle school curriculum can be deleted through cross-disciplinary approaches. In addition, the teacher should be continuously on the alert for those goals and objectives which can and should be deleted from each individual discipline.

The teacher, having decided upon those goals and learning experiences within and across disciplines which are necessary for all members of the class, may then look to deleted materials to ascertain which may be necessary or desirable for individual members of the class because of idiosyncratic needs and desires. Most of these goals and learning experiences should be reserved for the exploratory education of the emerging adolescent, but to delete from the middle school classroom all education except that needed by everyone would seriously hamper enrichment for the gifted and basic skills for the less able.

It should be noted that the development of interdomain and interdisciplinary objectives would be expected to add as well as subtract certain goals and learning experiences in the middle school curriculum. Each classroom teacher, team, and entire faculty must be aware of the need to add experiences based upon interdisciplinary objectives, so that the time saved by restructuring of content can be used most effectively.

Results of restructuring process. As a logical conclusion of the development of interdomain and interdisciplinary objectives and the restructuring of subject matter to meet the goals and experiences of those approaches a new type of middle school will certainly emerge. While the authors recommend a three-team organization (i.e., humanities, sciences, and psychomotor teams), it would certainly be within the domain of the faculty to determine the general format which a particular school would expect to utilize.

The authors of this work assume that learning skills which could be emphasized in this framework are the thought processes which expand upon basic skills learned in elementary school and which serve as the source for adult thinking. An emphasis upon thought processes throughout the various goals and objectives of the middle school must be stressed—rational, analytical, critical, synthetical, inquiry, multi-faceted logic, and creativity. With these the middle school pupil will be able to move forward into higher education with little difficulty. Without them he will be unable to complete the work of the middle school effectively.

Affective goals and experiences

Affective goals and experiences should be made available within the typical classroom, as well as in special opportunities and group guidance, homeroom, assemblies, and such. The topic is not so much the means as the ends to be achieved and the learning experiences which pupils might have to accomplish those goals. In general, it is assumed that the following four areas are matters of concern in affective education:

1. self-actualization,
2. education for sexuality,
3. education for valuing, and
4. education for moral development.

The four essential ways in which an emerging adolescent can grow affectively are concerned with the individual's growing knowledge and acceptance

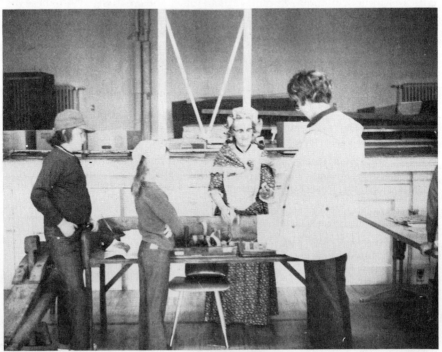

Emerging adolescents participating in an early American culture fair.
Berne Elementary Schools

(Courtesy of Berne-Knox-Westerlo, New York, Central School District)

of self. The teacher's role in this growth is best described as facilitative, aiding the pupil to move in an individualistic way toward these goals.

Self-actualization includes a knowledge of oneself and a satisfaction in being acceptable to others, but especially to oneself. Such self-acceptance comes through in intensive and rigorous self-examination which ordinarily occurs during the emerging adolescent years. A teacher can assist the development of such self-evaluation and acceptance in several ways. Every child should be encouraged to be as independent as possible in relations with others and the environment. Such independence can best be learned by having opportunities to practice it. Hence the teacher who manages a classroom in which independence is practiced is best facilitating such independence. Independence without responsibility becomes permissiveness and license, and cannot be permitted in the classroom. The pupil must, while exercising independence, practice individual responsibility. This age-old struggle between self-expression and acceding to the rights of others has been, is, and will continue to be one of the major developmental problems of attaining adulthood and, as such, requires great concern on the part of the teacher-facilitator. The climate of the classroom must be open, but the teacher must also indicate where the individual's rights end in terms of transgressing upon the rights of others.

Self-evaluation becomes an intensive problem in the middle school grades. It is insufficient for a teacher to express assessment of a pupil's work, personality, or habits. It is essential that the pupil be led toward a self-diagnosis. In order to achieve this goal it is essential that pupils establish, with the assistance of faculty, a set of realistic criteria for purposes of self-evaluation. It is in this respect that a teacher can be of most assistance, since such criteria can be seen as being objective with little sense of the punitive involved. Thus, as a teacher and pupil collaboratively establish these criteria the pupil is able to exercise personal independence and self-evaluation leading toward self-actualization.

Education for sexuality. Since sexual maturity is ordinarily achieved in the middle school years the role of maleness or femaleness within the individual pupil assumes a major importance. Certainly the physical, emotional, and social changes due to budding sexuality assume a major part of the emotional concern of an emerging adolescent. Since the social differences in sex roles have diminished so drastically in the last few years questions may arise concerning whether differentiated roles should be emphasized. Nevertheless, the teacher should recognize that sex, with its corresponding social complications, is critically important to emerging adolescents, even though it may not be perceived as quite so important several years later. Boy-girl relationships are seen

as a new and wonderful phenomenon. Physical development becomes extremely important. While curriculum may change toward reducing social
differences—e.g., all girls taking industrial arts, boys taking home economics,
coed p.e.—this should not be seen as negating the primary aspects of sexuality
as seen by emerging adolescents. Under these circumstances the understanding
middle school teacher should accept and encourage differences seen in the two
sexes.

In many instances in the curriculum common objectives will exist as noted
above. These should be emphasized in order that girls will not see womanhood
as a second-class existence. At the same time, teachers should emphasize those
differential objectives which indicate the advantages of both male and female
so that each can see himself/herself as a worthy individual because of this new
sexuality. Certainly all must have a knowledge of the basic sexual attributes,
hormonal development, and reproductive phases. Ordinarily this might and
should be taught in the elementary schools. If not, certainly it must become a
part of the middle school curriculum, whether in special classes in a formal
way, or in guidance in a less formal manner.

Education for valuing. In addition to learning what to value as inculcated
by home, society, and school, the emerging adolescent must learn how to
value—the valuing process. Adults, by virtue of their situations, are forced
into positions daily in which they must express their process of valuing. Children are ordinarily taught what to value. In the emerging adolescent stage it
becomes essential that the pupil remember the values inculcated in elementary
school, but begin to develop the valuing processes which must be utilized as an
adult. This can be done only if the teacher strongly encourages, both by exhor-
tation and example, the valuing process.

Values clarification techniques should be learned by all middle school
teachers, even more than elementary or secondary teachers, since it is at this
period of growth that children most need the help of teachers in this process.
Questioning techniques should be learned, source books read, audio-visual
materials viewed, all with an eye toward the development on the part of the
teacher of an ability to assist a pupil in clarifying currently held values so that
valuing can continue.

Certainly, while clarifying values of emerging adolescents and aiding in
the development of valuing processes, it is the social responsibility of middle
school teachers to present to emerging adolescents the values held by others.
The prevailing values of the community, the values of the school community,
and the values held by various cultures throughout history; all should be
appropriate subjects for the consideration of emerging adolescents who are
attempting to develop their own value systems.

Education for moral development. As with valuing, moral development may be encouraged by an accepting attitude on the part of the teacher. Developmental psychologists hold that moral development will occur at certain stages of an individual's cognitive growth. The development of a climate in which moral values are considered, discussed, and tentative conclusions drawn will certainly aid in such development, however.

Here also the moral ideas held by society must be considered in order to prevent disaster both for an individual pupil and a school system. The moral values of a community cannot be contradicted if the school intends to be a continuing positive factor in the affective education framework. In the midst of a society in which multiple subcultures are facing severe disagreements concerning moral values, it should be the role of the school and the teacher to clarify these roles to some extent for a pupil and to help that pupil to understand better the dilemmas arising from conflicting moral codes. In this way the pupil can grow to a stage in which moral problems can be met with the greatest degree of maturity.

Affective education in terms of the subjects discussed here is an extremely controversial topic in schools. But unless these matters are considered each individual pupil will move toward adulthood making decisions based upon an implicit and sometimes incorrect assumption as to the major values held by society. In an age where more and more fragmentation of society has created a situation in which the school has become a primary storage center for learning, the teacher must accept the responsibility for aiding emerging adolescents in their affective growth toward adulthood.

Deletion of unnecessary learning activities

One of the most difficult actions necessary to a middle school teacher's functions is the deletion of material which for any of a number of reasons may be unnecessary to the learning objectives of the emerging adolescent. General education, that needed by *all* children in order to prosper in the adult society, must be made coherent and systematic. The teacher may assist in the achievement of this goal by measuring each learning activity against objectives collaboratively established with pupils. Much of the material presented and experiences offered to *all* will be found to be extraneous or irrelevant.

To demonstrate this principle an example will be drawn from the field of mathematics. While individual teachers might consider the example debatable, the principle of systematic presentation of only those materials needed by *all* can be seen to be crucial. Mathematics in the middle school has been, in most instances, a review of arithmetic algorithms. Very few new concepts are presented at this stage of development. The mathematics teacher, under these circumstances, has one of three choices: to continue the review of previous concepts, thus to some extent wasting the time of the student; to move the student into algebra or some other form of conceptual advancement, for which the student may not be ready; or to lessen the time allotted to mathematics in the middle school. This choice between enrichment, acceleration, or diminution of mathematical activities is a prime example of the deletion problem.

The same decision rests with the teacher in all subject matter areas. The teacher of language arts is placed in a position of determining what degree of formal writing skills is necessary for *all* pupils, what reading level is necessary for *all*, and what conceptualization ability is necessary for *all*. The physical education teacher faces a similar problem. He or she must determine the utility of teaching of games to *all*, as opposed to the development of specific, individual psychomotor skills. In each case the basic question remains, should *all* children experience this activity. If not, the activity should be deleted from the entire class activity and be relegated to the exploratory curriculum devoted to the needs, purposes, and desires of individuals. At no time should this deletion of *activities* be considered as a deletion of *objectives* or a diminution of rigor. Both should be more emphasized under such a program.

Exploratory education is a necessary concomitant of the deletion of general education activities. If some two-thirds of the school day is to be allocated to general education with the remainder to be assigned to individual needs, purposes, and desires, then those needs, purposes, and desires must be made clear within the framework of objectives so that appropriate activities can be planned.

Such activities can be made available through elective classes, minicourses, independent study, and extra-class activities. The major implication for the teacher is that a commitment on the part of the teacher to participate in enrichment and acceleration activities both within and outside his or her particular discipline becomes essential. The teacher who is unwilling to work with pupils in a homeroom situation, group guidance, or outside of school activities will find middle school less than satisfying if a rich and varied curriculum is made available. Examples have been given of various types of enrichment and acceleration courses in another section of this chapter. Each teacher should determine which activities (not necessarily related to certification) are appropriate to his or her particular strengths and/or weaknesses and approach the situation in a positive light.

Homogeneous-heterogeneous activities

Each teacher must determine which activities should take place in a homogeneous class setting and which in a heterogeneous setting. Such decisions must be made not only in terms of intellectual ability but also in regards to sex, physical ability, and emotional maturity. For example, in physical education greater emphasis is being placed upon heterosexual groupings. If emphasis is to be placed upon individual motor skill development heterosexual approaches would be appropriate. If the accent is placed upon games, particularly those requiring greater weight or muscle, then the sexes should be separated in order to prevent the unfortunate situation of a five-foot-two-inch girl attempting to play basketball with a six-foot-two-inch boy. The same would apply to football and other sports involving physical contact.

As mentioned before, however, the emphasis in physical education might more appropriately be placed upon individual development, under which circumstance the physical differences between the sexes might not matter. Another area in which sex-heterogeneous activities might take place would be where interest determines the amount of participation in the activity. Chorus and band would certainly be equally interesting to boys and girls. More boys are becoming interested in homemaking, as girls are in industrial arts. When student needs, purposes, and desires are determined in an exploratory activity those purposes should take precedence over the question of sex as a basis for participation.

The same general principles apply to academic ability, physical ability, and emotional maturity. In academic work conceptual learning might well be approached from a heterogeneous organization, since the varying levels of conceptualization reached by poor, average, and brilliant pupils might lend a richness and depth to the final perceptions of individuals in the class. If sequential materials are being studied, however, homogeneous grouping might be more appropriate in order to move each group along at a different rate.

Varying interests of individuals would seem to indicate a necessity for homogeneous groupings at times based upon specific desires. Most extra-curricular activities in middle schools today are based upon this assumption. It becomes a teacher's task to identify those interests and to encourage and utilize them for the growth of the child rather than fitting the child into the present curriculum.

Physical ability also enters into the question of homogeneous-heterogeneous grouping since activities which are group oriented, such as team sports, might very well utilize both approaches, with "pick-up" teams in physical education, homeroom teams, etc., stressing the heterogeneous approach while the better athletes might wish to participate in some form of interscholastic field days and other activities. The same principle applies to individual activities. In most instances the pupil should be placed with those of relatively similar abilities so that he or she will be in a position of relative competitive competence. It is, however, salutary for the pupil to gain some idea as to his or her ability by being placed at relatively rare intervals with pupils who are better or worse at a particular individual sport. Thus a golfer who has a 45 handicap might very well be able to play golf with one who has a 25 handicap. This would give one student inspiration to move forward in his or her efforts, and give the other some idea of the problems inherent in that in which he or she has greater talent.

Lastly, emotional maturity must enter into any discussion of homogeneous-heterogeneous activities. Social activities should, in almost all cases, be heterogeneous except in those cases where individual interests would predicate the need for homogeneous grouping. For example, social dancing might be appropriate on an informal basis in a mini-course or some such informal setting (although not particularly desired for evening, formal occasions). But sixth and seventh grade boys probably would not be interested in such an activity. To place emphasis upon activities for which children are not emotionally mature is inappropriate. This indicates the necessity for careful scrutiny of all social activities on the part of teachers. Each activity must be evaluated in terms of the maturity evidenced by the class and the individual interests of those students involved.

REFERENCES

1. Robert W. Frederick, *The Third Curriculum* (New York: Appleton-Century-Crofts, 1959), p. 19.

2. William T. Gruhn and Harl R. Douglass, *The Modern Junior High School,* 2d. ed. Copyright © 1956 The Ronald Press Company, New York, p. 275.

RELATED READINGS

Cronbach, Lee J. "How Can Instruction Be Adapted to Individual Differences?" in Gagné, Robert, ed., *Learning and Individual Differences.* Columbus, Ohio: Merrill, 1967.

Henry, Nelson B., ed., *Individualizing Instruction.* The Sixty-First Yearbook of the National Society for the Study of Education—Part I. Chicago: University of Chicago Press, 1962.

Johnson, Rita B., and Johnson, Stuart R., *Toward Individualized Learning: A Developer's Guide to Self-Instruction.* Reading, Mass.: Addison-Wesley, 1975.

Wilson, L. Craig. *The Open Access Curriculum.* Boston: Allyn and Bacon, 1971.

UNIT IV

Instructional Procedures

The purposes of middle school education can be achieved only to the extent that teachers are able to implement programs that have inherent within them both general and specific objectives and appropriate instructional activities related to their achievement. Regardless of organizational structure, program goals, or objectives sought, instructional modes and strategies employed by teachers must be accurately perceived and accepted by pupils.

The philosophy of the middle school expressed here requires professional staff attention to a wide range of pupil needs, those demanded in affective and psychomotor growth and development as well as cognitive. Members of the staff need to be able to draw upon learner experiences and interests, and have the capability and imagination to achieve a match between these undeveloped, relatively unexplored areas and interests and the organized bodies of knowledge. Some purposes of the middle school may be met by experiences in a semi-departmental focus; however, many purposes and objectives will be achieved through a more open structure with attention to objectives which transcend the limitation of focus on substantive content in the cognitive domain.

The two chapters devoted to instruction view the teacher in two major roles: first, the planner and organizer of the learning experience, and second, the facilitator of the experience as it occurs. The strong teacher must be adept in both areas in addition to being a warm, enthusiastic human being to whom emerging adolescents can relate.

CHAPTER 12

Teacher as Organizer of Learning Environment

The conceptualization of teaching and instruction which best accommodates an emphasis on the interrelatedness of curriculum and instruction required for achievement of purposes focuses on various roles and functions for teachers and staff. A professional staff meeting requirements of these functions will effectively stimulate and facilitate growth in emerging adolescents. The functions incorporate roles in a number of different ways. None is entirely discrete or mutually exclusive. Divisions suggested are for convenience of discussion and are somewhat arbitrary. For example, Hough and Duncan described the following:

> Teaching is an activity—a unique professional, rational, and humane activity in which one creatively and imaginatively uses himself and his knowledge to promote the learning and welfare of others.[1]

They focused on teaching as a four-act phase with instruction more clearly delineated as one facet of the procedure: (1) curriculum planning, (2) instructing, (3) measuring, and (4) evaluating.[2] Actual instruction involves creating, using, and modifying instructional strategies and tactics to help children learn.[3]

In addition, the teacher's responsibilities include arranging the environment for learning and maintaining attention to the learning tasks connected with the requirements of both the social situation and school rules. Every social framework, including the school, possesses a set of mutually accepted social practices which members recognize and accept.

Dreeben observed that schools and classrooms have within them characteristic patterns of organizational properties in which socialization takes place, and that what children learn derives as much from the nature of their experiences in the school setting as from what they are taught. His concern was with the structural characteristics that distinguish schools from other settings and thereby contribute to socialization of pupils in unique ways.[4]

Emerging adolescents need a socializing environment which the middle school must provide. To serve such a function teachers are expected to perform in a multiplicity of roles. It is only for organizational purposes in this chapter that we have deliberately circumscribed the varying functions of the teacher within five roles which emphasize instructional procedures, including traditional teaching functions and a broader socialization environment. The five roles are: teacher as model, as planner, as diagnostician, as manager, and as guide to resources.

TEACHER AS MODEL

The period of emerging adolescence is characterized by alternating extremes of idealism and cynicism, so that adult models with whom middle school pupils associate are of prime importance. That teachers serve as models for a variety of adult roles is generally accepted. The developmental process is in part the inculcation both of teacher role models and values predominant in the society at large. Most individuals are susceptible to a variety of models and adapt their perceptions to their environment.

Self-discipline

Given the social-model effect, every teacher in a middle school should exemplify the self-discipline desired in a mature adult. Although each is a unique person with certain idiosyncratic behaviors, certain traits will still be present. While variations in degree are expected, teachers should be disciplined in approach to intellect, emotion, and appropriate health habits.

Intellectual self-discipline can be noted by the stance that the teacher takes as an inquirer after knowledge. The teacher does not accept factual knowledge as a never varying set of data. Rather, inquiry continues concerning content and processes in order to derive more information. A disciplined examination of data and opinions is conducted. The most effective learner is the most effective teacher. Self-discipline presupposes a knowledgeable teacher. A knowledgeable person is one who is familiar with the parameters of his or her learning. A teacher should know how to keep abreast of developments and do so, and, in addition, should be willing to admit to a lack of knowledge in areas beyond his or her competence.

An effective teacher is emotionally as well as intellectually disciplined. An emotionally balanced individual provides a stable learning environment. The teacher exercises self-control and can inspire others to emulate such control.

Emotional balance is the goal. The teacher with good mental health feels adequate, being compelled neither to dominate nor to be subservient.

The qualities of leadership are normally expected and required of teachers within the framework of a classroom setting. Such leaders can accept responsibility while building similar responsibilities into the actions of others. Independence rather than dependence is fostered in students.

The value of a sense of humor as a relief from tension and anxiety is well recognized. Emotional self-discipline is supported by the ability to see humor in oneself. An occasional laugh, often at oneself, has saved many a situation in classrooms. Further, life should be enjoyable and classroom life can be made so if children are encouraged to see humor in various situations.

An effective teacher exhibits self-discipline by being an example in health and physical well-being. Good health habits both in and out of school are evident. The individual will eat properly and get adequate exercise and sufficient rest to look and feel well. Smoking is a habit which may cause embarrassment, as may use of drugs (of which alcohol is one). Idealistic students may question such practices. Good health and a sense of physical well-being can create a poised individual who is able to react to various situations with élan. A person who is physically debilitated is less likely to exhibit such characteristics.

Teacher involvement

A teacher who is emotionally separated from pupils in class, who cannot relate to them and their needs, may be unable to identify their learning problems. An inability to stimulate pupils to become deeply involved in learning may result. Philip Jackson holds that "involvement" is the key to learning:

> More and more I have come to think of the teacher's work as consisting primarily of maintaining involvement in the classroom....The teacher hopes that involvement will result in learning. Learning becomes the by-product or secondary goal rather than the thing about which he is most directly concerned.[5]

Necessity for knowledge of the learning habits of pupils and of ways and means to advance those processes may be more important than the actual content which a child is expecting to learn. The child must do the learning if it is to occur. The task of a teacher is only to facilitate that learning.

In addition to involvement with learning processes of the pupil, a teacher must become involved with the students as human beings. Awareness of their strengths, weaknesses, and ambitions both for the future and in the present is a necessity. Each of them must be seen as a unique individual who is capable of being better than at present and who strongly desires to become that better self. The teacher must be perceived as prepared to assist in the ambitions of a pupil, while at the same time being far enough separate to be able to aid in a meaningful change in those ambitions when necessary. The fundamental hypotheses of this approach were most clearly stated by Bennetta B. Washington in the A.S.C.D. Yearbook, *To Nurture Humaneness*.

These hypotheses are:

1. The student's self concept is a significant factor in his ability to learn.
2. The student must be valued as an individual.
3. Every child wants to succeed.
4. The student's belief in himself must be nurtured if he is to grow emotionally and intellectually.
5. True learning will take place only if the student is an involved participant in the process.
6. The power structure and the learning situation must be understood and used to advantage because the child needs both the support of peers and the opportunity to differentiate himself from others.[6]

Teacher counseling

The role of the teacher as a model encompasses a counseling of students regarding their aptitudes, interests, goals, and values, as well as personal and educational problems. In both formal and informal settings a teacher serves as a model, constantly projecting beliefs and values to each child. Whether in the homeroom, group guidance, or classroom the teacher acting as counselor indicates in definite ways those values held most dear. In addition, the values held most important by society are represented.

In informal counseling the most common situations are those where questions come from pupils concerning their personal and educational problems. The task of the teacher is to accept and treat those problems as important. Any questions considered important enough by an individual pupil to be brought to the attention of a teacher should be considered. There are limits, however, beyond which any counselor cannot go in dealing with student problems since some problems will not have generally accepted answers. For this reason teachers should become skilled in exploring consequences of a wide variety of possible actions as well as techniques for categorizing opinions, feelings, and facts before seeking solutions.

Specific counseling procedures require appropriate settings. Structured counseling sessions may take place in the homeroom. Special group-guidance sessions in separate less-structured settings might be organized to serve other counseling functions which are identified as having relevance to interests of particular students.

Duties appropriate for the teacher-counselor have been recognized and recommended. According to Alexander, et al., planning for sessions should be characterized as follows:

1. Provide a secure and comfortable home-base environment for the assigned group;
2. Provide personal and educational guidance;
3. Plan and evaluate individual programs;
4. Coordinate all of the many parts of the total educational program for the students in the assigned group;
5. Develop with pupils a program of self-knowledge and understanding of the nature of adolescence.[7]

Within the framework of a homeroom a teacher-counselor may be involved in discussing many aspects of growth. Knowledge concerning cognitive development of pupils is a necessity. This should include information regarding criteria for intellectual development as well as school achievement. Social growth of individuals should be noted both within the framework of the homeroom setting and in school and community functions. Sophistication and skills in group and interpersonal relations should be stressed. Pupil reactions to others in both formal and informal settings should be noted, and assistance in social growth should be extended in appropriate and applicable situations such as school service and special out-of-school activities. Emotional development of each individual should be carefully observed. Since excesses of emotion seem common at these ages special attention must be given to the strengths and weaknesses of individual personalities.

Formal counseling in group-guidance settings should occur in middle schools. Some question exists as to whether such guidance should be conducted by guidance counselors, especially sensitive teachers, or all teachers. If ideal circumstances were to prevail every teacher should be involved in such an operation. But since some teachers are less emotionally prepared for such a setting the question must be settled within each school. It seems inevitable that student choice will determine to some extent which staff members will be trusted and helpful.

Group guidance should, within reasonable bounds, be based upon problems suggested by pupils rather than a carefully prepared statement of curricular purposes previously determined. Such a statement does not negate the possibility of preplanning, nor of teacher influence upon the development of such problems. Rather it indicates the importance of problems being those seen as relevant by the learner. The selection of problems for consideration should be of an overarching type related to the social life of the youth, the emotional problems engendered within that life, the physical problems of maturation, and the intellectual problems entailed by the educational setting of the school. These problems should be amenable to group discussion and should be of concern to most of the participating individuals.

Teacher-pupil planning

A fundamental premise of counseling and teaching is that growth is facilitated where cooperative endeavor is occurring with pupils. Having decisions imposed on pupils does not encourage growth toward decision making and responsibility. If cooperation is to be taught opportunities must be provided for decision making and commitment to cooperative endeavor. If responsibility is to be taught, emerging adolescents must have opportunities to demonstrate it. Deciding upon a plan of action to be accomplished on a cooperative basis requires that members of a group consider goals they wish to reach, possible plans for reaching those goals, and factors required to support selected plans. Once group members have made a decision they must be held responsible for accomplishment of the plan. Some authors refer to this planning in terms of a democratic classroom. Grambs and Iverson list the following characteristics for such a classroom:

1. Creation of freedom within rules.
2. Providing significant areas of choice. . . .
3. A democratic classroom also provides for participation by all members;
4. Creates a feeling of responsibility on the part of all members;
5. Creates a feeling of being valued;
6. Uses the experimental approach to subject matter.[8]

If students are to learn to assume individual responsibility for group action they also must learn how group decisions are most effectively reached. As they gain experience in shared decision making they will learn to expect alternative approaches and see that single approaches are rare. They will learn to compromise, to lose gracefully, to win without rancor.

In order to deal with planning processes a teacher needs definite skills. The following points of view and skills have been recommended by Gruhn and Douglass:

1. To employ cooperative planning very effectively, the teacher must be superior in his understanding of children and in the knowledge of his subject. . . .
2. The teacher must preplan his work more carefully as a basic for cooperative teacher-pupil planning than if he were to impose his own plan on the class. . . .
3. The teacher should stimulate and guide the planning of the pupils without imposing upon them a preconceived plan of his own. . . .
4. The teacher should retain a strong position of leadership in the planning of all units and learning activities. . . .
5. The teacher should not spend too much class time on cooperative planning. . . .
6. The teacher should realize that the concept of cooperative planning does not apply equally well to all subjects or to all topics within a subject. . . .[9]

Some of the problems of teacher-student planning according to Van Til, Vars, and Lounsbury are:

1. Cooperative planning is more difficult for the teacher than the traditional, teacher-dominated methods; therefore, a better-than-average teacher must be required.
2. The teacher must do more and better preplanning.
3. Students who are accustomed to being told what to do may not want to share in planning.
4. Time is spent in cooperative planning that could otherwise be used to cover more subject matter.
5. Students may choose the easiest problems or procedures rather than those that might promote optimum learning.
6. The individual may become dependent upon the group, unable to think for himself.
7. A teacher may go through the motions of cooperative planning while in reality manipulating the group to make it arrive at decisions he thinks best. Students may see through this Machiavellian "democracy" and become cynical of all democratic processes.[10]

Of all the advantages and limitations of teacher-pupil planning one particular issue stands out. It has been most clearly articulated by Rogers in the following statement.

It does not seem reasonable to impose freedom on anyone who does not desire it. Consequently it seems wise, if it is at all possible, that when a group is offered the freedom to learn on their own responsibility, there should also be provision for those who do not wish or desire this freedom and prefer to be instructed and guided.[11]

Throughout the emerging adolescent years differences between and among pupils necessitate consideration of individuals as individuals, rather than as members of groups. Some pupils will need teacher direction, others may more easily assume self-direction. A teacher cannot assume that all children are seeking independence, nor should it be assumed that all children need continuous direction. The prime task of the teacher as a model is to give each pupil the greatest possible degree of freedom, considering the degree of responsibility which the youth is able to assume.

Classroom climate

The teacher is responsible for establishing a classroom climate conducive to learning. Conditions may be set so that an approach may be highly structured or more open. Students may be encouraged to be active or passive, depending upon whether the teacher's style is facilitative or directive. While these conditions are neither good nor bad as such, their total effect on the learning of students as individuals and as a group should be evaluated. The prevailing pattern in many schools is that most classes are quite structured and directive, and pupils are more passive than is recommended. It is essential that a classroom climate which is most effective for the greatest number of pupils be established, while alternatives for individuals must exist in order to facilitate learning for those pupils who do not learn best under the prevailing structure.

TEACHER AS PLANNER

Teachers must become adept at developing objectives at varying levels of planning. They must relate to overarching purposes of education and translate aims and goals into viable programs for learners. Overarching purposes derive from society. As such, they may be stated by educational philosophers, interpreted by school boards, and codified by school staff. For example, good citizenship is a desired broad outcome. Most school boards would expect to achieve this aim as one of their broad school purposes. A problem arises when evidence of achievement of the purpose is sought. Developing a program for implementing broad purposes and evaluating the degree of their achievement is difficult. Such sets of goals are necessary, but they are not sufficiently specific. Teachers utilize these as guidelines, but the individual teacher in the planning of objectives must reduce them to more specific activities and statements of intended outcomes. Where clear statements of philosophy have been established, those statements must relate to long-range purposes as well as to specific learning situations which are to be designed for pupils in school.

There is a lack of understanding of relationships between objectives in education and behavior indicators which are required as data from which inferences for learning may be derived. Many teachers have focused on acquisition of content at the level of facts and statements as the main learning outcome from their teaching.

Obviously, the acquisition of content not previously known or recognized does represent a change in the student. But memory and recall of content do little good if other changes in behavior such as comprehension and use of what is known do not follow. Thus teachers must pursue objectives which extend to proposed changes in a learner which allow the manipulation of learned content in more complex patterns, a solution of problems and evidence of learning at higher levels of complexity.

The most common level for which teachers plan objectives on a systematic preteaching basis is the unit. Here a teacher establishes a series of objectives which he or she hopes can be achieved at the end of a certain relatively short period of time, during which a series of structured learning activities will have taken place. For example, as a unit objective to be met in studying the "Westward Movement" a pupil might be expected to understand and appreciate the hardships experienced by pioneers during the westward trek. Such an objective might conceivably contribute to an understanding of some aspects of good citizenship, a basic overarching purpose.

A problem in development of unit objectives is that while they can be implemented they are many times difficult to evaluate, especially if the language does not contain precise terms and operations. In order to ascertain whether objectives have been met they must be stated in specific language so that instructional strategies might be more appropriately selected. Learning activities designed to meet specific objectives in successive lessons will hopefully lead to improved learning situations and greater achievement. Achievement of a series of specific objectives should lead toward achievement of broader unit objectives which should contribute to the ultimate achievement of the overarching purposes of education.

A major problem in the development of objectives is that of perceived relevance in the eyes of pupils. The most carefully conceived set of plans developed by a teacher may or may not be relevant to the perceived needs of a class of pupils and almost certainly will not meet the perceived needs of every individual within the class. In order to deal with this problem it is essential that the teacher plan to relate objectives to pupils in order to stimulate learners so that they can learn what is needed to achieve a good education. Weinstein and Fantini suggested four causes of irrelevance in education which should be considered by the teacher-planner.

**Informal classroom settings encourage individual motivation.
John Baker School**

(Courtesy of Albuquerque, New Mexico, Public Schools)

1. Failure to match teaching procedures to children's *learning styles*. . . .
2. The use of material that is outside or poorly related to the learner's *knowledge* of his physical realm of experience. . . .
3. The use of teaching materials and methods that ignore the learner's *feelings*. . . .
4. The use of teaching content that ignores the *concerns* of the learners.[12]

With these principles in mind it should be possible to develop a series of objectives with alternative activities and methods to achieve them. Differing content, skills, and degrees of commitment might occur in a single class. Students who engage in different learning activities may come to learn the same concept. Thus, one pupil may choose to build a model of a Conestoga wagon, while another might prefer to gather data from various encyclopedias regarding the Conestoga wagon to lend authenticity to the model being constructed. Both could learn about the Conestoga wagon, while each was using his or her preferred activities to contribute to the common goal.

Objectives relevant to school purposes

The school is a microcosm of society. Strengths evident within society will probably be found within the school. Weaknesses inherent within the culture will certainly be noted in the school. For example, Macdonald has stated that the "problem with schools is not that they are irrelevant in the sense that they are odd cultural museum pieces, but that they are a living embodiment of the very shoddiness that pervades our general social experience . . . a rather faithful replica of the whole."[13]

Thus specific objectives must be conceived with an eye to overall functions of the school as a part of society. They must be selected with a view to what is appropriate for achievement within the school, and those areas where the school reinforces commonly accepted social learning experiences.

Some hold that school purposes should be focused on those areas where the school can be most effective. Objectives should be developed in areas where the school can directly perform in line with societal expectations. For example, student government can reflect political questions for pupils, and thus serve as an introduction to political operations in the broader society. This is an aspect of society which youth can experience in a limited way but is available within the school framework. Thus life within the school can reflect the democratic values of the society.

The middle school should be devoted to the maturational process of the emerging adolescent. Objectives should be developmental and dynamic in nature, and should be variable depending upon the situation and pupils involved. A teacher should plan objectives which may vary from day to day, season to season, and year to year according to the dynamic situation of the growth function. Changes in maturation may create a situation in which certain objectives might be appropriate in October but not in May due to changes in individuals in the class. What might be appropriate for one class in October might not be appropriate for another class at the same time due to differences in the maturational rate in individuals in the two classes. Planning must be flexible in order to permit variations because of this dynamic situation. In addition, objectives must be variable within the classroom because of the idiosyncratic nature of the individuals involved.

Objectives relevant to classroom purposes

The classroom is primarily a learning environment. A teacher plans a learning environment best adapted to the learning of each of the individuals involved in the classroom. In setting up objectives for a classroom the teacher must develop a set of instructional objectives with a great degree of specificity, and at the appropriate level. Robert Mager has established a set of criteria for objectives:

> 1) An instructional objective describes an intended outcome rather than a description or summary of content. 2) One characteristic of a usefully stated objective is that it is stated in behavioral, or performance, terms that describe what the learner will be *doing* when demonstrating his achievement of the objective. 3) The statement of objectives for an entire program of instruction will consist of several specific statements. 4) The objective...most usefully stated is one which best communicates the instructional intent of the person selecting the objective.[14]

Objectives must be stated in such clear terms that they can be understood, implemented, and evaluated in much the same way not only by one teacher but by fellow teachers, the administrator, parents, and pupils. Such specificity makes possible a clear delineation in order that pupils may not only understand but may add to or delete from a set of exploratory objectives according to their own perceived needs. This can be of great importance in the development of teacher-pupil planning in which pupils can relate an objective to their own particular perceived needs at that specific moment.

Objectives at the instructional level in the classroom must be appropriate, learnable, and carefully developed at an appropriate level of sophistication for the pupils involved. Objectives which are unrealistically high or low succeed only in leading to unreal aspirations on the part of pupils. Either situation can lead to disappointment at the time of final assessment.

The classroom should be seen as an environment for living as well as learning. Objectives should be set up with varying degrees of success expected. A willingness to accept failure should be emphasized. Objectives should be open to variation and social objectives should be particularly emphasized.

The teacher who establishes realistic objectives will not expect every objective to be achieved at a perfect level. Objectives should be arranged in which some pupils can achieve at a peak level, others at a very good level, and still others at a relatively poor level. For example, the model prepared by Frymier (see Fig. 12-1) graphically illustrates three dimensions of the learning activity; kinds of learning undertaken, degree of mastery required, and the significance of time as a variable. Thus 30 categories are delineated, each of which would indicate a different teacher expectation.

Probably the most significant of these dimensions is that of degree of mastery. The teacher should develop some idea of the degree to which the pupil is expected to achieve. The common misconception that every pupil should be expected to perform at a 100-percent level is easily refuted, but is still commonly held by many teachers.

There should be a willingness on the part of the teacher to accept the fact that some objectives may not be met by some pupils. There would be a clear delineation of objectives achieved by certain individuals, with as clear a statement concerning objectives which had not been reached. A teacher could then say to the next teacher of a pupil that certain objectives could and should be re-

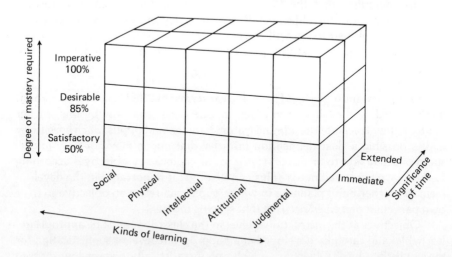

Fig. 12-1. Classification of Educational Objectives. (From *The Nature of Education Method* by Jack R. Frymier, Charles E. Merrill Publishing Co., Columbus, Ohio © 1965, p. 248.)

stated, hoping that greater maturation would assist in their achievement. At no time has a teacher ever been able to arrange a learning environment in such a way that total learning could take place. One aspect of the development of planning should be an acceptance of difficulties in facilitating the learning of all students to the highest level.

Objectives must be organized by teachers in relation to pupil development on a delineated set of criteria. Variations in plans should be possible as one moves forward through time. If teachers and students individually and in small groups are committed to achieving the most important objectives, they can alter sequence and time on agreement. Plans for another attempt following other experiences can be made. An agreement of teachers and students on the degree of importance of the objectives in question should be explicit. Achievement of objectives established in a preplanning phase before students and teachers began the year must be continually reevaluated, and perhaps revised in light of learning experiences, hopes, and aspirations of pupils and teachers working together during the school year.

TEACHER AS DIAGNOSTICIAN

The ability to evaluate is a necessity in the teaching function. Purposes for such evaluation are many, the primary one of which is to diagnose the learning situation as it exists at a particular time for a particular individual. To accomplish this fundamental task, evaluation must meet other requirements. One statement of these tasks is:

- Facilitate self-evaluation
- Encompass all the objectives
- Facilitate teaching and learning
- Generate records appropriate to various uses
- Facilitate decision making on curriculum and educational policy.[15]

To diagnose appropriate steps in the learning procedure a teacher must know where the pupil is located in the learning process regarding specific objectives. The teacher must then decide on procedures which seem appropriate to the learner's level of progress. Knowledge of the pupil and his or her learning patterns, personal style, and related problems are important in order to assist the pupil toward success on specific assigned tasks. Standardized tests for general intellectual development, personality profiles, and prior learning difficulties in addition to observations of individual achievement and interests are important for the development of such knowledge.

The teacher must be well grounded in a subject area, or may not be able to recognize learning difficulties a child is experiencing. He or she must be able to conceptualize expected progress along substantive paths for the child and design progressive steps in desired directions. Expectations must be reasonable as presented to a pupil. Unreasonable expectations, either too low or too high, are debilitating to a child.

Knowledge concerning the objectives of a lesson or unit is necessary to be able to make an evaluation at the conclusion of a specific learning experience. Such evaluation must include measurement of the achievement of specific objectives present in the unit. Thus the tasks of a teacher are to determine where a pupil stands before the unit begins, how much he or she can reasonably be expected to achieve, and what objective should be measured as a culmination of the learning experience.

One function of diagnosis and evaluation is the reporting task. Teachers are expected to report to parents concerning the achievement of their offspring. The teacher's role in these cases is to work with parents to develop an appropriate means of reporting. Another function which the teacher performs as a diagnostician is an evaluation of the learning experience. A curriculum should be a dynamic experience, continuously changing as the student body changes and as the opinions of the community and knowledge of subject matter change. At the conclusion of each learning experience pupils and teachers should attempt to determine what steps could be taken to improve that experience or whether it should be attempted again. In some cases this final exchange can be as effective a learning experience for those concerned as many procedures conducted during the experience.

Evaluation

Evaluation is valuable in that it helps pupils know the degree to which they have achieved those goals which they desire, and helps a teacher achieve those desired goals. Other supposed objectives of evaluation are valuable only insofar as they relate to these two overarching purposes. Thus pupils are enabled by evaluation to tell how well they are progressing toward commonly accepted goals. It is possible for a teacher to see how effective various strategies and techniques being utilized are in helping the child reach those goals. The following statement indicates times in which evaluation can be most useful.

1. When that evaluation is in terms of what is important to the learner
2. When it is a means which he can use for directing his future study
3. When it gives him feedback to help him know his competencies, where he is, to what point he has progressed

4. When he feels that the teacher is helping him evaluate himself and improve his perceptions as to his next needs
5. When it helps him see next steps and opens doors for him to move forward; *not* when it stops study and closes doors to future learning in the area
6. When it helps him gain personal meaning in an area of learning
7. When it helps him see progress and thus feel good about himself, even if he realizes he still has some way to go
8. When it encourages rather than discourages further learning
9. When it is set up so as to be a challenge (leading to what he believes he can do), rather than a frustration (convincing him he cannot succeed)
10. When in one form or another it is continuous
11. When the learner comes to see the behavior valued by the teacher to be his own realistic self-appraisal and self-direction, rather than convincing the teacher of the amount of information learned.[16]

A much more rigorous and exacting testing program must be developed to accomplish these purposes. Such a program will not evaluate pupil success and failure as a means of reporting to parents but will rather measure pupil success in terms of goals to be achieved. Testing has developed greatly in the last few decades. While not yet at a stage where its goals may be considered to have been met completely, certain gains have been noted in recent years.

1. Greater awareness of the objectives of education and the need to define these in specific terms
2. Greater awareness of the nature and extent of individual differences
3. Greater consistency and precision in measuring educational outcomes
4. Development of instruments by means of which educational hypotheses can be rigorously tested
5. Acceptance of the possibility of scientific demonstration of educational principles.[17]

Certain requirements are made of the teacher in order to achieve best results in diagnostic teaching. A strong statement of such demands was presented by Lee in the A.S.C.D. Yearbook of 1967.

1. It requires teachers to be aware of the skills—all the skills for which they have accepted responsibility, not just those arbitrarily assigned to any one grade or performance level, and not just those identified with the content of each area.

2. It requires the ability to see evidence of competence or lack of it in behavioral terms.
3. It requires awareness of concepts, understandings and generalizations
   which are important for learners in accomplishing their purposes and
   goals.
4. Again, it requires the ability to see evidence of the mastery or lack of
   mastery of these elements in behavioral terms.
5. It necessitates watching learners with a seeing eye and listening to
   them perceptively rather than merely "talking at" them or asking them
   memoriter kinds of "checking" questions.
6. It necessitates much self-evaluation and self-direction by learners on
   the basis of their awareness of their needs and purposes, which the
   teacher must help them to cultivate.
7. It requires teachers to look at the specific learnings, skills, competencies, concepts and applications of each learner rather than at general levels of learning, because the latter give little or no guidance in
   determining needed next steps.[18]

Assessment within the framework of diagnostic teaching performs a most
necessary function. Diagnostic tests must be developed for all processes and
concepts intended to be achieved. Such diagnostic tests should indicate specific
knowledges and skills possessed by the pupil at the beginning of a unit, and
what has been learned at the end of that unit. A pupil's progress is not
measured against a norm or his or her classmates, but rather according to what
has been achieved compared to previous knowledge, skills, and attitudes.
Such tests must not only be specific to knowledges presented within the unit,
but must relate to knowledges possessed by the pupil when the unit was begun.
Thus a wide range of conceptualization and processes must be measured with
each unit.

Anecdotal reports and case studies form an important aspect of the assessment function of a teacher. They present an opportunity to the teacher to
investigate in breadth in anecdotal reports and in depth in case studies. In
anecdotal reports a teacher is able to catch those unusual moments of learning
inspiration which may occur at infrequent times and are indicative of an insightful mind. In the case of a student who may learn either unusually rapidly
or slowly a case study may be utilized in order to determine the concatenation
of circumstances which fosters that learning.

The same principle applies to pupil logs, in which pupils record learning
activities and are encouraged to develop insights into their own learning processes. A lengthy review gathered over a considerable period of time should
help pupils gain insight into their learning. Such insight should greatly aid the
future learning process for the youth.

The teacher should be knowledgeable in the utilization of mechanical recording devices since these can be more objective in assessments than many other methods. Little can be done to rationalize the results of an audio-tape in reporting back to the performer the results of his or her singing, playing, or speaking. The same principle holds true in terms of video-taping of physical activities, plays, and other such activities. Such reporting can be useful in the development of interaction analysis. Not only does the number of comments enter into consideration, but also the amount of physical activity, the degree of assurance, and other such matters come to the forefront. The equipment which can be used in such assessment has come to be relatively available and inexpensive so that most classrooms could possess it if the teacher desired.

One of the more valuable tools of assessment is that of group evaluation. A group cannot be expected to evaluate any and all areas of pupil learning any more than a teacher can do this. Some learning is so internal that only the pupil can assess it. Nevertheless, certain aspects, particularly of the affective domain, can better be measured by a classroom group than by other means. Sociometric techniques, measurement of pupil acceptance of group determinations, and other such areas may and should be assessed by other members of the group in addition to those assessed by the youth or teacher.

Standardized tests

The utilization of standardized evaluative devices should be encouraged in addition to specific subject-area examinations. It is insufficient to know what specific concepts and/or processes the pupil is currently approaching. It is also necessary to have some idea concerning the general capabilities of the pupil, whether intellectual, psychomotor, or affective. In order to understand a level of performance, some knowledge of this general factor is necessary. General IQ tests of many sorts are available. Group IQ tests should be readily available to the teacher as diagnosis is being conducted. In some cases individual IQ tests such as the Stanford-Binet examination should be made available as should similar tests in the psychomotor and affective domains.

A word of caution should be given about the so-called "Pygmalion" effect. Pupils tend to perform at that level which is expected of them by their teachers and classmates. Thus in some cases a teacher who places too much faith in standardized exams can place a pupil in a position of low expectancy, thus creating a situation in which a pupil will achieve less than might normally have occurred. The purpose of standardized examinations is not to place pupils in a certain mold but rather to help the teacher understand the learning abilities and styles of individual pupils. A teacher must know all data which have been made available concerning a pupil in order to conduct the best diagnosis, and must be depended upon to be professional in appraisal of the data.

Summative tests

In addition to standardized exams to be utilized to determine general factors of intelligence and physical and emotional abilities, each pupil should take examinations based upon specific objectives of the learning experience. These summative examinations should be administered before the experience in order to discover what, if any, concepts and processes could be deleted from the pupil's experience due to prior knowledge. They should also be conducted at the end of the experience in order to determine whether further work is needed in any particular area. At no time in these evaluative experiences should any idea of praise or condemnation be considered. The only questions are what knowledges are considered necessary, and does the pupil have them.

Summative tests can be effective in evaluating development in processes; they are less strong in evaluating the development of conceptualizations. They are extremely strong in evaluating psychomotor development; with care they can be acceptable in the measurement of cognitive development; but they are rather weak in measuring affective development. It is necessary that the diagnosing teacher recognize inherent strengths and weaknesses of these measuring devices and utilize them only when appropriate.

Summative tests must evaluate objectives, and not the content involved in the unit. Objectives may be similar for all students, while content and techniques for achieving those objectives may vary. Summative tests would vary only to the degree that individual differences might make lesser achievement of certain objectives a viable alternative. This might occur where a student needed remedial work, or where he or she had advanced beyond what might be expected.

Variables in the mastery of objectives

Individual differences in abilities require that specific objectives also vary. A majority of pupils experiencing a unit should attempt to achieve similar objectives, but those objectives should be established on a basis where 100-percent achievement is not absolutely necessary. Hence a pupil might be able to achieve 50 percent of a certain goal and be permitted to proceed to the next unit with the understanding that remedial work could be done in the one area if other objectives have been met.

A major variable is the interplay of domains. The affective domain enters into achievement in the cognitive domain just as the reverse is true. Physical development may sometimes have an effect upon cognitive development as in the playing of a piano or typing. If the finger muscles do not operate in a competent way, the cognitive work can be of little avail. One of the more important problems a teacher must face in development and evaluation of objectives is the determination of degree to which the other domains may affect the particular one being measured.

Availability of learning materials makes a great difference in the degree of mastery of objectives possible to individual pupils. Seldom are all desired materials available. The teacher must be aware of which materials are available to the pupil, and what effect the unavailability of certain materials has upon the learning process before evaluating the achievement of goals.

Readiness to learn is one area of variability about which much has been said but little is known. Horrocks has described it as follows:

> A continuing concern of the schools lies in the readiness to learn of the children placed in their care. When children lack such readiness it is recognized that they will either fail to learn at all or that at best their learning will be slow and insufficient. Moreover, children who are encouraged to learn before they are ready are likely to meet discouraging failure, build work or study habits which must later be painfully unlearned, and they even endanger normal physical and social development. Readiness to learn the various kinds and levels of subject matter taught in school has many facets but may generally be defined as a capacity to learn accompanied by the wish and the skills and the proper background to do so.[19]

This readiness to learn is a conglomerate of many aspects, many of which are not measurable. For example, it is not yet possible to measure in any reliable way the effects of intellectual maturational readiness as considered in Piaget's concept of concrete to formal operations. Yet this concept must be considered seriously in the readiness to learn. Perceived relevance of material is strongly related to a pupil's approach toward readiness to learn. Environmental cues enter into the situation as does teacher encouragement or discouragement. These variables cannot be effectively measured, but can be considered by the teacher as carefully as possible. Certainly the content and process backgrounds necessary for such readiness can and should be evaluated most carefully.

Appraisal of pupil development

Appraisal of pupil development for the purposes of reporting progress both to the pupil and to the parent is an accepted part of the role of the teacher. Most pupil reporting is based upon normative data comparing the pupil to other children in the class who are of presumably equal caliber. Such a concept is obviously fallacious but has the weight of many decades of practice to support it. Reporting has been done in many ways, the most common being by means of a card with various subject matters delineated on it with a letter grade A-F, or percentage score 0-100 being assigned to each subject. Parents have come to recognize certain letters or numbers as indicating the level of their child in relation to other children and perceive this as being the important aspect of reporting. Rigorous efforts at re-education of parents to create a situation in which an evaluation of achievement of individual objectives is seen as being more relevant is necessary.

As a partial step in this direction, some schools give two grades for each subject, one being the normative grade based upon the average of the entire class, with a second grade being based upon a difficult-to-measure item classified as effort. Effort is perceived by some teachers to be an evaluation of a pupil's work as compared to what he or she could presumably be expected to do, thus being a rather naive but constructive approach to developmental evaluation.

Letters have been written with paragraph statements outlining strengths and weaknesses of pupils attempting to delineate more clearly the development of pupils to the parents. Such letters usually succeed in identifying particularly strong and weak points in the learning of the pupil. An administrative problem related to this approach is the large block of time required of teachers in writing such reports. Also these accounts do not always reveal a broad base of growth and development, but more often the teacher's value system. The parent conference poses the same set of problems. The teacher cannot meet with some 25-30-35 sets of parents, each for a considerable length of time. The parents also are not always able or willing to give this time. Such conversations may provide rather limited information and create situations for recrimination. If the school and staff have developed adequate sequences of behavior and intended outcomes, there is a basic framework for teaching, learning, and assessment. This requires a sequenced set of objectives, clearly delineated with measures to be used to assess progress along a continuum. It would then be possible to locate each pupil on such a continuum. Satisfactory, minimal, or unsatisfactory achievement could then be based upon change or progress and thus reported. The reporting system would be based upon the concept of individual progress rather than relative status or rank. In areas where such a process is not feasible, a letter or general statement could be utilized until these objectives could be developed into scope and sequence with appropriate criteria for assessment. In these circumstances reporting would emphasize the importance of objectives, criteria for diagnosis of their achievement, and not be based alone upon amount of subject-matter knowledge accumulated in a given time.

Self-evaluation

The evaluation of each youth's school achievement should be based upon his or her own purposes. Those purposes should be determined in cooperation with a teacher based upon the pupil's present rate and level of achievement. The pupil should be expected to view these goals with a degree of objectivity and personal thought which would make them relevant to his or her accomplishment. The task is to appraise the pupil's achievements, growth, and improvement upon definite previously determined criteria.

The pupil should have the assistance of peers and teachers in the development and assessment of these goals, since in some few cases they might be able to be more objective in their evaluation of an individual's work. Pupil achievement, whether teacher or student evaluated, should encompass review of other source data, tests, and a variety of objective measures.

The teacher role in stimulating growth and effective self-evaluation is that of helping in the selection of appropriate objectives and means for their achievement. A suitable evaluative device for the measurement of the achievement of objectives must be selected. Appraisal and redirection of effort should be based on more than subjective evaluation of abilities. Both over and underevaluating may be controlled to a degree through cooperative effort of teachers and students.

Evaluation of instructional procedures

The teacher as a diagnostician is concerned with how well individuals in the class are progressing. Hence an evaluation of instructional procedures is of concern. The general education curriculum experienced by the entire class must be evaluated as to whether specific experiences are best adapted to achieve the general objectives agreed upon between teacher and pupil. While aims and objectives may at times be cooperatively determined, activities designed to achieve objectives are more often designed primarily by the teacher on the assumption that a teacher knows the discipline more adequately. In other cases they may be left open to pupil negotiation. In any case, responsibility for results in general education rests with the teacher. If the objectives have not been met, if students haven't learned, the teacher must redesign activities for learning to proceed.

The exploratory curriculum for groups and individuals must also be carefully evaluated by the teacher in order to determine whether those experiences are best qualified to achieve the objectives cooperatively determined. The exploratory curriculum is determined by the needs, purposes, and desires of pupils. These may in some cases be evanescent, thus creating a continuing demand for evaluation of instructional procedures and programs.

TEACHER AS MANAGER

In addition to instructional roles, teachers face many tasks which are primarily managerial in nature. They must, for example, serve as disciplinarians, act as housekeepers of the rooms in which learning takes place, and keep appropriate records concerning activities of the pupils for whom they are responsible. These roles are an integral part of the broad range of teacher functions, and must be considered in an assessment of teacher competencies.

Learning is developed through motivated activities on the part of pupils. In the presence of such motivation discipline occupies a relatively small part of the conscious effort of the teacher. The existence of a universal motivation for all members of a class is remote. Nevertheless, the development of a sense of responsibility within pupils is a necessity. Each emerging adolescent must be able to act in the best interests of the learning group even though each individual may not learn at his or her peak capacity in each type of situation.

An attractive setting can alter learner attitudes so as to enhance and augment the learning which takes place within a classroom. A neat and orderly environment indicating purposeful activities is important. Minimal standards of cleanliness should be expected by a teacher. Responsibility of a pupil and necessary efforts on the part of a staff must be sustained to maintain such standards. Efforts to brighten classroom surroundings (e.g., bulletin boards and displays) should be a cooperative endeavor on the part of teachers and pupils. Pupils live in classrooms six hours a day. They should be encouraged to take part in the maintenance and enhancement of their environment.

One of the least popular managerial tasks undertaken by the teacher is that of record keeping, both administrative and assessment. While recording of scores on standardized examinations and other educational assessment such as pupil status and progress with periodic diagnostic data is seen as an integral part of a teacher's work, some teachers are less enthusiastic about recording various transactions which are a basic part of the social and physical framework of the school. Records such as lunch money, activity tickets, and such raise serious reservations in some minds. To appreciate the importance of these teacher tasks it is necessary to view the school as a small society where working and living together require a support system. Certain activities are a necessary part of that social setting, and the teacher's role in the maintenance function is vital to the school.

The classroom situation is a very complex one. It defies simplistic analysis. For example, Flanders noted that differing age groups relate to direct influence in different ways. Questions remain regarding the effects upon all pupils of specific actions of teachers. Depending upon their perceptions of the situation, pupils will react in their own unique ways to particular teacher-generated stimuli. Medley and Mitzel note:

Two behaviors are seldom identical in all observable respects. What would seem to be the same behavior can be quite different in impact according to who exhibits it....The setting or situation in which a behavior occurs also alters its effect....Moreover, when a particular teacher does a particular thing at a particular time, it does not necessarily have the same effect on all thirty of his pupils.[20]

It is difficult to predict the results of teacher actions. Actions and reactions must be interpreted as perceived by 30 independent learners, all of whom are at a much less sophisticated level of perception than is the teacher. As Stephen M. Corey pointed out, it is difficult to connect teacher actions directly with specific pupil learning.

The thought is that while teacher classroom behavior certainly occurs contemporaneously with some pupil learning, the relationship between the two is very difficult to establish and may be so slight as to suggest that classroom teacher behavior observation represents a somewhat unpromising search for the essence of teaching.[21]

One problem with many teacher-observation instruments and rating tools in use is that they have been based largely upon the role of the teacher as a purveyor of information, not as a manager of the learning environment. Various managing roles taken by a teacher are assumed in order to permit a pupil to achieve the most significant learnings possible. Each pupil will have different significant learnings depending upon his or her idiosyncratic values, abilities, and goals. It is crucial that teachers not limit their role to presentation of subject matter, or to tasks which are more easily measurable. Emphasis should be laid upon the development and management of a learning environment most conducive to learning for emerging adolescents.

TEACHER AS GUIDE TO RESOURCES

An important role of the teacher in the learning experience is that of a coordinator of the environment. Such coordination involves many aspects and knowledges, including the knowledge of how learning takes place and what resources are available to assist such learning. Pupils learn from their environment. That environment includes textbooks, group discussions, teacher lecture, audio-visual materials, peer teaching, independent study, and programmed learning. Since learning is idiosyncratic in nature, each pupil must be assumed to learn in a unique way ideally needing a different environment. Each pupil has his own preferred mode, rates, and physical circumstances.

Since such variations are ordinarily not available in a typical school a teacher's role as a guide to curriculum and materials becomes both crucial and complex.

Teachers have certain components of the environment within their purview. The primary resources involved in learning considered in this section are: (1) teacher resources, (2) human resources other than faculty, (3) community resources, (4) media resources, and (5) library resources.

Teacher resources

A teacher, as a resource for a pupil's learning, is ordinarily concerned with the focus of supervised study conducted by the individual in his or her idiosyncratic efforts to inquire, solve problems, and describe phenomena. This teaching role is usually accomplished through a judicious arrangement of learning assignments developed in cooperation with each pupil. These assignments ordinarily are divided into three types: supervised study, unsupervised study in school, and unsupervised study at home. While all are assigned with the assumption that their completion may improve the learning effectiveness of the individual pupil, each presupposes a differing degree of professional supervision. Supervised study ordinarily takes place in a classroom or in some place located so that a teacher may supervise the work of the pupil. This may be a library, a resource center, or a contiguous classroom. In unsupervised study a pupil may also utilize a classroom, library, or resource center, but is not expected to need as close a level of supervision. Another teacher or an aide might be expected to give whatever help is needed. A homework assignment is ordinarily given when supervision, as such, is felt to be unnecessary. Under these circumstances the accomplishment of a specific stated assignment is seen to be sufficient to accomplish the desired objective.

All learning activities should be based upon dual purposes—general education and exploration. Most general education should be subsumed under work done in class time, with some small part given over to supervised study in a classroom or study hall situation. Most exploration—that study conducted by the individual for his or her own unique purposes—should be most appropriately conducted in the home and/or resource center. Specific types of learning assignments have been developed in various school systems throughout the nation. One of the more complete listings was developed by the Philadelphia Public School system which stated the following as a recommended listing of home study activities:

- Studying for mastery of basic skills.
- Studying to remember certain significant content.
- Gathering information in preparation for a trip.

- Taking a trip on out-of-school time.
- Reporting a television program which has educational value.
- Reading to parents from books already read in class.
- Collecting, constructing, and classifying materials.
- Writing original stories, plays, poems.
- Constructing a model or doing an experiment.
- Participating in community activities.
- Practicing body-conditioning exercises and physical skills.
- Preparing a written report.
- Preparing for an oral report on literature, science, social studies.
- Listening to good music.
- Using arts and crafts skills to develop learning in other areas of the curriculum.
- Observing and reporting current happenings.
- Interviewing people.
- Solving significant problems.[22]

Certain fundamental principles should be adopted in establishing policies of learning assignments in middle schools. These are the following—

1. Assignments should be deleted where possible.
2. Assignments should be related to work in progress in the class.
3. Assignments should be supervised where possible.
4. Assignments should be based upon perceived needs when possible.
5. Assignments should be based upon cooperative planning.

A continuing debate rages over assigned homework for emerging adolescents. Arguments against homework assignments include those citing health needs of youth of this age for greater relaxation and rest during the period of accelerated growth, the inability of middle school pupils to study independently very effectively, homes which are not conducive to study, and the presence of other educational activities which might more advantageously occupy pupil time. Arguments in favor of home assignments are that school time is too limited, that pupils have differing needs for drill and practice, and that pupil motivation to continue independent learning should not be discouraged.

If and when home assignments are given, they should relate to work being conducted in class or by individual students. Assignments should be given only when individuals need or desire to learn particular aspects of a subject based upon their own idiosyncratic purposes. If all pupils need to learn the content it should be presented in school time. Assignments should whenever possible be scheduled in such a way that they can be conducted while the child is being supervised by a professional educator. When this is impossible due to teacher-student ratio, an aide might be called upon to assist. A qualified person should be available to assist pupils in their work when they are engaging in a learning assignment in school.

All learning assignments should be based upon cooperative planning. Work deemed useful and interesting by the pupil will elicit more interest and effort than will work arbitrarily assigned by a teacher. Such cooperative planning does not imply a lack of leadership on the part of a teacher. Cooperation implies more than one person working toward common goals. It is in this framework that cooperatively planned learning assignments should take place. Teachers should be able to give pupils the benefit of their experiences and knowledges in learning the subject matter intended, while pupils should be able to give teachers information concerning their own unique learning skills and interests.

Human resources other than faculty

A commonly unused resource in the learning experiences of a pupil and one which should be clearly and explicitly organized by the teacher is available human resources. These include teachers, fellow pupils, other school personnel, community-resource persons, and visiting dignitaries. A wide variety of available persons constitute a considerable reservoir from which learners can draw in their efforts to achieve their purposes.

Teachers are often overlooked as resources in areas outside the subject matter in which they are certified. A teacher who has been on a trip to Mediterranean lands could be utilized in geography and the study of ancient cultures; camping enthusiasts may teach some aspect of outdoor living to pupils; chess enthusiasts might teach some aspects of game logic—there are abundant possibilities. A teacher should be able to help pupils develop strengths in many areas in addition to the discipline for which he or she is certified. Team approaches can utilize the strengths of individual teachers through organization of units and invitation of individuals to contribute their special strengths through consultation, sharing special information, materials, exhibits, and commentary.

Pupils may serve as resources to other pupils through peer teaching, special presentations, preparation of exhibits, fairs, and other special projects. Such aid can serve not only to assist in the learning process itself, but can also help pupils to develop a degree of motivation since relevance is more likely to be seen when demonstrated by one's fellow students. School personnel—librarians, clerks, aides, bus drivers, custodians, cooks, gardeners, business managers, computer-center personnel—all have special knowledges in areas perceived as important by pupils. Where the strengths of these persons are added to the regular team to assist in the learning process they provide additional resources. Also, this use reinforces the awareness of pupils that learning takes place in different situations through the efforts of many persons. Thus learning can be experienced as a continuing process not dependent upon the traditional school setting alone.

Middle schools have utilized community people as resources for decades. A school administrator should assume responsibility for informing teachers of community resources available to the school. Many school leaders continuously build a roster of human resources in the community, people who can augment and supplement the school program of activities.

Community resources

Other types of community resources should be utilized in the learning experiences of a pupil. A teacher should be aware of natural resources available in the community and alert to ways in which these can supplement learning experiences provided by a classroom teacher. Rivers, farms, dams, buildings, business concerns, museums, and battlegrounds should be utilized, when available, to enhance learning. The utilization of the concrete is superior to verbal or literary stimuli in certain learning situations. Field trips, investigations, and studies of many types enrich learning and serve to tie community and school learning.

Community resources have relevance in many ways—in the academic disciplines, economics, politics, and social and personal living. For examples, mathematics classes can benefit from a trip to a computer installation; social studies classes can be enriched through a trip to the community governmental offices; science classes can visit commercial laboratories, docks, fisheries, and factories. Most disciplines should have connecting links to the surrounding community which can help pupils understand the dynamic processes of society, and how education is linked to the continuity of life.

Media resources

A media center can be of importance in the learning functions of children in a middle school. Many aspects of learning can be carried on more effectively through sight, by viewing pictures, either still or moving, or through sound, by means of recordings, in addition to books and journals. Certain fundamental principles should be considered when using audio-visual media. These have been summarized by Gruhn and Douglass:

1. Audio-visual materials should be selected and their use planned in terms of the particular contribution they are to make to the objectives of the unit being studied. . . .

Community service personnel aid in emerging adolescent learning.
Mount Hebron School
(Courtesy of Montclair, New Jersey, Public Schools)

2. Audio-visual materials should always be previewed by the teacher. . . .
3. The time for the presentation of the material should be well planned and economically used. . . .
4. The pupils should be prepared for the presentation of any audio-visual materials. . . .
5. The amount of audio-visual material which is employed should not be disproportionate as compared with other types of instructional materials. . . .
6. The teacher's plans for the use of audio-visual materials should be made weeks ahead.[23]

Audio-tape can be effectively used in two important ways. First, as a teaching aid—materials such as speeches, lectures, and other programs, recorded for retrieval on demand, permit a pupil to use them when needed. Second, as a self-improvement aid—an individual can monitor his own performance by retaping and replaying audio-tapes in such areas as music, instrument playing or voice, and speech. Utilizing recorded data the pupil can analyze performance weaknesses and strengths and repeat, each time improving where possible. This frees the teacher from time-consuming effort and the student from criticism before it is appropriate.

Filmstrips, slides, photographs, and films, are of use both in large-group and individual situations as aids to presentations. Their use presents a different orientation to the learning experience. New dimensions can be added through the use of these materials in both affective and aesthetic education. Aesthetic beauty is enhanced when visuals enliven what is seen, and audio carries sounds. A teacher can improve learning, particularly when wide ranges of media resources are available and utilized.

Programmed learning is a valuable method of achieving the individualized learning desired in middle school. The importance of programming rests upon its strength in presentation of material to the pupil when needed, rather than in conjunction with everyone in the class. Under these circumstances programmed learning could be utilized, not as a curriculum experience for an entire class, but as a resource intended to meet specific needs of a particular individual at a certain experiential level. Such a principle requires a teacher to be familiar with the curriculum of various learning programs so that excerpts from a particular program that might be needed by a pupil for a specific purpose can be utilized.

Library resources

Utilization of a broad selection of written materials depends upon available library resources. A wide range of materials on topics and areas being studied must be available to pupils. Articles in journals and periodicals as well as basic references such as encyclopedias are essential. Other resource materials, slides, single-concept films, full-length films, special publications and reports—all are important. Relationships conducive to cooperation in planning for projects and area studies are part of a broad range of assistance to be expected from librarians and learning facilities personnel. Hansen and Hearn have compiled a list of expectations for librarians in facilitating educational processes in schools:

1. Make readily accessible an unrestricted range of materials which are current, authentic, and pertinent.

2. Make available bibliographic materials in the professional fields of the teachers so they may keep informed of new materials.
3. Work with the teacher in constructing bibliographies related to a unit of study.
4. Assist teachers in selecting materials needed for teaching and plan with them methods for using them.
5. Facilitate the teachers' use of varied techniques by supplying a wealth of enrichment materials.
6. Work with teachers to provide meaningful experiences designed to stimulate students' interest in reading and research.
7. Plan with teachers experiences in library instruction related to units of study.
8. Be alert to providing assistance to teachers in learning effective use of all library resources.
9. Go to classrooms, talk to teachers, and make them aware of materials which may serve their various programs.
10. Watch for and follow changes in subject matter and teaching approaches.
11. Have materials ready for large groups of students as well as individuals.
12. Work with teachers to provide special services such as individual attention to a gifted student, assistance for an eager committee, an exhibit relating to classroom activities, or a visit from a resource person.[24]

The librarian is an important link in the curriculum development process. But teachers cannot utilize library services unless they have considerable knowledge in their subject fields. They combine this knowledge with the librarian's expertise in a partnership approach. A well-equipped library is a result of cooperative endeavor between all teachers and a library staff who cooperatively collect materials and augment the regular bibliographic functions of the librarian in maintaining an adequate library collection.

REFERENCES

1. John B. Hough and James K. Duncan, *Teaching: Description and Analysis* (Reading, Mass.: Addison-Wesley, 1970), p. 2.

2. Ibid., p. 3.

3. Ibid., p. 16.

4. Robert Dreeben, "The Contribution of Schooling to the Learning of Norms," *Harvard Educational Review*, vol. 27, 2 (Spring, 1967), pp. 211–237.

5. From Philip W. Jackson, "The Way Teaching Is," *N.E.A. Journal* 54 (November 1965), pp. 10–13. Reprinted with permission.

6. From Benetta B. Washington, "A Social Imperative: Respect for the Individual," *To Nurture Humaneness: Commitment for the '70's* (Washington, D.C.: Association for Supervision and Curriculum Development, N.E.A., 1970), p. 190. Reprinted with permission.

7. From William M. Alexander, et al., *The Emergent Middle School* (New York: Holt, 1968), p. 123. Reprinted with permission.

8. From Jean D. Grambs and William J. Iverson, *Modern Methods in Secondary Education* (New York: The Dryden Press, 1952), p. 65. Reprinted with permission.

9. From William T. Gruhn and Harl R. Douglass, *The Modern Junior High School*, 2d. ed. Copyright © 1956 The Ronald Press Company, New York, pp. 182–183.

10. From *Modern Education for the Junior High School Years*, 2d. ed., by William Van Til, Gordon F. Vars, and John H. Lounsbury, Copyright © 1961, 1967 by The Bobbs-Merrill Company, Inc., pp. 290–291. Reprinted by permission of the publisher.

11. From Carl R. Rogers, *Freedom to Learn* (Columbus, Ohio: Merrill, 1969), p. 134. Reprinted with permission.

12. From *Toward Humanistic Education: A Curriculum of Affect*, edited by Gerald Weinstein and Mario D. Fantini. © 1970 by The Ford Foundation. Reprinted by permission of Praeger Publishers, Inc., New York, pp. 21–22.

13. James B. Macdonald, "The School Environment as Learner Reality," *Curriculum Theory Network* (Toronto: Institute of Education, Winter, 1969–1970), pp. 45–54.

14. Robert F. Mager, *Preparing Instructional Objectives* (San Francisco: Fearon, 1962), p. 24. Reprinted with permission.

15. Fred T. Wilhelms and Paul B. Diederich, "The Fruits of Freedom," *Evaluation as Feedback and Guide* (ASCD 1967 Yearbook), ed. Fred T. Wilhelms (Washington: Association for Supervision and Curriculum Development, NEA, 1967), p. 234.

16. From Dorris May Lee, "Teaching and Evaluation," *Evaluation as Feedback and Guide* (ASCD 1967 Yearbook), ed. Fred T. Wilhelms (Washington: ASCD, NEA, 1967), p. 84. Reprinted with permission.

17. Clifford F. S. Bebell, "The Evaluation We Have," *Evaluation as Feedback and Guide* (ASCD 1967 Yearbook), ed. Fred T. Wilhelms (Washington: ASCD, NEA, 1967), p. 31. Reprinted with permission.

18. From Dorris May Lee, "Teaching and Evaluation," *Evaluation as Feedback and Guide* (ASCD 1967 Yearbook), ed. Fred T. Wilhelms (Washington: ASCD, NEA, 1967), p. 75. Reprinted by permission.

19. From *Assessment of Behavior: The Methodology and Content of Psychological Measurement*, by John E. Horrocks, Charles E. Merrill Publishing Co., Columbus, Ohio © 1964, p. 418. Reprinted by permission of the publisher.

20. Donald M. Medley and Harold E. Mitzel, "The Scientific Study of Teacher Behavior." From A.A. Bellack, ed., *Theory and Research in Teaching* (New York: Teachers College Press, 1963), pp. 85–86.

21. From Report of the Seminar on Teaching, *The Way Teaching Is* (Washington, D.C.: Association for Supervision and Curriculum Development and The Center for the Study of Instruction, National Education Association, 1966), p. 79. Reprinted with permission.

22. From *Policy of the Philadelphia Public Schools on Homework Assignments* © 1962 The School District of Philadelphia, pp. 3, 4. Reprinted with permission.

23. From William T. Gruhn and Harl R. Douglass, *The Modern Junior High School,* 2d. ed. Copyright © 1956 The Ronald Press Company, New York, pp. 192–193.

24. From John H. Hansen and Arthur C. Hearn, *The Middle School Program* (Chicago: Rand McNally, 1971), pp. 272–273. Reprinted with permission.

RELATED READINGS

Bellack, Arno, ed. *Theory and Research in Teaching.* New York: Teachers College Press, 1963.

Belth, Marc. *The New World of Education: A Philosophical Analysis of Concepts of Teaching.* Boston: Allyn and Bacon, 1970.

Dreeben, Robert. "The Contribution of Schooling to the Learning of Norms," *Harvard Educational Review* 27, 2, Spring, 1967, pp. 211–237.

Frymier, Jack R. *The Nature of Education Method.* Columbus, Ohio: Merrill, 1965.

Horrocks, John E. *Assessment of Behavior: The Methodology and Content of Psychological Measurement.* Columbus, Ohio: Merrill, 1964.

Hough, John B., and Duncan, James K. *Teaching: Description and Analysis.* Reading, Mass.: Addison-Wesley, 1970.

Hutchins, C.L.; Dunning, Barbara; Madsen, Marilyn; and Rainey, Sylvia I. *Minicourses Work.* Berkeley, Calif.: Far West Laboratory, for Educational Research and Development, 1971.

Kibler, Robert J.; Barker, Larry L.; and Miles, David T. *Behavioral Objectives and Instruction.* Boston: Allyn and Bacon, 1970.

Mager, Robert F. *Preparing Instructional Objectives.* San Francisco: Fearon, 1962.

Medley, Donald M., and Mitzel, Harold E. "The Scientific Study of Teacher Behavior." *Theory and Research in Teaching.* Edited by Arno A. Bellack. New York: Teachers College Press, 1963.

Mills, Belen Collantes, and Mills, Ralph Ainslee, eds. *Designing Instructional Strategies for Young Children.* Dubuque, Iowa: William C. Brown, 1972.

Olson, David R., ed. *Media and Symbols: The Forms of Expression, Communication, and Education.* The Seventy-Third Yearbook of the National Society for the Study of Education—Part I. Chicago: University of Chicago Press, 1974.

Searles, John E. *A System for Instruction.* Scranton, Pa.: International Textbook Company, 1967.

Weinstein, Gerald, and Fantini, Mario D., eds. *Toward Humanistic Education: A Curriculum of Affect.* New York: Praeger, for the Ford Foundation, 1970.

CHAPTER 13

Teacher as Learning Facilitator

This function of the teacher must vary more from the traditional than those previously delineated. The teacher must assume a subordinate role in the learning experience. The pupil learns because of the total environment. The teacher as a learning facilitator assists in the changing of the environment in such a way that the pupil can most effectively develop as a human and thus learn. The teacher will accept a low profile in which the purposes and readiness of pupil development become most important, and the teacher assists and facilitates in the learning which takes place because of this need and desire.

In this approach the teacher becomes an expert in many different teaching techniques. Listening, hearing, and reflecting to the group what is heard become vital techniques. Capabilities are extended beyond lectures, subject-centered discussions, and reviews, or recitations on what was studied. Certain areas of development and learnings are promoted by the utilization of particular teaching techniques. It is the teacher's responsibility to determine which technique should be utilized at what times, for which purposes, in what situational settings, and for which children.

Social learning and communication skills are important. Psychological support from teacher to pupil is vital. Empathy and unconditional willingness to accept each child are crucial factors. Carl Rogers has outlined the responsibilities of the facilitator role in teaching in the following statements:

1. The facilitator has much to do with setting the initial mood or climate of the group or class experience. . . .
2. The facilitator helps to elicit and clarify the purposes of the individuals in the class as well as the more general purposes of the group. . . .
3. He relies upon the desire of each student to implement these purposes which have meaning for him, as the motivational force behind significant learning. . . .

255

4. He endeavors to organize and make easily available the widest possible range of resources for learning. . . .
5. He regards himself as a flexible resource to be utilized by the group. . . .
6. In responding to expressions in the classroom group, he accepts both the intellectual content and the emotionalized attitudes, endeavoring to give each aspect the approximate degree of emphasis which it has for the individual or the group. . . .
7. As the acceptant classroom climate becomes established, the facilitator is able increasingly to become a participant learner, a member of the group, expressing his views as those of one individual only.
8. He takes the initiative in sharing himself with the group—his feelings as well as his thoughts—in ways which do not demand nor impose but represent simply a personal sharing which students may take or leave. . . .
9. Throughout the classroom experience, he remains alert to the expressions indicative of deep or strong feelings. . . .
10. In his functioning as a facilitator of learning, the leader endeavors to recognize and accept his own limitations. . . . [1]

He stated that the most significant learning has five elements. These are: (1) a quality of personal involvement, (2) self-initiation, (3) pervasiveness, (4) evaluation by the learner, and (5) essence is meaning.[2]

The most significant learning takes place within the pupil, with the teacher serving as a facilitator of that learning. Such facilitation depends upon the individual idiosyncratic learning styles and abilities of the learners in the educational setting. For example, a teacher may help emerging adolescents gain insights into the self-evaluative ability in two ways: (1) by helping them see themselves better, and (2) by a focused objective evaluation. The ultimate goal is to assist the students in the establishment of a capability for self-evaluation.

The practice of Rogerian principles is based on a specific philosophy regarding what is important to be learned. Rogers bases his conceptualization of how teachers should operate on his knowledge of what should be learned and how that learning is best facilitated. He does not deny use of other techniques, roles, or strategies, but assumes that the primary determiner of the appropriateness of these other techniques should be recognized need on the part of learners who have become more aware of their own needs while experiencing the psychologically supportive climate created by the teacher facilitator.

LEARNING PURPOSES

If a child-centered approach is accepted, the needs perceived by the child and the relevance of externally determined subject matter become central in importance. Readiness to learn is a concomitant of any learning act: readiness must be determined by the facilitator in his or her assessment of the pupil's engagement with various elements of the learning environment.

Available means of learning must be explored by the facilitator and brought to bear in order to assist the pupil in the learning function. A knowledge of ways in which a learner is perceiving and giving meaning to various elements of a situation are data which the facilitator gathers to determine readiness as well as depth of engagement of pupils. Once the learner is involved in the situation and committed to achieving certain outcomes a wider variety of learning acts may occur. For example, if a need to know something is perceived and assistance is requested, a programmed unit might quickly be completed which otherwise might have been rejected. The facilitator will learn what types of knowledge can most effectively be learned by what means. Means selected for involving a learner may range from strategies derived from classical conditioning at one extreme to problem solving and creative endeavors at the other. The means are not so important as the pervasive supportive attitude expressed by the teacher-facilitator.

Instructional strategies

Many possible instructional strategies are available for use in learning situations. Some focus on the role of the teacher (such as orientation structuring, giving information, etc.) and are generally accepted appropriate models of teaching, depending upon objectives. Learning may also be structured to focus upon resources as a basic approach. Learning activity packages, programs, films, and such serve as a source of direction in the learning situation in this environment. A third mode focuses on the learning situation in which a student pursues learning and meanings through peer and self-selected materials, activities, and leadership.

Teacher-oriented instructional processes

In the lecture, recitation, and discussion types of learning the teacher assumes responsibility for the structure, substantive element, and direction of the class. These approaches are effective in dealing with knowledge at lower levels of awareness and knowing. Their use should continue when they are the most effective way to achieve stated purposes. Their weakness is that a pupil may assume a less active role in learning, and may not be required to utilize higher-level thinking processes. Overuse of those methods limits the student's role in learning and precludes learning how to learn for oneself.

The lecture is a valid teaching technique and should be used when a teacher wishes to motivate pupils, when an introduction to a unit is needed, when a summary is appropriate, and at other selected times. The primary criticism of the lecture as a teaching method is not that it is ineffective, but that it is used in many cases to meet inappropriate objectives.

According to a series of principles developed by Howard, among the purposes which might be best met by lecture are motivation, succinct information presentation, and classification.[3] Lectures have been unfairly condemned, and should be evaluated upon criteria preset by the teacher in a review of objectives to be achieved.

Recitation—a "re-citing" of materials which have previously been learned—is an important means of helping pupils ascertain that they have indeed learned the material at hand and a chance to put forth ideas for criticism. It should not be used as a means of evaluation on the part of the teacher, and is criticized only for its utilization at inappropriate times.

Group discussion should be used when questions may have more than one answer, or when discussion of alternative answers may lead the class to the most appropriate response. Interpersonal reactions of various pupils within the class should be noted, and individuals should be encouraged to recognize a range of reactions as appropriate within a group framework. Disapproval and condemnation should not assume any significant portion of the emotional atmosphere since they weaken the framework of willing cooperation and contribution. Contributions should be welcomed and encouraged inasmuch as group discussion is involved with a series of questions and answers for which preestablished conclusions have not been reached.

Discussion involves questions and answers to either narrow or broad topics. Where goals are unclear, open dialogue can be used to great advantage. For example, questions should be asked by both teacher and pupils in a climate of exploration where definitive answers are not sought. The raising of questions which become the basis for next steps in the learning sequence is one desired end of this strategy. Teacher-pupil planning of assignments, activities, and responsibilities demonstrates one effective use of question and answer sessions.

Resource-oriented instructional processes

Instruction may be conducted through use of a variety of media. Where appropriate resource materials are available learning is inherent within the media. Varieties of media, such as single-concept films, film strips, documentaries, and full-length feature films, are available which can utilize different sense modalities as inputs to individuals. Their selection and use depend upon the appropriateness of the content to meet the intended learning outcomes of the curriculum under consideration. Resource-oriented learning must be as carefully planned as other instructional activities. Cooperative pupil-teacher planning can help insure that appropriate materials have been selected. It is the responsibility of the teacher to insure that selected materials are readily available so that the time and effort of the learner are productive.

Programmed learning should be utilized in two areas: first, where individualized learning can be most effective; and second, where drill and/or directed practice is prescribed. Since individual rates of learning vary, use of self-pacing programs can most effectively meet individual needs. Self-paced learning can be utilized in areas where students need specific knowledge and can acquire it without direct supervision. Both programmed instruction and learning activity packages can provide for the self-pacing option. Repetition included in drill and practice can be facilitated through some type of self-directed learning. Professional staff should designate appropriate materials and prepare others necessitated by diagnosed learner needs. Commercially prepared materials as well as those prepared by school staff can be used to free a teacher from routine duties and repetitious activities, thus allowing more time for work with individuals and groups of children who need special help.

Pupil-oriented instructional processes. Small-group work, tutorial and peer teaching, and other activities which require pupil involvement serve a variety of learning purposes. Pupils learn from others; they develop a sense of continuity where learning can be recognized as a continuing process to be furthered in a number of ways. Pupils who have special knowledge or skills may make presentations to the class. They may demonstrate processes over which they have gained control or where they have special talents. The social and emotional climate developed by emerging adolescents who see themselves as determiners of the learning process has desirable consequences for motivation, self-direction, self-evaluation, and satisfactions which are rewarding for many students.

Peer teaching, where one pupil tutors another individual or small group of pupils, helping them develop skills and understandings in basic areas, is beneficial not only for the students taught but for the student who is doing the teaching. It is not always the more advanced or accomplished pupil who is teaching; however, advanced pupils may learn by tutoring someone else. Where pupils are very strong in certain academic areas, they may serve as peer teachers for the entire class under the general supervision of the classroom teacher.

Peer teaching is effective for emerging adolescents.
Iroquois Middle School
(Courtesy of Niskayuna, New York, Central School District)

The teacher acting as a learning facilitator can benefit from the admonition to center learning in the student. "Put the problems before him and let him solve them himself. Let him know nothing because you have told him, but because he has learnt it for himself."[4]

The teacher's role is that of assisting pupils to experience for themselves so that what is learned is relevant for them. Leadership serves a facilitating function. Supervised activity assists the pupil in developing skill in social relations as well as cognitive knowledge. "Children do not necessarily learn to be cooperative, unselfish and respectful of the rights and feelings of others through free play alone."[5]

The learning facilitator exercises leadership which can be perceived and understood by the learner. The humanity with which the teacher approaches the learning act determines the way learning will occur. The questions below present guidelines for teachers who wish to guide pupils toward more effective learning.

- Will your questions increase the learner's *will* as well as his capacity to learn?
- Will they help to give him a sense of joy in learning?

- Will they help to provide the learner with confidence in his ability to learn?
- In order to get answers, will the learner be required to make inquiries? (Ask further questions, clarify terms, make observations, classify data, etc.?)
- Does each question allow for alternative answers (which implies alternative modes of inquiry)?
- Will the process of answering the questions tend to stress the uniqueness of the learner?
- Would the questions produce different answers if asked at different stages of the learner's development?
- Will the answers help the learner to sense and understand the universals in the human condition and so enhance his ability to draw closer to other people?[6]

Capability for implementing these guidelines and ability to organize the learning environment along with expectations for student success should lead toward achievement of learning particularly where purposes have been established with learner and teacher in agreement concerning pupil needs.

IMPLICATIONS FOR TEACHERS

Diagnosis

The term "diagnosis" includes the processes necessary to make judgments prior to "prescribing" next steps. This is a necessary part of the educational process, which is continuous on a day-to-day basis throughout the formal schooling of individuals. Because the process encompasses far more than can be the responsibility of one teacher within a classroom, we make the point that the total staff and administration from principal to superintendent are involved. Total district and school policies determine both content, process, and socialization measures and standards and, therefore, the total assessment process.

The most desirable way to set up a school's total approach is to arrange a series of workshops to determine what cognitive (intellectual), affective (attitudinal), and psychomotor (physical) goals are desired. From these aims and goals, benchmarks can be established for larger blocks of time, allocated to certain groups of staff for determining situations within which the objectives can be realized in smaller segments. Thus what is to be achieved, the ways in which progress toward those ends will be made, and the ways in which data will be taken can be made explicit. For example, if students are expected to be able to read at specified levels when they enter middle school, the testing program should establish whether each student is on the mark (as expected) or slightly above or below the mark. The prescription then contains information for those who will be responsible for assisting that pupil to continue progress.

Each teacher and staff member contributes to the reinforcement process. If a teacher ignores reading problems, the student may assume that reading is not a part of mastering that particular subject matter. On the other hand, if the math teacher takes time to ascertain that students are able to read well and determine the information in a word problem, pupils can see that part of the ability to succeed in mathematics is dependent upon the ability to read. The same is, of course, true in other subject areas.

For each goal the long-range diagnosis-prescription process must be worked through by the total staff so that there is sequence, focus, and continuity in the developmental profile of students. We see the greatest need initially for focus on fundamental processes, study habits and skills, learning skills, and transitioning into learning to use these in achievement of the ultimate goal—that of each pupil gaining command of these processes and becoming a continuing learner.

The diagnostic-prescriptive efforts of the total staff toward broader dimensions of a program are vital to efforts which must be followed by all teachers and school staff personnel. This implies the necessity for systematic planning so that the scope and sequence of activities which follow from pursuit by the staff of specific objectives make a desirable total program for the pupils in the program.

The tolerance levels of individual pupils must be ascertained. Learning to cope with and alter these relationships is important for staff as well as for pupils. The mutuality of this need shared by both pupils and teachers should make up a part of the entire school effort to maintain the highest quality learning environment so that socio-emotional growth goals are achieved as well as cognitive and psychomotor aims and goals. The difficulty of building appropriate measurement devices for many of these areas is accepted. But to expand upon the diagnostic-prescriptive analogy we borrowed from medicine, the fact that the physician may have inadequate data, questionable knowledge of precise causes of symptoms, and even insufficient expertise and skill to predict exact outcomes does not deter us from taking the medicine given, following procedures prescribed, and even submitting our lives into the care of physicians. This is the same set of knowns/unknowns, hunches, hopes, and expectations for growth and life-giving prescriptions that all of us face so that the educational prognosis (degree of predicted success) will be as high as our best professional efforts can make it for each pupil.

Group process

Certain areas of social and intellectual growth involve individual relationships with small groups and with the larger society as a whole. There are groups of skills which can be learned which, once learned, are useful in a wide range of adolescent and adult activities. Exercising group skills involves learning how we perceive others and some of the ways they seem to experience contacts with us. Effective working in groups is necessary if broader purposes are to be achieved within families, groups, communities, or even the entire country. Our society is made up of a tremendous number of groups of people all working toward ends which taken together make up private and public worlds. The school itself is an example of this set of principles. We gradually come to see that individuals can actualize their own purposes, needs, and interests only as they become a part of a broader group. Artists need audiences to confirm their artistry, businesses need customers, leaders need groups to lead, followers need groups to develop a sense of belonging, and so on.

Learning to work in groups requires an understanding of the importance of groups to us as individuals. It is necessary to understand and practice behavioral and conceptual skills and receive feedback to know how well we are developing these skills. These skills must be continuously performed and practiced in a wide variety of settings in order to gain full command of them so they can be ready when working in groups is appropriate.

One of our first tasks is to know ourselves and our needs, purposes, and interests so that we can come to understand how they can be realized, modified, altered, or achieved. In order to share with others in goal setting and achievement we have to master the processes through which we solve or resolve our problems. Among the necessary skills are:

1. selection of leaders,
2. definition of goals,
3. collection of appropriate information,
4. discussion of value positions, and
5. consideration of proposed avenues for meeting needs.

In order to work in groups there are a number of tasks and functions which must be performed so the group can continue to search for the solution or resolution of these problems. For example, group members must:

1. gather the information,
2. share opinions and feelings,
3. allocate responsibilities for gathering or grouping data,
4. summarize data,

5. channel energies,
6. test whether information is adequate,
7. develop ways to test readiness for final conclusion, and
8. share responsibility for participation.

Role model

Adults in school are working with each other and with pupils continuously. Even though we may not know exactly how or when pupils are copying behaviors, observation and imitation are inevitable. Pupils compare and contrast a variety of behaviors with those observed out of school—behaviors of parents, relatives, and members of the broader community. Teachers should be aware of the need for pupils to have more adequate models for many of the adult roles of which they gradually become aware. For example, it is important that the staff provide role models which may be less accessible in other settings. Social skills can be part of a program of planned experiences in a number of different ways. These would include planned encounters in human-relations areas, learning of manners, and learning how to cope with problems that arise in daily contacts. If encounters among and between adults which students observe are comparatively smooth, or are in a dissonant mode, the staff can demonstrate their competence in communication facilitation and problem resolution by example. It seems important that human differences which occur not be discounted or treated as unnatural, but that staff members see these differences as examples of daily opportunities for demonstrating how to communicate and understand counter points of view so that a better solution for human problems can be found.

The use of role-playing methods in regular classroom or small-group experiences will provide both training and skills, along with the understandings for staff and students so that this recommendation can be a reality. In any case, many current problems of adults and emerging adolescents lend themselves very well to consideration by role-playing methods. Briefly, the teacher-leader has three major responsibilities as pointed out by Chesler and Fox:

1. Understand bases for selection of problems for consideration and teach the group how to proceed.
2. Set the stage and provide guidelines for discussion and interpretation of role-playing acts.
3. Provide for evaluation in final stages of the sequence.[7]

The teacher should take several sessions to acquaint students with role-playing procedures, the way in which these are carried out, the roles which they can assume, and the outcomes which can be achieved. There are audience roles, participant roles, and a wide variety of situational factors which can be explored through these activities. These methods have been found to benefit personal, social, and academic learning. Classroom social-interaction problems and group-relations problems are appropriate target situations if the teacher or team has the skills and understandings for utilization of these methods.

Counseling

It is essential that teachers and students be able to engage in discussions where current issues and problems of personal interest and long-range implications for both student and staff are at issue. While some members of a middle school staff may be reluctant to engage in discussions concerning personal problems, there should be a number of staff members who can engage in these counseling-type activities when students express needs. Early in the school year both staff and students should have sessions in which the basic "rules of the game" and procedures are fairly well understood. Thus when problems with emotional content and particular personal involvement occur, students are schooled in coming to grips with them adequately even though some students may be more personally involved than others.

If there are opportunities provided as a part of the regular curriculum for consideration of implications for personal choice-making and for consideration of consequences of decisions, students can develop habits of considering both the impetus and the situations out of which problems arise. Hopefully, over time, students will learn how to avoid difficulties earlier and to handle unanticipated problems more easily.

Effective thinking

Middle school teachers must become fully aware of the need to introduce and deliberately direct attention on a systematic basis to the processes involved in thinking. This includes the examination of written material for assumptions, statements which will be verifiable, and value statements. The nature of belief, values, attitudes, and opinions, as well as forms of language used in making these statements, are important elements in the capability of a teacher of emerging adolescents.

The relationship between concrete logical and symbolic logical thought is important because some middle school pupils will be in the concrete stage of thinking, beginning to emerge and utilize more abstract thinking abilities. They will still be dependent upon concrete situations and on concepts which must be carefully developed if they are to use more abstract concepts in various subject matter areas. For example, as the term "community" comes to include greater numbers of defining attributes and to include the broader social context, the teacher must be aware of the need to make this set of broader attributes clear. Piagetian questioning to assess what students think some textbook passages mean can sensitize teachers to conceptual problems in various subject areas.

The necessity for development of processes of inquiry and a sense of current structures within the various disciplines does not obviate the importance of the pupil's learning the best that is known at this time so that decisions can be made daily which take that knowledge into account. The present lack of knowledge about interactions makes a case for the lack of a definitive position upon which to base decisions, whether they be individual decisions or decisions for the broader society.

Learning skills

The development of learning skills is based upon the understanding of the difference between them and basic skills. Learning skills are linked to thought processes which utilize basic skills to achieve educational purposes. In order to operationalize these skills for a middle school learning setting it becomes necessary to determine how such skills can be utilized in a pragmatic classroom environment. For example, creativity is considered to be important, and references for its use have been included elsewhere, but a question still remains as to how it can be translated into individual learning. The same dilemma seems evident with other learning skills.

Thus the question to be considered is the nature of learning problems to be faced by the pupil in which teacher-encouraged learning skills can be effective. It would seem that the following problems would fit in this category.

1. Investigating.
2. Problem solving.
3. Planning.
4. Human-relations conceptions.
5. Discussion.
6. Group dynamics.[8]

As pupils take part in each of these classroom activities, some cognitive, others affective, it becomes incumbent upon them to exercise learning skills in confronting the problems inherent within them. Due to these student tasks, the teacher's function as a leader in development of learning skills, in knowledge of contexts in which they are essential, and their interrelationships becomes essential.

REFERENCES

1. Carl R. Rogers, *Freedom to Learn* (Columbus, Ohio: Merrill, 1969), pp. 164–166. Reprinted with permission.

2. Ibid., p. 5.

3. Alvin W. Howard, *Teaching in Middle Schools* (Scranton, Pa.: International Textbook Company, 1968), p. 71.

4. Jean Jacques Rousseau, *Emile* (London: Dent, 1911), p. 131.

5. Bruce L. Bennett, "Recess is Not Enough," *Childhood Education*, May 1959, 35: 398–402.

6. From Neil Postman and Charles Weingartner, *Teaching as a Subversive Activity*. Copyright © 1969, Delacorte Press, New York, p. 66.

7. Mark Chesler and Robert Fox, *Role-Playing Methods in the Classroom* (Chicago, Science Research Associates, Inc., 1966). (This is one of the Teacher Resource Booklets on Classroom Social Relations and Learning.)

8. Florence Damon Cleary, *Blueprints for Better Learning* (Metuchen, N.J.: The Scarecrow Press, 1968), 262 pp.

RELATED READINGS

Gall, Meredith D. "The Use of Questions in Teaching." *Review of Educational Research* XL, no. 5, Dec. 1970, 707–721.

Hunkins, Francis P. *Questioning Strategies and Techniques.* Boston: Allyn and Bacon, 1972.

Joyce, Bruce, and Weil, Marsha. *Models of Teaching*. Englewood Cliffs, N.J.: Prentice-Hall, 1972.

Zahorik, John A., and Brubaker, Dale L. *Toward More Humanistic Instruction.* Dubuque, Iowa: William C. Brown, 1972.

Diagnosis

Banathy, Bela H. *Instructional Systems.* Palo Alto: Fearon, 1968.

Block, James H., ed. *Mastery Learning Theory and Practice.* New York: Holt, 1971.

Gagné, Robert M., and Briggs, Leslie J. *Principles of Instructional Design.* New York: Holt, 1974.

McAshan, H. H. *The Goals Approach to Performance Objectives.* Philadelphia: Saunders, 1974.

Raths, Louis E.; Wasserman, Selma; Jonas, Arthur; and Rothstein, Arnold M. *Teaching for Thinking, Theory and Application.* Columbus, Ohio: Merrill, 1967.

Group process

Johnson, David W., and Johnson, Frank P. *Joining Together Group Theory and Group Skills.* Englewood Cliffs, N. J.: Prentice-Hall, 1975.

Counseling

Howe, Leland W., and Howe, Mary M. *Personalizing Education: Values Clarification and Beyond.* New York: Hart, 1975.

Raths, Louis E.; Harmin, Merrill; and Simon, Sidney B. *Values and Teaching.* Columbus, Ohio: Merrill, 1966.

Simon, Sidney B.; Howe, Leland W.; and Kirschenbaum, Howard. *Values Clarification: A Handbook of Practical Strategies for Teachers and Students.* New York: Hart, 1972.

Learning skills

Carpenter, Helen McCracken, ed. *Skill Development in Social Studies.* The Thirty-Third Yearbook of the National Council for the Social Studies. Washington, D. C.: National Council for the Social Studies, N.E.A., 1963.

Cleary, Florence Damon. *Blueprints for Better Learning.* Metuchen, N.J.: Scarecrow Press, 1968.

CHAPTER 14

Organization for Learning

Facilitation of learning is the major purpose for the development of the various organizations found in schools. Certain types of learning can most effectively be achieved with structured organizations while others can best be achieved with less structured approaches. Hence the middle school administrator who seeks certain objectives will give particular emphasis to the form of organization which might best achieve those specific purposes. Curriculum balance can be significantly influenced by the ways in which classes are organized. Grouping and grading practices are also affected by organizational patterns. Instructional strategies are particularly affected as instruction in the classroom is directly dependent upon organization. Hence an interdisciplinary team of teachers could be expected to utilize significantly different approaches to instruction than teachers functioning in self-contained classrooms. The organization of classes should be predetermined by the fundamental purposes established for the school. Thus each school's faculty, administration, school board, and patrons must consider the educational purposes to be attained before determining the organization to be utilized.

The organization of a school is usually a combination of several subsets. Thus a particular environment might contain some aspects of any (or all) of the organizational concepts outlined in this chapter. The most effective arrangement would probably be eclectic in nature since schools, due to their social character, rarely are developed along singular lines. For purposes of clarification each of five organizational considerations will be discussed in this chapter in separate sections. Rarely, however, will they be seen in school in such isolation. They are the most commonly utilized procedures in the middle school, and are recommended in order to achieve the various purposes of emerging adolescent education. Two organizations, the departmentalized classroom (commonly found in senior high schools) and the self-contained classroom (commonly located in elementary schools), are relatively traditional in nature, and so will not be included in the organizational analysis since most faculty members are aware of their strengths and weaknesses. The five modes to be considered are nongraded organization, core, team teaching, modular scheduling, and resource centers.

NONGRADED ORGANIZATION

A nongraded organization is one in which grade structures are not utilized—grades six, seven, eight, and/or nine are not considered as separate entities. Instead, pupils are divided according to individual growth along any one of several continua. Examples of such criteria are achievement, sex, interest, physical development, maturation, and even heterogeneity. The focus of this work is on curriculum and instruction, and hence the concept of curriculum sequence based upon continuous learning and ability grouping will be followed. Thus, a child could enter the middle school after having completed the appropriate elementary educational sequence, and would leave upon completion of those learning units required within that organization. Upon completion of certain objectives in the psychomotor, affective, and cognitive domains the pupil would be evaluated according to a broad range of factors for ability to profit from a more advanced level of experiences more typically found in the secondary school.

Learning experiences could be based upon one of two accepted rationales, continuous progress and ability grouping. In the continuous-progress procedure pupils are placed in a preplanned sequential curriculum. Each pupil is expected to achieve at least the minimum objectives in individual units along a continuum with the primary variable being the amount of time necessary to achieve those objectives. This type of nongrading is ordinarily found in elementary schools. Ability grouping, which occurs more often in the secondary school, is concerned with a multiplicity of experiences as a primary focus. Here units of an accelerative or enriching type are introduced to various and differing pupils, thus providing more varied types of learning experiences based upon differences in pupils. Thus objectives are seen to vary from one pupil to another creating an organizational need for groupings of like interests and abilities. Middle schools, in serving the transitional function, would utilize some aspects of both of these types of nongrading.

Continuous progress

The rationale for such an organization can be found in the tremendous variability in characteristics within and among emerging adolescents in the middle school. Goodlad and Anderson noted the variance in pupils starting at the beginning of elementary school and increasing as children progressed up to and through the middle school.

By the time children reach the intermediate elementary grades, the range in intellectual readiness to learn and in most areas of achievement is as great as or greater than the number designating the grade level.[1]

Thus by the time children reach the sixth or seventh grade their cognitive ability varies in such a way that some are capable of doing ninth-grade work while others are still struggling with third-grade work. Such statistics do not include the outermost one or two percent, but indicate only the statistically significant portion of middle school classes. To illustrate, in *The Nongraded Elementary School* Goodlad and Anderson included the diagram shown in Fig. 14-1.

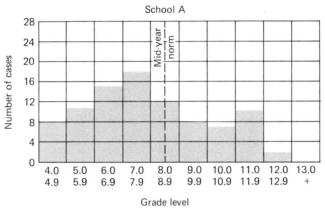

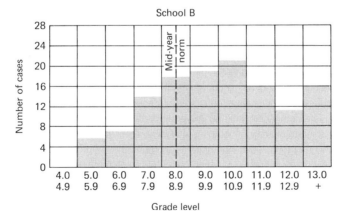

Fig. 14-1. Range in reading achievement among eighth-grade pupils of two schools in a large city. (Copyright © 1959, 1963 by Harcourt Brace Jovanovich, Inc., and reproduced with their permission from *The Nongraded Elementary School*, Revised Edition, p. 26, by John I. Goodlad and Robert H. Anderson.)

From these statistics it becomes evident that the variability among pupils at a certain grade militates against the utilization of grade standards, along with the concomitant idea of a set of curriculum experiences appropriate only for a specific grade. Rather the way is open for a school which establishes a series of objectives appropriate for shorter time segments, with each pupil being assisted to achieve those objectives at his or her own speed and depth. Each pupil would then receive evaluation of a summative nature indicating his or her achievement on a series of objectives rather than a normative evaluation based upon achievement as compared to a supposed normal expectation of the child's agemates.

One of the basic tenets upon which nongradedness is based is the concept that pupils learn more effectively when experiencing a series of short units where promotion from one step to the next is a relatively nontraumatic event. If a pupil fails to pass the evaluative section of a particular unit, it is not a great blow, and the pupil can expect to receive a diagnosis of reasons for the failure. With this diagnosis he or she is theoretically able, with only a relatively short delay, to achieve the objectives of the unit, and move on to the next segment of the curriculum. The fundamental assumption upon which this procedure is based is that nonpromotion in itself does not improve school achievement. Low-achieving pupils do not seem to make any greater gains when non-promoted, and at times achieve even more when promoted.[2] Thus a non-grading practice which lessens the trauma and delay occasioned by failing grades can be strongly recommended.

Smaller curriculum units are not intended to change either the scope or the depth of the experiences of the emerging adolescent. Goodlad and Anderson have pointed to one of the main differences between a graded and a nongraded school as:

> ...the learning experiences follow a less rigid time schedule. Objectives are therefore modified principally in terms of timing. Over the total span of the elementary school period a child in a nongraded school has essentially the same aggregate of experiences, involving the same instructional materials and approaches and aimed at the same major goals, but he will have these experiences on a more flexible time-schedule.[3]

In order to achieve the goals of the nongraded organization, the curriculum content within each subject matter area must be more clearly stated. Concepts, learning skills, and learning modes must be identified in specific objectives so that faculty will be able to evaluate each individual pupil's development in specific units of study. For example, Sidney P. Rollins described the English curriculum in the following words:

The field of English, for example, has been broken down into 111 concepts and skills, ranging from the first ("taking part in conversation") and second ("listening for information") to the one-hundred and eleventh ("writing a full length research paper with footnotes, preface, and bibliography").[4]

Such specific objectives are amenable to measurement and to diagnosis so that a pupil having difficulty with some particular portion of the unit may receive the help of a teacher who has been able to understand more clearly the problem faced by that particular pupil.

Ability grouping

An emphasis has occurred in some schools on ability grouping as a base for nongrading. In this organization students are placed in particular classes based upon their ability in the particular subject. They are then permitted to move ahead in that subject area at their own rate of speed. For example, a gifted pupil may be placed, along with other such youngsters, in a curriculum segment involving more intellectually demanding topics. This grouping permits students to study various subjects based upon their ability rather than according to a time element, as in the continuous-progress approach.

A nongraded school utilizing ability grouping would be organized on a subject matter basis, with a series of units based upon expected age achievements. These units would be experienced by a majority of the student body, with only the slow or disadvantaged students being excused from the basic sequence. Those students capable of working either faster or more in depth would be expected to register for experiences beyond the normal. The structure would be more complex than that experienced in a continuous-progress school since more alternatives would be available to the pupils.

One of the earliest schools attempting such an organization was the Nova High School in Broward County, Florida. In speaking of the experiences of students in Nova High School, Kaufman and Bethune note that:

When students enter Nova they undergo area examinations and all information coming from their former schools is considered. The student is then placed in the appropriate units *in each discipline*. The class to which he is assigned may have students at various levels within the unit. For example, some students in the group may be working to considerably more depth than others in the same group. . . .

A student whose interest is in science may elect to go far beyond what is required, while in English he may pursue a less time-consuming pattern.

On the other hand, he may devote extra effort to languages and do a minimum of science and math.[5]

The primary concept to be noted is that such a schedule may be arranged to allow a pupil gifted in one subject area and less so in another to move forward to the greatest degree in each. This may be achieved either by permitting advanced-placement classes for acceleration or special classes for enrichment.

An important factor in the decision of many high schools to utilize ability grouping in their nongraded framework rather than continuous progress is the problem of age ranges. If pupils were given univariate paths the age ranges within a class would be immense by the eighth grade. Some students would be capable of twelfth-grade work whereas others would be doing fourth-grade work. This would create the unfortunate anomaly of a ten-year-old youngster possibly working with an eighteen-year-old adolescent in the same class due to differences in cognitive development. While such variations might create relatively few problems in elementary school, middle school and high school pupils would find such a setting unfortunate due to socio-emotional problems which might arise. Hence a nongraded organization in the middle school probably should contain some facets of both continuous progress and ability grouping in order to be most effective in the utilization of nongradedness in education for emerging adolescents.

Individualized study

The nongrading method of organization is used to permit a greater degree of flexibility within the instructional practices of the school. As an ideal a nongraded organization would maximize personalization of education. Individual pupils would be permitted to move forward in areas of their own choosing at their own speed, according to their own unique purposes, desires, or needs. Individualization in instruction is one step along the path toward such personalization. Most nongraded organizations stress a system in which pupils are allowed to work at their own rate of speed toward pre-established goals. Such goals are ordinarily established in the various domains with appropriate concern for the structure of subject matter.

Thus the two primary variables in this arrangement are time and curriculum. If pupils move rapidly through the established procedures they may either move sooner into the next phase or, with teacher advice, select enrichment procedures.

Individualized study is characterized by several factors among which are the changes in roles of the teacher and the student, and the need for a systems-analysis approach. A teacher will need to be able to diagnose and develop programs for individual children. Pupils will face the necessity of more responsibility for their own learning, in addition to the possibility of helping other pupils with their learning. A learning center approach will become typical in this type of learning and will require a systems approach in which many alternatives are available to individual pupils.

A particular advantage of nongradedness is the emphasis placed upon the learning of the individual rather than upon group activities. While individualized learning procedures can take place in groups, this framework is not necessary. Although the pupil may learn from interaction with the group when appropriate, the emphasis is where it belongs—on the experiences of individual pupils.

CORE PROGRAMS

The development of core programs in the past and their continued utilization indicates a viability for this organization which recommends consideration for its practice in a middle school. Core curriculum was originally conceived to serve the purposes of general education for junior and senior high school youth. It was concerned with those experiences thought to be necessary for all learners in a democratic society. In addition, core programs have been noted for their group-oriented instructional approaches. For example, relevance is heightened when pupils are permitted to discuss problems they perceive as being important.

What characteristics most typical of core might be found in such an organization? Faunce and Bossing developed the following statement of fundamentals which they felt to be necessary to the core program.

1. The core idea is based upon the fundamental psychological principle that learning involves change in behavior brought about through experience. . . .
2. The core is organized around the types of problems of personal and social concern common to all youth in our democratic society.
3. The core seeks to draw upon a wide range of informational sources, materials, and appropriate activities necessary to the solution of these vital problems of personal and social concern. . . .
4. The core emphasizes the utilization of genuine problem-solving procedures and techniques in the solution of personal and social problem situations.
5. The core involves and provides for a wide range of cooperative curriculum planning by teachers. . . .
6. The core involves joint planning by pupils and teachers for the solution of vital problems.

7. The core makes individual and group guidance an integral part of teaching. . . .
8. The core idea involves a recognition of the over-all organization of the curriculum into two highly integrated and interrelated divisions, namely, (a) the core program devoted to the types of problems common to all youth and the common competencies all must possess to function successfully in our democratic society, and (b) the section of the curriculum devoted to the development of the special concerns of pupils. . . .
9. Administratively important to the success of the core idea is the provision of large blocks of time in the day's schedule to facilitate the maximum use of problem-solving processes and the use of community resources.
10. Administratively important to the success of the guidance function of the core is the need to provide for longer spans of association between core teachers and pupils in order that teachers may know the pupils better. . . .[6]

Of basic importance to the core concept is the delegation of responsibilities to the classroom teacher which are not ordinarily found in a more traditional classroom. Thus the teacher becomes responsible for assisting pupils in the determination of group decisions rather than making personal decisions, gives more attention to the affective domain than in traditional classrooms, and serves as a counselor more than a single-subject teacher. It is in the latter area that core teachers might find their traditional tasks changed most dramatically. A core teacher would be more committed to the personal problems and needs of pupils because of the nature of programming of the core. Van Til, Vars, and Lounsbury indicated some of the advantages of centering guidance functions in a core program. These follow:

I. The teacher comes to know each individual student better because:
   A. Teacher and student are together during a longer block of school time.
   B. The teacher sees the student in a greater variety of situations.
   C. The teacher deals with fewer different students per day.
   D. The kind of teaching common in the core tends to reveal more personal information about each student, his needs, interests, problems, and values.

II. Problems growing out of interpersonal relations can be worked out through:
   A. Studying units of work built around real problems of adolescents.
   B. Participating in group work of various kinds.

    C. The catharsis that comes from learning that one's peers have similar problems.

    D. Actually working on problems of this type in a group of friends, both adults and peers.

    E. Sharing beliefs and values in an atmosphere that encourages respect for other people.

III. Counseling is more effective because:

    A. Student and teacher know each other better.

    B. Counseling is more natural, growing out of group problem-solving situations.

    C. The longer time block and more flexible scheduling tend to make it easier to find time for conferences.

    D. Shifting some of the responsibility for discipline to the group frees the teacher to some extent from his punitive role, thereby improving rapport.

IV. Core-centered guidance is more sound administratively because:

    A. Major responsibility for guidance is spread among several teachers, not concentrated in the hands of one specialist. Yet guidance is not so diffuse as to be nonexistent. Core teachers accept guidance as an important part of their job.

    B. Guidance and curriculum are combined in the same person.

    C. Guidance is made possible in the school where resources are too limited to provide for the services of specialists.[7]

Types of core

Basic concepts of core curriculum can be organized in a number of differing manners. During the approximately sixty-five years of junior high school existence a multitude of such variations have been instituted with some still existing today. These varying programs have been divided into four basic categories by Grace Wright.

Type A. Each subject retains its identity in the core; that is, subjects are correlated but not fused. The group may be taught both subjects [e.g. American history and American literature] by one teacher or each subject by the appropriate subject teacher.

Type B. Subject lines are broken down. Subjects included in core are fused into a unified whole around a central theme.

Type C. Subjects are brought in only as needed. The core consists of a number of broad pre-planned problems usually related to a central theme.

Problems are based on predetermined areas of pupil needs, both immediate felt needs and needs as a society sees them. Members of the class may or may not have a choice from among several problems; they will, however, choose activities within the problems.

Type D. Subjects are brought in only as needed as in "C." There are no predetermined problem areas to be studied. Pupils and teachers are free to select problems on which they wish to work.[8]

In Type A, the correlated-subjects approach, a teacher would teach two general subjects, ordinarily language arts and social studies, to one class during a larger block of time than would be customary for each class individually. For example, one-third to one-half of the day for such a correlated class might be appropriate. Each of the two subjects would maintain its integrity, with the teacher correlating where such action seemed advisable—e.g., oral or written reports which might be evaluated from the standpoints of both clarity of communication and conceptualization within the subject matter. While language arts and social studies are the most common subjects to be correlated, other areas sometimes combined are arithmetic and science, art and music with language arts, and home economics and industrial arts. Correlation between subjects is a generally accepted curricular procedure at the present time. The idea of one teacher working to correlate is but one additional step in the general conception.

In Type B, fused subjects, those subjects which are included are no longer taught as definable areas. Units are usually selected by the instructor which contain sufficient material from the subject matter areas concerned. In addition, however, such subjects will possess an interest for the pupil which is intrinsic to the unit. For example, space travel as a unit subject might draw content from almost any subject area in the curriculum. In fused core, however, the important aspect is the achievement of conceptualizations concerning space travel, not specific concepts from individual subject areas. In this way it differs markedly from Type A, correlation, in which subject matter is still preeminent.

Type C core, pre-planned problems, goes a step further than fused subject areas. In this approach subject areas, as such, are relegated to a relatively unimportant position. The important center for curriculum planning is the problem predetermined by faculty and staff involved with the needs and purposes of pupils. For example, in an election year a topic concerning voting and elections might be appropriate. A pupil entering a certain school would certainly be interested in a unit concerning orientation to that school. Such units become the center for study with subject areas entering the picture only as they present information appropriate to the central issue. Under these circumstances language arts, arithmetic, social studies, and science are no longer of such great import as subject areas per se, receiving emphasis only in relation to their importance to predetermined problems.

Type D core, unplanned problems, is similar to Type C core in its general impact. In this approach, however, problems are not predetermined by the faculty but rather are brought to surface by a series of teacher-pupil relationships within the classroom. In this situation the teacher would not predetermine that elections are important, but would rather, by adroit questioning, bring out from the pupils their concerns which might or might not have to do with the election process at that particular time. While such concerns may be more ephemeral the selection factor involved predicates a great degree of motivational force.

Unit development

Central to all types of core programs is the unit approach to curriculum development. In contradistinction to many traditional classrooms in which the textbook or other similar resources serve as a center around which the curriculum for the classroom is developed, all types of core programs are dependent upon units. A unit is ordinarily developed around a specific topic drawing from a systematic survey and organization of possible resources derived from various subject areas. Ordinarily a unit consists of the following sections:

1. a statement of the problem and its significance to pupils,
2. a list of learning experiences,
3. a list of resources appropriate to those experiences,
4. an evaluative approach, and
5. a bibliography of materials.

In all types of core except for the unplanned variety a resource unit may be prepared for each topic planned by the instructor prior to the inception of the learning experience. In determining the construction of such a resource unit certain criteria for the inclusion or exclusion of materials should be planned. Faunce and Bossing suggested the following criteria for the evaluation of a resource unit:

1. The resource unit should recognize students' needs and interests
2. It should include specific ways in which students can participate in planning, developing, and evaluating the work
3. It should provide suitable socializing activities

4. It should explore community resources that will be useful in developing the learning unit
5. It should be based upon sound principles of learning
6. It should be practicable under prevailing school conditions
7. It should stimulate professional growth in democratic ways of working with students
8. It should provide the students with experiences that call for reflective thinking
9. It should be organized for easy use by the teachers
10. It should be based upon a definite philosophy of education
11. It should be developed by several teachers representing as many subject fields as possible
12. It should contain many more suggestions than any class is likely to use
13. It should be suited to the students' maturity.[9]

A considerable amount of study was conducted concerning the development of resource units, particularly in the Type C, pre-planned problems approaches to core programs. Lurry and Alberty, after extensive investigation, outlined sixteen problem areas which they stated could be utilized as a basis for the scope of an adequate core program. These were:

1. Problems of School Living
2. Problems of Self-Understanding
3. Problems of Finding Values by Which We Live
4. Problems of Social Relationships
5. Problems of Employment and Vocation
6. Problems of Using and Conserving Natural Resources
7. Problems of Education in American Democracy
8. Problems of Constructive Use of Leisure
9. Problems of Family Living
10. Problems of Communication
11. Problems of Democratic Government
12. Problems of Community and Personal Health
13. Problems of Economic Relationships in a Democracy
14. Problems of Achieving World Peace in the Atomic Age
15. Problems of Intercultural Relations
16. Problems of Critical Thinking[10]

These problem areas were intended to serve as a guideline for faculties and students who would then select more specific topics derived from these general areas. Those topics could then serve as centers for curriculum development within the classroom setting. The utilization of such topics for units, and the subsequent utilization of unit approaches to curriculum have experienced success in junior high schools and middle schools throughout the United States for several decades. Their continued use and an increase in the number of middle schools utilizing such approaches is encouraged.

Eight-Year Study

Seldom have efforts been made to evaluate the results of a particular organizational approach on a broad spectrum of criteria. The core curriculum is one of the few structures thus evaluated. Both the research design and the conclusions of the study are noted here since they present a solid research rationale for the resurgence of core programs in middle schools. A longitudinal study was conducted in the period from 1932 to 1940 under the direction of Ralph W. Tyler. The graduates of 30 schools were selected. These students attended more than 300 colleges and universities which agreed to suspend the usual college entrance requirements for the experimental students. Each of the 30 secondary schools was permitted to develop its own experimental curriculum which in most cases utilized some element of the core curriculum. From the experimental secondary schools 1,475 graduates were matched with graduates of other secondary schools who attended the same colleges. They were matched according to similarities in several variables including age, race, sex, aptitude, and others. In 1940 the evaluation report at the end of the study indicated that graduates of the experimental schools:

1. earned a slightly higher total grade average;
2. earned higher grade averages in all subject fields except foreign languages;
3. received slightly more academic honors each year;
4. were more often judged to possess a high degree of intellectual curiosity and drive;
5. were more often judged to be precise, systematic, and objective in their thinking;
6. were more often judged to have developed clear or well-formulated ideas concerning the meaning of education;
7. more often demonstrated a high degree of resourcefulness in meeting new situations;
8. had about the same problems of adjustment as the comparison group, but approached their solution with greater effectiveness;
9. participated somewhat more frequently in student groups;
10. earned a higher percentage of nonacademic honors (officerships, athletic awards, etc.);

11. had a somewhat better orientation toward the choice of a vocation;
12. demonstrated a more active concern for what was going on in the world.[11]

At the conclusion of the Eight-Year Study core programs were at a peak in relation to numbers of schools utilizing such an approach. The number of schools continuing core practices slowly diminished until the advent of Sputnik in 1956. At that time a U. S. Office of Education survey revealed that almost one-fifth of the junior high schools in the nation were offering block-time courses (Type A of core curriculum).[12]

Varying pressures upon the schools coming from such diverse sources as societal pressures for more subject orientation, and college efforts to develop more discipline-oriented content brought about a continuing decline in the use of the core program. Recently revised societal emphases have created a renaissance of the core program philosophy with an attendant growth in block-time and other phenomena of the core. Interdisciplinary studies, an integral aspect of core, has increased in recent years along with a demand for pupil-oriented teachers in middle schools. Emphasis upon these aspects of middle school education would indicate the increasing importance being given to the core program approach to the development of instructional methodologies best suited to the emerging adolescent.

Advantages of core

Advantages in the core program are evident both in theory and practice. Certain educational principles seem to be inherent within the core concept. A list of these was prepared by Faunce and Bossing:

1. The core is in harmony with the best we know about the nature of learning. Learning is recognized as an active process. . . .
2. The core centers around vital problems of personal and social concern to the learner. . . .
3. The core, with its problem-centered emphasis through experience learning, provides a superior opportunity for pupils to learn such essential social skills as cooperative planning and working together. . . .
4. The core makes possible greater attention to the individual differences of children. . . .
5. The use of the multiple period now commonly associated with the core organization, combined with the emphasis upon personal-social

problems as basic in the core, provides an excellent opportunity for the teacher to exercise the guidance function now accepted as the central activity of teaching. . . .

6. The lifelike activities and purposeful atmosphere of the core curriculum are most conducive to the serious motivation of pupils. . . .

7. The core curriculum provides for a natural integration of school, home, and community living. . . .

8. The core concept makes the so-called extracurricular activities a natural, integral part of the curriculum. . . .

9. In the core concept teachers take on a new status. Under the subject curriculum concept teachers were essentially drill masters. . . . The core teacher . . . becomes a guide to meaningful learning in the personal-social areas of concern to the pupil. . . .

10. The core curriculum provides the theoretical bases favorable to the establishment of rapport and cooperative efforts within the school staff. . . . [13]

In addition to fundamental principles noted above, a series of advantages to be derived in a practicing educational situation can be noted. Here the emphasis would be upon strengths to be found in a classroom practicing core program techniques. While such strengths may not be inherent within the structure, they are quite often characteristically found in such an organization. In a study in 1951 Cramer found the following advantages for a core program:

1. A smaller number of pupils for each teacher of common learnings to understand;

2. Fewer pupils for each teacher to know;

3. Smaller gap between the elementary and junior high schools;

4. More opportunity for supervision and curriculum construction on school time;

5. More time and better school organization for guidance and adjustment;

6. Greater amount of group and work-type procedure within the classrooms;

7. More convenient to plan projects which concern the welfare of the pupils in the whole school; and

8. Wider use of community resources in the curriculum. [14]

The advantages thus noted in theory and in practice, in addition to those noted in the Eight-Year Study, seem to indicate great strength for the core program movement in achieving effective instructional stances. However, a question occasionally arises as to the effectiveness of core in the inculcation of subject matter. Vars found from a review of over 50 studies that those studies:

> ...consistently show that in learning subject matter and basic skills, pupils in block-time and core programs do as well or better than pupils in separate-subject classes. Loss in the learning of subject matter, feared by some, simply does not occur. Opinionaire studies reveal further that teachers, pupils, and parents usually approve of the newer programs.[15]

In the final analysis most schools which have discontinued core programs have done so for practical reasons, for the most part having to do with teacher preparation. For example, a survey by Gruhn and Douglass indicated two reasons as being significant for discontinuance of core. More than three-quarters of the schools discontinuing core programs did so because qualified and interested teachers were difficult to find. Another third of the reporting officials indicated that teachers objected to teaching more than one subject.[16]

Since the core program seems to be theoretically and practically a viable approach to organization for instruction in the middle school, a strong program of teacher preparation to qualify teachers to work within such a framework is appropriate. In addition, stronger orientation to such programs is important within the teacher preparation program so that prospective teachers may see advantages to be derived from core techniques.

TEAM TEACHING

Team teaching is a method of organization used in many middle schools throughout the United States. It has three major variations (in addition to other minor ones): disciplinary team, interdisciplinary team, and hierarchical team. These three types of teams vary in basic purposes for organization but have certain things in common. Olson has defined team teaching as:

> ...an instructional situation where two or more teachers possessing complementary teaching skills cooperatively plan and implement the instruction for a single group of students using flexible scheduling and grouping techniques to meet the particular instructional needs of the students.[17]

Thus, while disciplinary team teaching might stress greater capabilities and efficiency within a particular subject, and interdisciplinary teaming emphasize the correlational impact of two or more subjects, the basic fundamental premise of two or more individuals working cooperatively toward the achievement of instructional objectives is still present. The original premise of team teaching as presented by Trump,[18] that the primary purpose of team teaching was to improve instruction, still holds true no matter the particular type of team utilized.

Disciplinary team teaching

Disciplinary team teaching is an organization in which two or more teachers in a particular subject matter team together in order to present more effectively the fundamental framework of their particular discipline. For example, three teachers of history might agree that the unique strengths of each might lead them to divide an American history course into political history, economic history, and intellectual history of the United States. Thus each person could be more competent to teach within the narrower confines of his or her specialization in addition to assisting the other two in less specific sections of their work.

The original organizational framework suggested a flexible organization of large-group, small-group, and independent study periods in order to facilitate the work of the individual instructors. Large-group instruction could consist of any size class from 50 upward, while small-group classes were conceived as ranging from 12 to 15 members, and independent study as an individual operation.

Purposes. Since the primary purpose of disciplinary team teaching is to improve instruction and to lead to more specific statements of the framework of the discipline, the purposes of the various organizational arrangements may vary slightly from a typical classroom. A large-group setting may be particularly valuable due to its motivational force, the amount of information given, and the impetus in the direction of further study presented.[19] While these three factors may appear in a typical classroom, the power with which they are carried by the large-group arrangement may be crucial. Thus a well-prepared lecture, supplemented by films and/or other audio-visual devices, may carry more motivational impact than the typical less thoroughly planned classroom approach would. Just as importantly, the amount of specific information available in a lecture where additional teacher time has been allocated for careful planning should outweigh that of a classroom where less advance planning would be possible. The carefully planned series of thoughts presented in such a lecture also might contain more directions for future study than might be found in a traditional classroom. All of these assumptions presuppose a degree of advance planning made possible through the team teaching arrangement. Such a degree of planning has been found to be more difficult when attempted in a traditional departmentalized classroom.

The small-group classroom is seen as a subdivision of the large group, ranging in number from 12 to 15. This number has been suggested based upon the functioning and study of group dynamics and on knowledge of learning. Members of a group of this size can be expected to participate more effectively than is possible in the classroom with 25 or more students where less interaction is expected due to larger numbers of individuals. Nevertheless, groups can be smaller or even somewhat larger in number than 12 to 15 subject to purposes sought at a particular time. Very small groups of 3, 4, or 5 may be appropriate, and the organizational pattern in team teaching should be flexible enough to permit many different temporary arrangements. The primary purposes of small-group instruction, according to Trump and Miller,[20] are the development of communication skills and improved human relations with other members of the group. In these circumstances, the teacher's task is not only to present further information concerning substantive content, but also to facilitate the development of these skills and relationships. Such techniques do not denigrate the importance of the subject matter being considered, but express the importance of differing learning modes.

The constituency of the small group should vary from time to time, depending upon purposes of the group at that particular meeting. If the purpose is to consider controversial issues a different set of pupils might be organized than if the topic were values clarification, analytical thinking, or other substantive content or process. If the purpose is the facilitation of discussion, one set of pupils for the group might be appropriate. If its purpose is debate, a different set of pupils might be appropriate. At times homogeneous grouping might be employed, while at other times heterogeneous grouping would be most effective. Girls and boys might meet together according to some purposes and separately for others. Thus at all times one planning task of a team teaching faculty is to determine the basic purposes of each small-group session and select the grouping which can most effectively meet those objectives.

The third segment of disciplinary team teaching is independent study. The library, resource center, and study room, as well as the classroom serve as environments in which a pupil might conduct his or her own independent study while surrounded by other pupils. Such independent study may be the result of a specific assignment presented by a teacher, the result of an independent research project conducted by the student for his or her own purposes, may come from ideas suggested by the unit being experienced, or from suggestions of peers.

Teacher functions. Certain functions of teachers in disciplinary team teaching create built-in advantages for an organization. While such functions are not guaranteed by an organization, they are found more characteristically in team teaching, and hence should be noted. Teachers are ordinarily brought into closer working relationships with their colleagues in a team approach. Two or more teachers are brought into an organization which by its nature causes them to consider the ideas, attitudes, and desires of other professionals. The opinion of a colleague can be ignored only with difficulty when two or more people are working closely as teachers in a team teaching organization. Attitudes toward discipline and motivation tend to be less arbitrary in such circumstances. Homework assignments usually become less disparate. Teachers who work closely together usually tend to come closer in their ideas of appropriate teaching techniques.

Ordinarily such teachers begin to plan together for more effective learning experiences for their pupils. Such plans involve homework assignments, test assignments, and report assignments, in addition to more important facets of learning such as common objectives and evaluative criteria. Large-group instruction provides a beneficial side-effect of permitting some teachers to observe the presentation of other teachers. This has fine effects both upon the observer and the observed. Observers may learn much from attendance at the lecture of a colleague who has had sufficient time to prepare a well-organized, well-conceived presentation on a particular topic. Lecture techniques, unknown information, and resources may all become available due to such observation. In addition, the observed teacher has the motivation of presenting before informed colleagues as well as to the pupils in the class. He or she also has the opportunity to inquire as to methods of improving the presentation in future lectures.

Sharing of information concerning students is one of the most important advantages to be derived from the team teaching approach. Such information may be personal or class related. It may be in the cognitive, psychomotor, or affective domain. Such information belonging to one member of the teaching team should be common knowledge to all unless unusual circumstances dictate otherwise. In this way, learning difficulties may be foreseen and possibly forestalled. Individual emotional problems may be diminished, as may teacher-pupil personality clashes. The better informed a teacher is concerning the pupils as individuals, the more effective he or she can become.

Joint evaluation of the work of individual pupils becomes possible in a team operation. If a group of teachers can take conference time to consider evaluation of various facets of a pupil's progress the results should be beneficial. Such evaluation would include test scoring, assignment checking, discussion evaluation, classroom motivation, and others. Such evaluation presents a compilation of the views of several teachers, and lessens the effect of a possibly biased view of an individual teacher.

Administrative factors. Certain factors involved in team teaching need to be considered in determining the efficacy of this organization for middle school. A teaching team conducts three activities on an organized basis. They plan, teach, and evaluate together. In order to accomplish those tasks it is necessary for certain administrative aspects to be considered. For example, more time is consumed in group planning in a team teaching organization than in a departmentalized operation. Planning for improvement of instruction, care for individual differences, and other concerns should be encouraged, but sufficient time for teachers to plan both as individuals and in groups is an absolute necessity if team teaching is to be successful.

Team teaching may also serve as a focus for an administrative unit that is more convenient and effective than an individual teacher or a principal responsible for an entire school. Hence, a leader of a teacher team might reasonably be expected to assume a more humanized approach to the needs of some hundred or more pupils when compared to a principal who is responsible for many times this number. The more effective administrative structures within middle schools are those in which teams are permitted a great deal of latitude in their administrative decisions within the general framework of policies established for all teams within the school. In other words, the teaching team should be responsible for the education of the students in their team under general conditions laid down by the school administration. Thus the degree of responsibility given to the team can determine to a great extent their degree of success.

Interdisciplinary team teaching

Interdisciplinary team teaching is a relatively common organization in the middle schools of the United States. Although recent in conceptualization, many middle schools have adopted this structure within the last decade. It has been defined as:

> ...a combination of teachers from different subject areas who plan and conduct the instruction in these areas for particular groups of pupils. The aim of the interdisciplinary team approach is to promote communication, coordination, and cooperation among subject matter specialists so that students benefit from instruction planned by specialists, but lacking the fragmentation which characterizes many departmentalized plans.[21]

The communication and cooperation mentioned above, while stressing the subject matter of the disciplines, are not limited only to those. Communication regarding developmental needs, social problems, and other matters conceivably of more concern to pupils than subject matter is seen as being an integral function of the interdisciplinary team. Thus two teachers of different subjects might be found discussing a pupil with a social problem just as frequently as they might be found discussing another student with a learning problem.

Types of teams. In the relatively short span of time during which interdisciplinary teams have become popular in the middle schools, several variations of this theme have become evident. The following list is intended to be representative of those types of interdisciplinary teams which are most often found in middle schools. While not inclusive, they contain the vast majority of practicing interdisciplinary teams in middle schools at the present time.

1. Language arts, social studies, arithmetic, science
2. Language arts, social studies, arithmetic, science, reading
3. Language arts, social studies, arithmetic, science, guidance
4. Language arts, social studies
5. Language arts, social studies, guidance
6. Science, arithmetic
7. Language arts, social studies, music, art (humanities)

By far the most common of these types of interdisciplinary teams is the four-person team, with each teacher specializing in either language arts, social studies, science, or mathematics. The four individuals form a teaching group which ordinarily works with approximately 100 to 120 pupils in an instructional setting. They meet regularly to plan cooperatively for this instruction and to organize learning activities for the group of students for whom they are responsible. Commonly, the four teachers also have a homeroom activity period arranged where each meets one-fourth of the large group.

When the reading teacher is associated as a fifth member of the team, this individual functions in one of two ways. Reading is treated as either a separate and distinct subject matter area to be taught in a group situation similar to the other four subject areas, or the reading teacher acts as a consultant and counselor to the team, working with planning for the large group, while concurrently working with individuals on idiosyncratic reading problems. The same situation applies when a guidance teacher becomes involved with the four-person team. Here again group guidance and homeroom activities are organized and supervised by the guidance teacher. Other circumstances may dictate the guidance counselor serving as a consultant to the four teachers while working with pupils on an individual counseling basis according to the particular needs and purposes of the persons involved. Most of the other interdisciplinary teams listed are permutations of the four-man team noted as being most common. The varying purposes of different schools might make one such variation more appropriate than another, but most stress the importance of the four disciplines basic to middle school general education.

A strongly recommended variation on this plan is the humanities-team approach to interdisciplinary teaching. In this organization four teachers would be working with 100 to 120 pupils but the curriculum balance and purposes would differ considerably from the more typical arrangement. Here, a language arts, social studies, music, and art teacher would develop a curriculum based upon a humanities orientation. A conceptual approach on a less sequential base to learning would be encouraged. Arithmetic and science, with more sequential bases, would be scheduled outside the framework of this team. Under these circumstances, a greater emphasis in curriculum balance is given to humanistic views of life, rather than a more traditional approach to the curriculum.

A type of teaming which was not listed above is highly recommended by theory. Its practice is not yet fully achieved, hence it should be seen primarily as a theoretical conceptualization. Such a team would consist of several faculty members equally divided between conceptualization approaches and learning skills approaches to the curriculum. For example, some aspects of language arts are sequential in nature, having to do with learning skills. These could be acquired in a learning center. Other knowledges which would need to be derived from a conceptualization base could be learned in more typical classroom settings with teachers who specialize in such an approach. The same situation is found in most disciplines. Thus teachers could be committed either to skills development, working in learning centers devoted to those, or to conceptualization approaches, working in classrooms devoted to those. Such an approach would exemplify the often expressed idea that teachers should be specialists in the learning process in addition to the subject matter which is the vehicle of that process. Some learning skills bridge several disciplines. Such skills could be taught and practiced in the learning center with a specialist teacher. Similarly some concepts hold across disciplines making the same situation applicable to a teacher working with students in conceptual learning.

Basic purposes. Most middle schools utilizing the interdisciplinary team approach do so for one of two basic reasons in addition to others. Some visualize the interdisciplinary team primarily facilitating pupil learning in the instructional process through the development of units correlated across subject fields. Others see such a team as aiding in the overall development of individuals in the middle school through a concern for socio-emotional growth within and among pupils. It is highly unlikely that those who espouse either of these two fundamental premises would argue for the negation of the other. Nevertheless, the emphasis carried by one would place it in comparative dominance in a hierarchy of purposes. Thus a principal concerned with improvement of instruction would not argue against overall development, but would see the development of subject matter expertise as being more important.

Those who would defend the improvement of instruction as the fundamental purpose of interdisciplinary teaming would contend that interdisciplinary teaming would permit greater flexibility in the learning process, more variation in aspects of instruction, better planning for instruction and evaluation, and more effective coordination of various subject matter areas. The assumption implicit within these contentions is that the learning environment would improve as cooperation between team members increases. The "cross-pollination" involved with different individuals planning together for the curriculum and instruction of a group should necessarily occasion greater effectiveness in the learning process.

Those who espouse the overall developmental approach as a rationale for interdisciplinary teaming would argue that intellectual work is only one aspect of the developmental growth of the individual. Under those circumstances the affective development of the emerging adolescent is seen as being extremely important. Teachers would be able to assist each other in counseling, companionship, and other such helping phases—thus a student creating disciplinary problems for one teacher might be approached by another teacher with whom his or her personal relations are in better order to resolve the situation. Under these circumstances counseling would be as carefully considered as lesson plans. The goal of such activities would be the development of a solidly functioning community of learners who have certain commonly agreed upon goals, some cognitive, others affective, others psychomotor, all devoted to the overall development of the emerging adolescent.

Advantages. Interdisciplinary team teaching has certain built-in advantages. For example, the sharing of information concerning pupils among teachers enables teachers to be more conversant with the idiosyncratic strengths and weaknesses of each individual. To further strengthen this situation a guidance counselor, if not regularly assigned to the group, could meet with the team occasionally during planning sessions in order to strengthen their work through the dissemination of further information concerning individual students.

Administration is eased since in most cases classes are scheduled in a block of time. Teachers may plan accordingly for more flexible opportunities such as field trips and other activities which would consume a period of time longer than a typical class period. In addition, this same flexibility of scheduling permits a correlation between subject areas. The language arts and social studies teachers might be able to schedule classes together with both teachers serving in a simultaneous instructional capacity. Teachers will certainly get to know each other to a fuller extent. The interaction of planning together would enable them to become not only more cognizant of attitudes different from their own but also more tolerant of such attitudes.

One facet of interdisciplinary team teaching which can be an advantage when adequately utilized is the time ordinarily set aside for planning. According to Olson:

> Sufficient planning time is vital to the success of a team. If a team does not have adequate planning time or if the members of the team do not devote the necessary time to planning, the team will fail.[22]

While Olson has placed this necessity for planning in a negative sense, the positive elements of the possibilities entailed in cooperative planning must also be emphasized. Most team teaching schedules allow some time for the planning function since it is considered to be so important. Since group planning is ordinarily an integral part of the team teaching process it has a considerable advantage over the typical classroom-planning system in which less time is ordinarily relegated to this function.

Flexibility is the most noticeable advantage to be derived from the interdisciplinary team teaching process. To the extent that team teaching, either within or between disciplines, aids in the development of flexibility of structure and instructional practices it furnishes strength to the middle school. As the degree of flexibility becomes greater, so the educational environment of the middle school is improved.

Hierarchical team teaching

The differentiated staff is a concept which may be organized in conjunction with either disciplinary or interdisciplinary team teaching. The basic purpose of such an organization is to free the professional person for that task in the instructional framework for which he or she is most fully qualified. Thus an experienced, expert teacher should be working in instruction, and should not be doing clerical work. Rather, this could be conducted by an assistant who, while knowledgeable in education, would not need the degree of expertise necessary to the senior teacher. Such a staff hierarchy would relate the teacher's work more to the learning function than to the mastery of subject matter alone.

Trump and Miller noted six levels of differentiation in their hierarchical team plan.

1. Professional teachers
   (teacher specialists)
   (general teachers)
2. Instruction assistants
3. Clerical aides
4. General aides
5. Community consultants
6. Staff specialists[23]

Allen in his work on differentiated staffing went another step in further subdividing teachers while continuing the utilization of paraprofessional personnel. In his staff organization he outlined the following:

1. Curriculum associate.
2. Senior teacher.
3. Staff teacher.
4. Associate teacher.
5. Para-professional personnel.[24]

Hierarchical team teaching as a concept is a valuable addition to the various structures devoted to the improvement of instruction since it permits a degree of differentiation as to duties. Differing tasks include varying lengths of time developing materials, classroom teaching, and clerical work. For example, a curriculum associate in Allen's plan could be concerned with research in curriculum and methodology with correspondingly less attention to the physical act of meeting a group of students. Very little time would be spent on clerical tasks. At the other extreme academic assistants would be expected to be skilled paraprofessionals who would work with students in special areas but who would also be expected to grade papers and supervise resource center activities rather than assume major responsibilities in the planning of pupil learning. Higher prestige and salary would be accorded to upper echelons in such an hierarchy. Attention would be given to teaching skills and knowledges in order to determine appropriate placement of teachers on such a professional ladder.

MODULAR SCHEDULING

In order for personalization of education to take place an organization for instruction must be flexible. Various means of achieving this flexibility, such as nongrading and core, have already been discussed. Another way to achieve this goal is through the use of flexible or modular scheduling. Rather than the short units suggested in core along with block-time or nongraded segments of time which must be considered in terms of weeks or months, modular scheduling works on the basis of time allocation to pupils within a day's schedule. The underlying assumption is that the traditional schedule featuring 45 to 55 minutes per subject per day is an ineffective one. Information concerning the characteristics of emerging adolescents indicates such a period to be too long for most learning activities. Even if this were not true variations in time schedules might be appropriate due to the particular learning responsibility encountered by a middle school pupil on a particular day. For example, physical education with its attendant dressing problems might well consume an hour, whereas a course stressing specific learning skills, such as foreign language, might be appropriate for two short 15-minute sessions each day. The time consumed in a class should be that which is optimal in terms of learning time for the particular subject. Thus a pupil might consume only 15 minutes in music on Monday, not attend the class at all on Tuesday, and then take an hour on Wednesday if such time allocation was appropriate for the learning activity undertaken by the pupil at that time.

In order to achieve such an outcome the class-day schedule may be divided into a larger number of units than in the traditional schedule. Rather than a six-hour day divided into eight or nine periods of approximately 45 minutes each, the flexible day might be arranged into 24 modules of 15 minutes each, or 18 modules of 20 minutes each. Thus various classes could be scheduled for varying periods of time for the purpose of greater flexibility in the school day. A typical school day might see the schedule shown in Table 14-1 for a middle school child.

Such a schedule permits the utilization of time appropriate to the concerns of a homeroom while at the same time permitting physical education to consume the time necessary for that course. In order to create a valid curriculum balance schedules can and should be changed from day to day.

Other variations in modular scheduling not only permit schedules to vary from period to period during the day and from day to day during the week, but also permit completely different schedules to occur on a revolving basis. For example, Monday might be classified as "A" day, with Tuesday classified as "B" day. Such a schedule would permit a slightly more structured schedule than the typical modular schedule but would be considerably less structured than the traditional day. Thus on "A" day a pupil might be scheduled for one

---

Table 14-1. Illustrative Daily Class Schedule

Module Class   (Each module equals twenty minutes.)

1	Homeroom
2	Sciences (includes mathematics)
3	"
4	Exploration (based upon individual pupil needs and desires)
5	"
6	Physical Education
7	" "
8	" "
9	Lunch
10	Recreational Period
11	Group Guidance
12	" "
13	Exploration (based upon individual pupil needs and desires)
14	Humanities (includes language arts, social studies, etc.)
15	"
16	"
17	Fine and Practical Arts (includes music, art, industrial arts, home economics, etc.)
18	" " " "

Note: Sciences, physical education, group guidance, humanities, and fine and practical arts are devoted to those aspects of education needed by all. Homeroom, exploration, and recreation should be devoted to individual needs and desires.

hour of physical education; on "B" day not at all. On "A" day one might be scheduled for two 15-minute periods of foreign language, on "B" day a 45-minute period. In such a way the schedule could become more flexible than under the traditional arrangement.

The primary purpose of modular scheduling is similar to the purposes of block-time, interdisciplinary teaming, and nongraded schedules. The underlying fundamental root of all these programmatic arrangements is the development of the most complete degree of flexibility possible within the framework of education for emerging adolescents.

RESOURCE CENTER

Resource center learning is placed within the context of organizational structure because administrative approval and facilitation are necessary in order to achieve its most effective functioning. A well-equipped, well-staffed, and well-utilized resource center is a necessity for an effectively organized middle school. Whether the school is based upon nongraded strategies, core curriculum approaches, team teaching bases, or a combination of any or all of these, the resource center becomes a center for the learning process. It is in this center that learning can occur in a personalized manner, either in individual or group processes.

Open space

As with the learning center, open-space education is ordinarily based upon a structural arrangement determined by the architectural preferences of school boards, patrons, and, at times, faculty and administration of middle schools. While noting this, the advantages and disadvantages of such a setting must be noted. Open-space setting has ordinarily been identified as a room with dimensions equal to or larger than two typical classrooms. In many schools utilizing interdisciplinary teams the open-space classroom contains sufficient space for all four teachers to work in a common setting. Where individualized learning is emphasized, a large resource-center type room is utilized.

Some advantages of open space are noted:

1. Flexibility—teachers may utilize larger or smaller amounts of space as needed, various parts of the room may be used at different times according to need, and so on.
2. Cooperation—teachers may work with more than one class at a time, teachers may work cooperatively if desired, and so on.
3. Efficiency—the setting can be made more aesthetic, specialized areas of study not so easily organized in a traditional classroom can be arranged, and so on.

Certain disadvantages have been noted:

1. Disagreements among teachers can be exacerbated by proximity.
2. Noise levels can become distressing if acoustics are not considered in the construction of the room.

Neither the list of advantages nor the list of disadvantages is intended to be exhaustive; they are, rather, suggestive of possible areas of concern. In summation, open space would seem to be an architectural arrangement which shows promise for organizational settings to facilitate instruction.

Independent study encourages diversity of interests.
Iroquois Middle School
(Courtesy of Niskayuna, New York, Central School District)

Individual learning

Individualized learning is the learning undertaken by each emerging adolescent on a singular basis within the framework of the educational environment imposed by the school setting. It can be categorized as either directed learning or independent learning. Directed learning includes the various assignments made to the individual either separately or as a member of a class requiring his or her particular work. Independent study includes that realm of concern which the pupil selects and pursues free of most class restraints. Objectives of independent study according to one source are:

1. To develop creativity, adaptability, responsibility, and habits of inquiry in students.
2. To permit different rates of progress.
3. To enable students to pursue elective interests on their own.
4. To encourage and facilitate development of good study habits.
5. To permit program adaptation to individual student needs.
6. To permit program adaptation in individual student problem-solving skills.[25]

Both directed learning and independent learning take place in the learning-resource center through a variety of means of which three will be investigated: contract plans, programmed learning, and audio-visual devices.

Contract plans vary both in complexity and length of assignment. The basic underlying purpose of the contract, no matter what its intricacy, is to lay at the door of the pupil the responsibility for determining the degree to which his or her particular learning will occur. A simple contract stating only that a pupil agrees to finish a specific assignment on a particular day is an example of this framework. A complex unit which requires many hours over a several-week period, while admittedly more rigorous, may meet the same basic purpose.

The contract plan usually begins with a teacher explaining the system to a group of pupils, and then assisting them to determine the objectives which they may wish to achieve within the framework of a particular unit. After cooperative consideration the pupil will agree to accept some significant portion of responsibility for the specific unit. After contracting with the teacher, the pupil will go to the resource center and, with the help of center personnel, select appropriate resources to achieve the objectives of the contract. After the study has been completed to the satisfaction of the pupil, the contracted work is transmitted to the teacher, at which time teacher and pupil jointly determine the degree to which the contract has been fulfilled.

The most noted contract plan conducted in the United States was the so-called Dalton Plan.[26] This plan was carried on quite successfully for several years in Illinois during the 1920s. After a lapse of a few decades during which the contract plan was utilized sporadically and in relatively isolated subject-matter fields, a resurgence of interest in this particular type of plan seems to be occurring.

Contract plans are of most effect when teachers are able to plan contracts in advance, along with notations of available resources. This enables pupils to go to the center with some initial information which lessens the amount of time requisite to achieving the contract assignment. The individual learner is better able, under the contract plan, to enrich his or her own experiences since alternatives are open. While specific reading and/or audio-visual resources are presented, the pupil is permitted to pursue in an independent manner the interests aroused by a contract. Hence the contract is limited only by the amount and degree of motivation displayed by the pupil after he or she has had opportunity to explore the contract topic. Peripheral learnings which might not occur in a typical classroom become important within the framework of such a setting. Learning is limited only by lack of resources, or lack of imagination of either the pupil or teacher involved in the contract.

Programmed learning will assume a major role in individual learning occurring in a resource center. It consists of a series of specific pieces of information which follow sequentially one from another. The logical distances between a given question and the ones immediately preceding and following it are short enough so that one answer will tend to lead toward the next. The basic rationale for such a learning sequence is that many carefully graduated, sequentially arranged questions and answers should constitute a viable learning program.

There are two basic types of programs, linear and branching. The linear program is based upon one line of thought moving directly toward a preconceived conclusion. Each answer should ideally lead to a next question with the progression continuing until a final solution is reached. A branching program, on the other hand, gives a pupil a series of multiple-choice possibilities for a selected answer, thus leading toward alternative choices. Branching programs tend to offer more choices, providing for curriculum differentiation but should ordinarily lead the pupil to the preordained conclusion.

Programmed learning has many advantages. Parker and Rubin[27] have noted the following:

1. Machines are consistent and optimally efficient.
2. Educational costs can be reduced.
3. Teacher shortage can be relieved.
4. Instruction can be individualized to a tailor-made program.
5. The pupil may detect learning errors immediately and hence localize difficulties.
6. Learning occurs more thoroughly and rapidly.
7. Content and methodology are more consistent.

Programmed learning may take place most effectively in those learning tasks which have specific answers or solutions, and where the methodology to achieve those answers has been accepted. In many learning skill areas and other curricular approaches the utilization of programmed learning as an instructional strategy in the resource center has much to recommend it.

Audio-visual devices may serve a valuable and necessary function within the framework of the resource center. Whether used as part of a contract plan, or as an aspect of the programmed learning approach, audio-visual devices (e.g., film loops, film strips, video cassettes, and CAI) present a degree of individuality to the learning efforts of pupils difficult to achieve through other means. Certain types of machines facilitate study by individuals in areas in which they are uniquely interested. For example, pupils might be able to achieve a degree of mastery of a concept through the utilization of a film loop which would permit them to review a single idea on their own, and for their own needed length of time. Utilizing the same rationale, tape recordings may prove effective in presenting information especially designed to aid individual learning. Also, tapes can be made of class discussions or lectures and reviewed by students who have had unavoidable school absence. A pupil would be enabled to take time arranged for study to view work the rest of the class has completed. Special projects could be taped and stored for future use.

Individualized learning in groups

Individuals participating within classes and other large groups can find a resource center extremely useful as they increase their learning parameters. In conjunction with, and utilizing the coordinative function of resource center personnel, teachers should consider the advantages of the rest of the school building, grounds, immediate community, and other areas within the immediate vicinity available for field trips. In addition, resource people should be brought in to the school from the surrounding community to aid in the conduct of education for pupils in a group setting.

A resource center usually keeps a library of films and kinescopes to be made available to classrooms within the middle school. Films present an opportunity for visual enrichment of a pre-planned experience unavailable at times by any other means. In addition, a depth of conceptualization is made possible from visualizing the experience rather than just hearing about it from the teacher. Such films should be used only after a preview of the film has made it evident that the particular objectives of the class period can best be met with this medium.

Educational television can be utilized either through continuing attention to a pre-planned series concerning a certain subject, or through individual programs which fortuitously match the needs and purposes of a particular class.

These chance weddings of school purposes and television scheduling occur more often than expected, and careful note should be taken of educational television scheduling where available in order to accomplish this goal most effectively.

Purchase of a relatively inexpensive television camera can open up an entire new field of interest for middle school youngsters. The production of programs, plays, daily news broadcasts, and other such programming can develop both a sense of responsibility and an appreciation of television as an educational tool. Van Til, Vars, and Lounsbury noted the following advantages of television as an educational medium.

1. Instruction presented via television is everywhere the same....
2. Instruction by a very talented teacher is available to all students....
3. Equipment, materials, and specially trained personnel are available to help the television teacher....
4. Classroom teachers may improve...by watching master teachers on television....
5. School television provides an outlet for student talent....[28]

Field trips should form an integral part of group learning in an ideal middle school. Coordination for such trips should be the responsibility of resource center personnel. Field trips may be either of the formal type in which pupils go to a specific scheduled spot as a part of the established curriculum, or may be of the type in which a very informal learning experience can occur. No matter the type, the fundamental purpose of broadening the educational environment remains the same. A pupil restricted to classroom and book experiences has a learning environment more hampered than one who is able to utilize the resource center and other parts of the school building.

An ideal learning situation is one in which the emerging adolescent is able to see the entire community as a part of his or her learning environment. School buses should be made available for such expanded community experience. In cases where groups are smaller, making bus transportation uneconomical, cars may be made available for use. Field trips should be of a type which permit emerging adolescents to obtain experiences which are either unavailable or less effective within school boundaries. The extra expense of such trips can be justified, but only in the context of a richer learning experience. The opportunity to see a massive computer at work, to see a different socio-economic setting, to see a newspaper being published—these and many others are experiences which are unavailable in a school building. Such experiences tend to be more meaningful than a vicarious experience intended to achieve the same learning objective.

**Education occurs outdoors in addition to inside school walls.
Berne Elementary Schools**

(Courtesy of Berne-Knox-Westerlo, New York, Central School District)

One of the more important seldom-used resources available to a middle school are human resources that are available in every community. Such resources should be compiled and catalogued within resource center files. These human resources are individuals in the community who possess specialized knowledges and skills which make them better qualified to present specific information to the middle school pupil. Their continued presence in the classroom is not necessary, but an occasional visit with such information as they possess is extremely effective. Thus the amount of specific information available to pupils becomes greater than if restricted to that obtainable from the faculty.

A stock broker, an automobile mechanic, and a storekeeper are examples of people who can present meaningful information to emerging adolescents concerning the broader life of society, while at the same time presenting specific information concerning topics of educational concern. Any effort either by visitors or faculty which can broaden the scope of the learning environment for pupils of this age should be encouraged.

REFERENCES

1. John I. Goodlad and Robert H. Anderson, *The Nongraded Elementary School*, rev. ed. (New York: Harcourt, Brace Jovanovich, 1963), p. 28.

2. Walter H. Worth, "Promotion or Nonpromotion?" *Educational Administration and Supervision*, vol. 46, Jan. 1960, pp. 16–26.

3. Goodlad and Anderson, *The Nongraded Elementary School*, p. 104.

4. Sidney P. Rollins, *The Middletown Project: The Development of a Non-Graded Secondary School* (Providence: Division of Graduate Studies, Rhode Island College, 1962), pp. 18–19.

5. Burt Kaufman and Paul Bethune, "Nova High—Space Age School," *Phi Delta Kappan*, Sept. 1964, p. 11. Reprinted with permission.

6. From Roland C. Faunce and Nelson L. Bossing, *Developing the Core Curriculum*, © 1958, pp. 59–60. Reprinted by permission of Prentice-Hall, Inc., Englewood Cliffs, N.J.

7. From *Modern Education for the Junior High School Years*, 2nd ed., by William Van Til, Gordon F. Vars, and John H. Lounsbury, copyright © 1961, 1967, by The Bobbs-Merrill Company, Inc, pp. 432–433, reprinted by permission of the publisher.

8. Grace S. Wright, *Core Curriculum Development: Problems and Practices*, U.S. Office of Education Bulletin 1952, no. 5 (Washington, D. C.: Government Printing Office, 1952), p. 8. Reprinted with permission.

9. Faunce and Bossing, *Developing the Core Curriculum*, pp. 241–242. Reprinted with permission of Macmillan Publishing Co., Inc. from *Reorganizing the High School Curriculum* by Harold Alberty. Copyright © 1947, 1953, 1962 by Macmillan Publishing Co., Inc.

10. Lucile L. Lurry and Elsie J. Alberty, *Developing a High School Core Program* (New York: Macmillan, 1957), p. 60. Reprinted with permission.

11. From *The Story of the Eight-Year Study* by Wilford M. Aikin. Copyright © 1942 by McGraw-Hill, Inc., p. 144. Used with permission of McGraw-Hill Book Company.

12. Daniel Tanner, *Secondary Curriculum: Theory and Development* (New York: Macmillan, 1971), pp. 65–66.

13. From Roland C. Faunce and Nelson L. Bossing, *Developing the Core Curriculum*, © 1958, pp. 61–64. Reprinted by permission of Prentice-Hall, Inc., Englewood Cliffs, N.J.

14. From Leonard V. Koos, *Junior High School Trends* (New York: Harper, 1955), p. 72. (Adapted from material: Roscoe V. Cramer, "Common Learnings Program in the Junior High School," *Bulletin of the National Association of Secondary School Principals* XXXV [April 1951], pp. 163–166.) Reprinted with permission.

15. From *Modern Education for the Junior High School Years*, 2nd ed., by William Van Til, Gordon F. Vars, and John H. Lounsbury, copyright © 1961, 1967, by The Bobbs-Merrill Company, Inc, p. 191, reprinted by permission of the publisher.

16. William T. Gruhn and Harl R. Douglass, *The Modern Junior High School*, 2d. ed. (New York: Ronald, 1971), p. 115.

17. Carl O. Olson, Jr., "Why Teaching Teams Fail," *Peabody Journal of Education*, vol. 45, no. 1 (July 1967), pp. 15–20. Reprinted with permission.

18. J. Lloyd Trump, *Images of the Future: A New Approach to the Secondary School* (Washington, D. C.: The National Association of Secondary School Principals, 1959).

19. J. Lloyd Trump and Delmas F. Miller, *Secondary School Curriculum Improvement: Proposals and Procedures* (Boston: Allyn and Bacon, 1968), p. 275.

20. Ibid., p. 283.

21. William M. Alexander, et al., *The Emergent Middle School* (New York: Holt, 1968), pp. 107–108. Reprinted with permission.

22. From Carl O. Olson, Jr., "Why Teaching Teams Fail," *Peabody Journal of Education*, vol. 45, no. 1 (July 1967), pp. 15–20. Reprinted with permission.

23. Trump and Miller, *Secondary School Curriculum Improvement*.

24. M. John Rand and Fenwick English, "Towards a Differentiated Teaching Staff," *Phi Delta Kappan*, vol. 49, no. 5 (Jan. 1968), pp. 264–268.

25. William Rogge, "Independent Study is Self-Directed Learning." From the volume *Independent Study* in the series *Bold New Venture* edited by David W. Beggs III and Edward G. Buffie. Copyright © 1965 by Indiana University Press. Reprinted by permission of the publisher.

26. Helen Parkhurst, *Education on the Dalton Plan* (New York: Dutton; Renewal, 1950, by H. Parkhurst).

27. J. Cecil Parker and Louis J. Rubin, *Process as Content: Curriculum Design and the Application of Knowledge* (Chicago: Rand McNally, 1966) (Rand McNally Curriculum Series, ed. J. Cecil Parker).

28. From *Modern Education for the Junior High School Years*, 2nd ed., by William Van Til, Gordon F. Vars, and John H. Lounsbury, copyright © 1961, 1967, by The Bobbs-Merrill Company, Inc, pp. 486–487, reprinted by permission of the publisher.

RELATED READINGS

Aikin, Wilford M. *The Story of the Eight-Year Study*. New York: McGraw-Hill, 1942.

Alberty, Harold, *Reorganizing the High School Curriculum*. Rev. ed. New York: Macmillan, 1953.

Faunce, Roland C., and Bossing, Nelson L. *Developing the Core Curriculum*. 2d. ed. Englewood Cliffs, N. J.: Prentice-Hall, 1958.

Frymier, Jack R. *A School for Tomorrow*. Berkeley, Calif.: McCutchan, 1973.

Goodlad, John I., and Anderson, Robert H. *The Nongraded Elementary School*. Rev. ed. New York: Harcourt, 1963.

Lurry, Lucile L., and Alberty, Elsie J. *Developing a High School Core Program*. New York: Macmillan, 1957.

Myers, Donald A., ed. *Open Education Re-examined*. Lexington, Mass.: Heath, 1973.

Rollins, Sidney P. *Developing Nongraded Schools*. Itasca, Ill.: F. E. Peacock, 1968.

Trump, J. Lloyd. *Images of the Future: A New Approach to the Secondary School*. Washington, D. C.: The National Association of Secondary School Principals, 1959.

Wright, Grace S. *Core Curriculum Development: Problems and Practices*, U.S. Office of Education Bulletin 1952, no. 5. Washington, D. C.: Government Printing Office, 1952.

APPENDIX A
Units as Learning Experiences

One focus of organization for learning experiences for emerging adolescents is the unit approach. Units may be utilized within most organizational contexts, team teaching, core curriculum, departmentalization, and so on. In the unit approach emphasis is placed upon broad overarching foci for study which may utilize subject matter from one or more disciplines. It will ordinarily be scheduled in a two- to six-week time block based upon the objectives and content appropriate to such a unit.

Examples of unit building and finished products are available in several sources ranging from "The Oregon Trail" to "Democracy as a Form of Government." Such examples are not present in this text due to their length (ranging from 20 to 50 pages). The following books, however, contain material about unit planning with examples and are recommended for your further perusal.

RELATED READINGS

Faunce, Roland C., and Bossing, Nelson L. *Developing the Core Curriculum.2d. ed.* Englewood Cliffs, N.J.: Prentice-Hall, 1958.

Leese, Joseph; Frasure, Kenneth; and Johnson, Mauritz, Jr. *The Teacher in Curriculum Making.* New York: Harper, 1961.

Lurry, Lucile L., and Alberty, Elsie J. *Developing a High School Core Program.* New York: Macmillan, 1957.

Nerbovig, Marcella H. *Unit Planning: A Model for Curriculum Development.* Belmont, Calif.: Wadsworth, 1970.

Van Til, William; Vars, Gordon F.; and Lounsbury, John H. *Modern Education for the Junior High School Years.* 2d. ed. Indianapolis, Ind.: Bobbs-Merrill, 1967.

Vars, Gordon F., ed. *Common Learnings: Core and Interdisciplinary Team Approaches.* Scranton, Pa.: International Textbook Company, 1969.

APPENDIX B
Diagnosis and Evaluation

The major emphasis in this text has been expressed in terms of optimizing the development of each individual student on a number of dimensions: basic skills, general education needs for participation in society, psychomotor development, encouragement in the development of intellectual capabilities, exploration of special interests, and so on. Some dimensions are in the domain of general education and as such would be common to all students; some are in areas unique to individual students; others are more akin to potentials which may arise as interests of students, some lasting and some quite transient and ephemeral.

Implications for measurement and evaluation are usually specific to each special area, and most instructional planning has been based upon sources external to individual students. What has been proposed in this text has been a movement toward more attention to measurement and diagnosis based upon individual growth and change in behaviors and performances over time with check points identified at regular points and recommendations for next steps being made on the basis of each student's progress on identifiable skills, knowledges, and abilities.

To make decisions upon the basis of data obtained from a variety of measurement and assessment devices, many not now in use, will require a staff-development effort to acquaint the total district staff with both requirements for selection of instruments and identification of information and data now available. Further, clarification of goals and objectives and how the district effort can be marshalled toward growth and development of more students will be useful for support of these efforts.

Even though goals in each area have many levels, and a wide range of differences exist among students in every age group; when considered in the ideal or theoretical sense, we recommend that the professional staff charged with responsibility for education for emerging adolescents begin to inform themselves regarding the issues and problems in tests and measurement, and that they come together to find ways to combine the use of existing instruments currently used state-wide and district-wide. After consideration of what is currently used and at what levels, the professional staff will be in a position to determine new needs in terms of selected priorities, aims, and goals.

Steps which the professional staff could take would probably include some or most of the following suggestions.

1. Convene workshop-type meetings to assess the major areas of knowledge and competence among themselves.
2. Determine who among them can share special knowledge and technical competence on issues and problems likely to be experienced in adapting and extending the school program to include more attention to growth and development goals and objectives.
3. Conduct an early discussion including a shared reading and discussion of material on more recent literature connected with individualization, mastery learning, domain-referenced and criterion-referenced testing, a review of teacher-made test requirements, norm-referenced tests, and school data-processing capability.
4. Develop an analysis of current testing program and scoring services provided, uses of information currently provided, consideration of goals and objectives not covered by current testing program, and identification of goals and objectives not systematically measured and appraised up to now.

Some questions which might be raised are indicated in the following examples.

1. Are we maximizing our use of currently available information and data?
2. What are the strengths and advantages of our current testing program?
3. What additional analyses might be available from scoring services provided with the standardized tests we now use? Would use of any of these be advantageous in connection with assessing changes and in diagnosing specific needed instruction for individual students?
4. Is data being provided in line with our district, school, and classroom goals and objectives? Are our goal statements clear enough to give direction to the staff?
5. Is our district-wide testing program adequate to the assessment of effectiveness of allocation of resources on the higher-priority goals? Are the priority goals of various groups of professionals congruent with those of other groups? Are there problems of articulation between and among levels of schooling across the district? Do our students have relatively "trouble-free" transfer from school to school? Do our students move from elementary to

middle or junior high school without major gaps in goal achievement becoming alarmingly evident?

6. In instances where data show gaps in program effectiveness within grades, between grades, across grades, or across schools is there a mechanism for coming to grips with these difficulties?

7. What new measures do we need and for which goals and objectives: direct measures? indirect measures? observation scales? check lists?

8. For areas of our program not systematically measured or assessed by standardized tests, are we making adequate judgments of the effectiveness or absence of observations, measurements, examinations, and analysis, and working to develop or improve our evaluation efforts?

9. Do we have measures to assess the incremental effects of our efforts on our major goals? Are students increasingly able to handle problems in the discipline-centered curricular areas? Are our eighth graders achieving more than they did by seventh grade, and seventh graders more then they did as sixth graders? Have we identified the areas of satisfactory progress as well as those of less satisfactory change? Have we considered both grouped data and data on individuals?

10. Do our tests, scales, and instruments include criteria for showing growth on a variety of dimensions? Are students increasingly able to discipline themselves? Can individual students develop their own projects, share in group efforts, contribute to school projects? Have growth patterns on socio-emotional as well as psychomotor dimensions been recorded? Do individual student profiles exist from which reports of progress and parent reporting can be based?

11. Have teams of professional staff met to consider curriculum sequence and balance in relation to short-term, intermediate, and long-range goals? Are these reflected in day-to-day, week-by-week, term-by-term planning and development by staff? Have parents and students been represented in these planning efforts? Have targets been set so that a progress report can be made on success of change efforts of the staff as well as change efforts of students and groups of students?

12. Have program developers within professional staff utilized district specialists, state department of education specialists, and professional association competence in supporting their efforts? Does the district professional library have up-to-date materials on special and general goals and on technical issues and problems entailed in diagnosis and evaluation?

13. In the absence of a concerted school-wide or district-wide effort, are the efforts of individual teachers and groups of teachers who wish to work toward improvement of their instructional efforts encouraged? Are they supported tangibly with resources?

RELATED READINGS

Block, James H., ed. *Mastery Learning: Theory and Practice*. New York: Holt, 1971.

Block, James H., ed. *Schools, Society, and Mastery Learning*. New York: Holt, 1974.

Bloom, Benjamin S.; Hastings, J. Thomas; and Madaus, George F. *Handbook on Formative and Summative Evaluation of Student Learning*. New York: McGraw-Hill, 1971.

Gagné, Robert M., and Briggs, Leslie J. *Principles of Instructional Design*. New York: Holt, 1974.

Green, John A. *Teacher-Made Tests*. New York: Harper & Row, 1963.

Johnson, David W., and Johnson, Roger T. *Learning Together and Alone*. Englewood Cliffs, N.J.: Prentice-Hall, 1975.

McAshan, H.H. *The Goals Approach to Performance Objectives*. Philadelphia: Saunders, 1974.

Payne, David A. *The Specification and Measurement of Learning Outcomes*. Waltham, Mass.: Blaisdell, 1968.

Popham, W. James, ed. *Criterion-Referenced Measurement (An Introduction)*. Englewood Cliffs, N.J.: Educational Technology Publications, 1971.

Popham, W. James, ed. *Evaluation in Education: Current Applications*. Berkeley, Calif.: McCutchan, 1974.

Popham, W. James, and Husek, T.R. "Implications of Criterion-Referenced Measurement." *Journal of Educational Measurement* 6, Spring, 1969, 1–9.

Tyler, Ralph W., ed. *Educational Evaluation: New Roles, New Means*. Sixty-Eighth Yearbook of the National Society for the Study of Education, Part II. Chicago: University of Chicago Press, 1969.

Tyler, Ralph W., and Wolf, Richard M., eds. *Crucial Issues in Testing*. Berkeley, Calif.: McCutchan, 1974.

Webb, Eugene J.; Campbell, Donald T.; Schwartz, Richard D.; and Sechrest, Lee. *Unobtrusive Measures: Nonreactive Research in the Social Sciences*. Chicago: Rand McNally, 1966.

APPENDIX C
Middle School Practices

Theories propounded in this text are, to a great extent, authenticated by practices of middle schools throughout the country. These practices have proved effective in schools and have been recommended for utilization in other schools by the school people who have used them.

Homeroom

The homeroom program in the Keokuk Junior High School[1] in Keokuk, Iowa, assumed an important role in the affective development of the emerging adolescent for many years (see Tables C-1 and C-2). Homeroom practices were expanded beyond use of typical administrative techniques common in many schools using this organization. While assisting the pupil in orientation to the school, handling routines, and various administrative problems, such as taking roll and making announcements, the homeroom program was developed to serve as a base for social activities, school business, discussion center, and student government. Thus, pupils were given a real sense of belonging—the "home-away-from-home" atmosphere—which is strongly recommended, as well as real feelings of participation in school planning and decision making. Although revisions have occurred in this program in recent years due to various factors, the original premises are still held as a theoretical base.

While some time was taken each day for necessary routines such as attendance, listings of activities in which pupils were involved in the homeroom indicate that a majority of the time in the homeroom was scheduled for student-government activities and organized games which promoted a social climate recommended for the middle school. Some time was given to the study of common emerging adolescent concerns with assemblies devoted to films concerning learning practices, social amenities, and topics of interest to the students. Topics were covered substantively and later discussed during homeroom period. Even the few days specifically designated as being concerned with administrative problems were not devoted to problems usually placed in this category. For example, much of the time devoted to administration purposes was given to exploratory concerns that youngsters might have in their

Table C-1. Homeroom Program—Keokuk Junior High School. (Table used with permission of the Principal.)

Activities		Number of Meetings During School Year	Percentage
Administration		18	9
Explanatory sessions	12		
Progress report conferences	6		
Business		49	29
Student government	13		
Homeroom government	36		
Interest		36	19
Assemblies	21		
Orientation	4		
Publicity for future events	11		
Games		62	33
Free Periods		21	10
		186	100

Table C-2. Homeroom Program—Keokuk Junior High School—Illustrative Six-Week Schedule. (Table used with permission of the Principal.)

Week 1	Week 4
M Discussion of School Handbook	M Free period
T Student Council election	T Variety show publicity
W Homeroom business	W Homeroom business
Th Games period	Th Games period
F Games period	F Progress report conference
Week 2	**Week 5**
M Basketball season publicity	M Film "Habit Patterns"
T Honors assembly	T Film discussion
W Homeroom business	W Homeroom business
Th Games period	Th Games period
F Free period	F Games period
Week 3	**Week 6**
M Film "Social Courtesy"	M Student Council report
T Film discussion	T Games period
W Homeroom business	W Homeroom business
Th Games period	Th Games period
F Games period	F Free period

relationships to others in the school. A handbook was developed which served as the basis for many of these discussions. Another common administrative approach was a review with a child and homeroom teacher privately discussing the grades received by the pupil during each six-week grading period. Thus, it was possible for the homeroom teacher to discuss and understand grading practices and their implications more thoroughly through assistance to the pupil.

The homeroom period was seen by the staff and administration of the Keokuk Junior High School as a period during which one teacher comes to know the child better by focusing on different areas and interests, some of which are intellectual in nature but many of which have emotional and social connotations. Thus this teacher could at times serve as a counselor, at times as parent surrogate, at times as a fellow in adversity, and at all times as an understanding adult in relationship to an emerging adolescent in an often confusing world.

Elective courses

In order to meet most effectively the more personal needs of the many and varied types of emerging adolescents many middle schools have developed mini-courses. The purpose of these courses is to expand and augment the general curriculum by presenting many alternative topics for study. These are planned to meet the specific needs, purposes, and desires of the middle school pupil.

Such a program was initiated at the St. Cloud Middle School[2] in St. Cloud, Florida. Until recently students met in regular classes in block time arrangements from 8:25 a.m. until 1:21 p.m. In the period from 1:21 p.m. to 3:17 p.m. (a total of one hour and 56 minutes) pupils selected various enrichment activities. This approximately two-hour period of time was divided into four segments during which students elected a variety of topics. With a list of 51 offerings in the area of vocational enrichment (see Table C-3), in addition to other types of enrichment, there was a richness and diversity of possibilities offered at this forward-looking school. Due to a recent shortening of the school day and opening of a new building the activity period has recently been limited to one hour, but the philosophy has remained the same.

Period for relaxation

The growth of the human body and the increase in the metabolic rate during adolescence creates a need for periods of relaxation for emerging adolescents during the school day. Such a practice is exemplified by the "cool-it" period in the Barnstable Middle School[3] in Hyannis, Massachusetts.

Table C-3. St. Cloud Middle School—Vocational Enrichment. (Table used with permission of the Principal.)

1. Advanced sewing	27. Florida history
2. Art enrichment	28. French
3. Arts & crafts	29. Future Teachers of America
4. Astronomy	30. Guitar
5. Audio-visual	31. Gymnastics
6. Beginning German	32. Handwriting
7. Beginning sewing	33. Independent study
8. Cartography	34. Intramurals
9. Ceramics	35. Knitting & crocheting
10. Chorus	36. Latin
11. Crafts	37. Leathercraft
12. Creative writing	38. Library Science
13. Criminology	39. Math enrichment
14. Culinary arts	40. Natural resources
15. Current events	41. Nature study
16. Debate	42. Newspaper
17. Developmental reading	43. Personal grooming
18. Directed study	44. Photography
19. Dramatic reading	45. Reading
20. Dramatics	46. Red Cross water safety
21. Ecology	47. Science enrichment
22. Educational games	48. Slim and trim
23. Embroidery	49. Social studies enrichment
24. English enrichment	50. Southern history
25. Etiquette	51. Spelling
26. Fine Arts	

Midway through the morning a period has been set aside in which pupils are permitted under broadly construed guidelines to enjoy a ten-minute break. Students may congregate in classrooms to talk, walk leisurely through the halls, or just sit, according to their individual needs and desires at that moment. This semistructured time provides a relief-rest-relaxation period. Students can go back to work with more enthusiasm than if they had been attending classes continuously three, four, or five hours at a time. While this practice is relatively unused in middle schools, it is strongly recommended. It corresponds closely to the elementary school recess time and to the adult coffee break. Reported results have been very good. Few discipline problems have resulted from this semistructured situation, while greater attention and direction of ability and enthusiasm toward later in-class efforts have been the rule.

De-emphasis of competition

Many progressive middle schools have developed a philosophy which de-emphasizes competition both in classroom work and on the sports field. A few athletic conferences have also limited competition. For example, the Suburban Council[4] in the environs of Albany, New York, agreed that interscholastic athletics in middle schools should be curtailed and that extramural and modified interscholastic programs should take their place. Assumptions underlying this decision were that children in emerging adolescence should not be placed in stressful situations, either emotional or physical. High school athletics in these schools have not been adversely affected. The various schools in the conference seem to achieve in the various sports on a level equal to the best in the state.

Intramural sports assume a position of great importance with students. Homerooms and/or halls (school-within-a-school) receive some smaller portion of their loyalty which had previously been given to official all-school teams. The number of students permitted to compete in the intramural and field day competitions is far greater and there is less stress upon competitive aspects of the sports. This current policy of the Suburban Council has been in effect for several years, is generally accepted by administrators and boards as being beneficial, and is, in general, applauded by most educational theorists, doctors, and school practitioners.

SUBURBAN COUNCIL
REPORT OF JUNIOR HIGH PRINCIPALS ATHLETIC COMPETITION

The following recommendations are designed for schools with grades 6, 7 and 8. Districts may participate in all or parts of this program.

Definitions:

Intramural events are athletic activities open to all boys and girls and held within the school program.

Extramural events are athletic activities open to all boys and girls, and held after school in field or playday arrangements in limited competition with other schools. (Broad based participation of boys and girls—rotation of all boys and girls, etc.)

Interscholastic events are athletic activities open to gifted boys and girls who have passed a physical examination, engaged in a regular training program and are responsive to a coach's directions, such events occurring in officiated competition scheduled with other league schools. (No uniforms, no cheerleaders, no spectators, or publicity.)

Recommendations:

1. No form of interscholastics or extramurals for grade 6.
2. A broadly-based intramural program for grades 6, 7 and 8.
3. A seventh grade program should involve extramural activities but no interscholastics.
4. Limited interscholastic competition for grade 8. We suggest the following factors be considered as means for limiting the competition.
   a. length of season
   b. game rules and conditions (portion of activity in which any one student may participate)
   c. number of games and practices
5. Except for *unusual* circumstances it is not recommended that eighth graders participate in ninth grade competition. (Unusual—average, oversized)

Encouragement of independence

A developmental task of the emerging adolescent is the transition from dependence upon others to a more independent attitude. This can be achieved in several ways. The Ballston Spa Middle School[5] of Ballston Spa, New York, has attempted to meet this particular need through the development of an individualized learning center. In this arrangement individuals are scheduled to meet two hours a day in a large learning center for the purpose of working toward the objectives of mathematics, language arts, social studies, and reading. Work in humanities and science is arranged in other rooms. The following statement by the Ballston Spa administration gives some idea of the depth of effort devoted to this means of developing independent study.

Individualized Learning Center:

A. Academic methodology—Academic methodology in relation to school organization: In order to meet the concrete objectives of mathematics, language arts, social studies, and reading the school will establish an individualized learning center to which pupils will come for at least two (2) hours a day. The centers will be staffed by teachers of the appropriate subject matter field and they will assist students individually. The materials in these centers will consist of: programmed materials, tapes, filmstrips, films, and any other materials for instruction which lend themselves to individualization. The learning center will operate in the following manner:

1. Each pupil will work through a sequence of instructional units which have been prescribed for him according to prior achievement and individualized learning habits. This means that pupils will be working on different materials at their own pace.

2. Each pupil will spend at least 70 per cent of his time learning on his own; 30 per cent of his time will be spent in small group and/or tutorial learning experiences.

3. In working through a sequence of instructional units, no pupil will be permitted to start work on a new unit until he has acquired a specific minimum degree of mastery of the material in the units identified as prerequisites to it.

4. Frequent evaluations of pupil progress will be the basis for the development of individualized instructional prescriptions. The frequent evaluations will be accomplished by a monitoring system based on the students' progress through the instructional units.

5. Professionally trained teachers in each academic area will primarily perform the tasks of instructing individual pupils or small groups, diagnosing pupil needs, and planning instructional programs. Additionally, aides will be employed to carry on the routine tasks in the centers (checking, monitoring, testing, helping youngsters understand the system, etc.).

6. Each pupil will assume more responsibility for planning and carrying out his own program of study. The system will encourage students to help each other in the learning process (tutoring, etc.).

The degree of independence offered to students during more than one-third of their school day is rewarded by a growth in responsibility on their part, a feeling of support for the school on the part of the students, and a general acceptance of the requirements of learning. Teachers are enthusiastic because their task becomes that of aiding pupils in their learning rather than transmitting information by lecture or materials in which students have little interest. While the scheduling of such an activity requires a major reappraisal of school objectives, the results in Ballston Spa have been extraordinary.

REFERENCES

1. Further information may be obtained from the Principal, Keokuk Junior High School, Keokuk, Iowa. Material used with permission of the Principal.

2. Further information may be obtained from the Principal, St. Cloud Middle School, St. Cloud, Florida. Material used with permission of the Principal.

3. Further information may be obtained from the Principal, Barnstable Middle School, Hyannis, Massachusetts. Material used with permission of the Principal.

4. Further information may be obtained from the Director of Physical Education, Shaker High School, Loudonville, New York. Material used with permission of the Director.

5. Further information may be obtained from the Principal, Ballston Spa Middle School, Ballston Spa, New York. Material used with permission of the Principal.

Indexes

Author Index

Subject Index